FOUNDATIONS OF CODING THEORY

EPISTEME

A SERIES IN THE FOUNDATIONAL,

METHODOLOGICAL, PHILOSOPHICAL, PSYCHOLOGICAL,

SOCIOLOGICAL AND HISTORICAL ASPECTS

OF THE SCIENCES, PURE AND APPLIED

Editor: MARIO BUNGE

Foundations and Philosophy of Science Unit, McGill University

VOLUME 1

FOUNDATIONS OF
CODING THEORY

Edited by

WILLIAM E. HARTNETT

Dept. of Mathematics, State University College, Plattsburgh, N.Y., U.S.A.

D. REIDEL PUBLISHING COMPANY

DORDRECHT-HOLLAND / BOSTON-U.S.A.

ISBN-13:978-94-010-2300-9   e-ISBN-13:978-94-009-2298-9
DOI: 10.1007/978-94-009-2298-9

Published by D. Reidel Publishing Company,
P.O. Box 17, Dordrecht, Holland

Sold and distributed in the U.S.A., Canada, and Mexico
by D. Reidel Publishing Company, Inc.
306 Dartmouth Street, Boston,
Mass. 02116, U.S.A.

TABLE OF CONTENTS

PART III / TESTS AND CONSTRUCTIONS

PREFACE

During the sixteenth century, Cardano wrote a fascinating work called *The Book on Games of Chance*. In it he gives an extremely candid recounting and personal appraisal of some aspects of his most remarkable life.* One feature of the book is striking for the modern scientist or mathematician accustomed to current publishing practices. It is brought out during Cardano's discussion of his investigations of certain special questions of applied probability, namely, the question of how to win at gambling. His technique is simplicity itself: in fine reportorial style he reveals his proposed strategy for a particular gambling game, giving marvelous motivating arguments which induce the reader to feel warm, heartfelt support for the projected strategy. Then with all the drama that only a ringside seat observation can bring, Cardano announces that he tried the strategy at the casino and ended up borrowing his taxi fare. Undaunted by failure, he analyzes his now fire-tested strategy in detail, mounts new and persuasive arguments, and, ablaze with fresh optimism and replenished resources, charges off to the fray determined to now succeed where he had so often failed before.

Along the way, Cardano developed a number of valuable insights about games of chance and produced useful research results which presumably would be of interest in our present-day society. However, he could never publish the results today in journals with all the flair, the mistakes, the failures and minor successes which he exhibits in his book. Journal editors rarely give page space to a recounting of mistakes, no matter how charmingly told. They are even reluctant to publish papers which seek to provide a developmental account of the thinking which eventually led to the results being reported. All of which seems remarkable in view of the simultaneous efforts to attract and train new workers in the field: one almost has the impression they feel that the proper way to equip

* A translation by Sidney Gould of this work on gambling by Cardano appears in *Cardano, The Gambling Scholar* by Oystein Ore, Princeton University Press (1953).

the neophyte worker is to shield him from the work of others and provide him with only the "latest" research results of such work.

Any attempt to report the work of a group of people presents difficulties, particularly if the work has been carried out over a period of time with shifts in group membership. The usual outcome of such attempts is either a polished and somewhat sterile version of the final results or a more or less personal history of the group's work habits: the flavor of individual contribution and the benefit of a developmental overview are lost. In the first case, the emphasis is on the results of the group; in the second, on the group to the detriment of its findings. In rare cases, an opportunity exists to present important technical results obtained by a group in a fashion which makes clear how the concepts developed and yet maintains the individuality of the contributors.

Such is the case with the Coding Group at Parke Mathematical Laboratories, Incorporated in Carlisle, Massachusetts, U.S.A., which was occupied with various problems in Coding Theory from 1957 until 1968 when the work terminated. Membership in the Group changed during the eleven years and the range of effort varied. The last four years of this period saw a concerted and systematic attack on the basic problems of Coding Theory in a context more general than that which had been reported in the literature. What emerged from these efforts has been termed Abstract Coding Theory and this book is devoted to an exposition of the foundations of that theory.

Five individuals were concerned with this study: Lorenzo Calabi who directed the effort, John Riley, Lester Arquette, Theodore Hatcher and the writer, William Hartnett. In a long series of some twenty-seven separate and joint papers and memoranda they explored the properties of codes, formulated theoretical foundations for a study of Abstract Coding Theory, fashioned important tools for the study, and constructed specific families of codes with desirable properties. A few but not all of the papers have been reported in the literature. Our aim here is to organize ten of the more important of these papers into a sequence of chapters which reflects the temporal development of the concepts studied and which provides an intellectual framework for an understanding and appreciation of the generality of the approach used and of the results obtained. The book is divided into three parts: the first is introductory and mainly expository, the second presents the extensive theoretical work on abstract codes, and the third provides tests of code properties and certain constructions of families of codes. The first chapter, separately written by the editor, introduces the four basic problems dealt with in the later chapters and provides a general background for the papers. The overviews for Parts I and II summarize the basic content of the parts. The editorial notes which precede the chapters describe the historical and conceptual framework in which each paper was written. A reference of the form [PML 21] refers to item 21 of the Parke Selected Bibliography; [21] would refer to the usual references.

It seems worthwhile to comment briefly on the composition of the group because of its influence on the development of Abstract Coding Theory. With the exception of Arquette whose basic training was in electrical engineering with secondary work in mathematics, all members of the Group were pure mathematicians applying mathematics, its conceptual framework and its arsenal of techniques, to the problems of Abstract Coding Theory. With contractual affiliations with communication engineers at Air Force Cambridge Research Laboratories, Bedford, Massachusetts, the Group functioned with a foot in each of two worlds. Living and working in the world of mathematics, the Group maintained a constant awareness of the differences in approach of the two worlds and made consistent and strenuous efforts to relate its results with the needs and interests of a broader audience. In practice, this meant that care was given in the exposition of the work to make a mathematical approach to the problems meaningful and attractive. It would be pleasant to report that our efforts were unqualified successes but we are not at all sure that such is the factual situation. However, even modest success would amply reward our efforts. After all, we did enjoy the work. It is our fond hope that others may find some pleasure in reading this account of our work.

WILLIAM E. HARTNETT
for the PML Coding Group

Plattsburgh, New York, U.S.A.
June 1974

ACKNOWLEDGEMENTS

To the Air Force Cambridge Research Laboratories for sponsoring our research on Abstract Coding Theory under contracts AF19(628)-3826 and F1962867COO30 during the years 1964–1968.

To *Information and Control* for permission to reprint the material of Chapters 7, 8, and 9 and to IEEE *Transactions on Information Theory* for permission to reprint the material of Chapters 10 and 11.

To all of the staff at Parke Mathematical Laboratories for making life there so pleasant but especially to Georgia Smith and Betty Millward who skillfully and lovingly typed the original versions of the papers and to Dorothy Moran who carefully edited them.

To my colleagues and collaborators without whom there would be no book. In particular I thank Lorenzo Calabi for many things which cannot be described and cannot be repaid.

W. E. H.

CROSS REFERENCES FOR THE CHAPTERS IN
THE PARKE SELECTED BIBLIOGRAPHY

Note: The versions of the papers in this book are sometimes slightly edited versions of the originals.

Chapter 2 = PML35
Chapter 3 = PML43
Chapter 4 = PML44
Chapter 5 = PML46
Chapter 6 = PML47
Chapter 7 = PML59
Chapter 8 = PML34
Chapter 9 = PML42
Chapter 10 = PML55
Chapter 11 = PML48

Numbered references refer to the general bibliography.

PART I

INTRODUCTION

CHAPTER 1

BASIC PROBLEMS OF ABSTRACT CODING THEORY

W. E. HARTNETT

1. The setting for the study

It might be well to begin by setting down in general terms some of the basic problems and considerations that motivated the PML Coding Group. Later we can and will elaborate on these problems and considerations and give a more formal treatment of them. Still later we shall furnish a detailed formulation of topics of interest. Finally, we shall re-examine the problems and considerations from the vantage point of our results and attempt to summarize gracefully the essence of our concerns.

As part of Information Theory, Coding Theory deals with the transmission of information. Specifically, it deals with codes designed to facilitate such transmission and it does so by studying codes and their properties. For the most part, and in its simplest form, one assumes that he has a transmission channel which accepts certain inputs and produces certain outputs, the inputs and outputs representing information. In such a scheme we can always replace the sets of inputs and outputs by sets of 'words' formed from specified alphabet symbols; we simply use different words to represent different inputs and outputs. We can then speak of a transmission channel which accepts words and produces words. Because transmission channels using words are the prototypes for general channels, it is traditional that one consider only such schemes and so we limit ourselves to that setting.

If A is a set of words (written in some alphabet), we may form sentences of these words, say, $(a_1, a_2, ..., a_k)$ consisting of k words. By assumption, our channel only accepts words and not sentences and so cannot transmit the sentence just written. However we can form a new word by writing

W. E. Hartnett (ed.), Foundations of Coding Theory, 3–15. All Rights Reserved.

the letters of a_1, followed by the letters of a_2, and so on until we follow with the letters of a_k. Our new word x will be written as $a_1 \, a_2 \, ... \, a_k$ and we can now transmit x. After transmission, our channel produces a permissible output word y. Schematically, we have the following diagram.

$$\text{Sentence} \longrightarrow \text{input word of the sentence} \xrightarrow{\text{channel}} \text{output word}$$

The basic aim of information transmission is now easy to state: determine sets A such that whenever a particular word y occurs as output of the channel, we can construct the unique sentence the transmission of whose word gave rise to y, that is, we can always recover the information (= the sentence) sent. A few moments thought convinces one that it is necessary to say something about what the channel does to the words being transmitted if we hope to accomplish this aim. Traditionally, one does this by specifying a model of the behavior of the channel. Put another way, one assumes that the channel has a certain behavior and then deals with sets of words which permit transmission of information through channels with such behavior.

The usual description of channel behavior rests on the observation that in practical situations there may be 'noise' in the channel; indeed, the presence of noise is to be expected. Without being precise about what noise is, one says that the effect of possible noise is the occurrence of errors in transmission. If the word x is transmitted and no noise is present, then no errors occur and x is produced as output; in the presence of errors any one of a set of words may occur as output depending on the errors which are caused by the noise. Essentially, one specifies a model for channel behavior by stipulating the kinds and numbers of allowable errors; in brief, one describes the permissible error pattern for the channel. Because we shall be concerned only with models of channels, we shall identify the model (= the error pattern) and the channel and study sets of words, called *codes*, suitable for transmitting information for various models.

The study of codes involves four major problem areas: description, definition, characterization, and construction. One must find useful and, if possible, pleasant ways to describe the various error patterns to be considered. At the same time one must identify the important properties which codes suitable for information transmission must have, and then give precise definitions of these code properties. Having formulated descriptions and definitions, one then has to discover statements which characterize codes possessing the properties; explicitly, one must find necessary and sufficient conditions that a code have a specified code property. Finally, one has the problem of constructing codes which possess desirable properties with respect to specified models.

It is apparent from a consideration of the above that any study of codes will involve a mixture of the false starts, wrong directions, misplaced emphasis, and a suitable portion of plain stupidity and the study being reported here is no exception. It is of course possible and indeed presently even in fashion to present the results of such a study in a fashion which stuns the reader into believing that the beheld magnificence and generality sprang full-blown and in elegant form from the agile and gifted mind of the writer. An approach like that would be a dreadful mistake in reporting the PML effort. Not only would we lose the historical record of successive refinements but we would also lose most of the intermediate results which furnished motivation for what became our final formulation.

The end result of such a course of action would be a smooth, polished presentation of results most of which would be ignored or unappreciated. Although it may be trite to observe, it should be remarked that one aim of the study was to provide new and more mathematical directions for Coding Theory and this can only be done if the reporting of the study clearly indicates what makes the directions new and more mathematical. In view of our earlier remarks, it would appear that the only sensible approach to reporting the study would be a historical one and this is the path we have elected to take.

The problems of description and definition precedes that of characterization which in turn precedes the problem of construction. For that reason it seems profitable to give a preliminary and somewhat general discussion of models and code properties before we present the detailed treatment of these notions. At the end of the conversation about definitions, we give a brief guide to the chapters which follow. Each of them was originally written as a PML Scientific Report. Five of them have appeared in the literature.

For simplicity we deal here only with two basic code properties although later we shall deal with six properties of interest. -

2. MODELS

Suppose that J is an *alphabet* with $g \geqslant 2$ letters and suppose that Σ is the set of nonempty finite sequences of elements of J, written as strings. Then, for $g = 2$, the sequence 1, 1, 0, 1, 0) belongs to Σ and would be written as the string 11010. The strings in Σ are frequently called *words over the alphabet J* (or *with letters in J*).

If A is a finite nonempty set of words over J, then we can form the set $\Sigma(A)$ of nonempty finite sequences of words in A. We shall call such sequences *sentences over A* and our first consideration involves Σ and $\Sigma(A)$. The problem is this: if we assume (as usual) that our transmitter accepts and delivers words over J, then in order to transmit a sentence $X = (a_1, a_2, ..., a_k)$ we must first form the word $\hat{X} = a_1 a_2 ... a_k$ by writing the words of X together in order as a single word and then transmit that word. If we call $\hat{X}$ the *message* of the sentence X, then (as expected) we transmit messages rather than sentences. It is obvious that if X and Y are distinct sentences with the same message, then after transmission there is no hope of recovering the sentences, that is, the information transmitted. So all usable codes must be such that different sentences have different messages.

But we need to worry about other problems also. Suppose that X is a sentence over a usable code A and that the word $\hat{X}$ is transmitted. If transmission is perfect, then the word $\hat{X}$ is received and yields the completely determined sentence X. If transmission can be impaired, then we receive a word $\hat{X}'$ which may differ greatly from $\hat{X}$. How $\hat{X}'$ differs from $\hat{X}$ will depend upon the kind of impairment involved. The obvious possibilities for misspelling $\hat{X}$ in transmission seem to be: (1) certain letters in $\hat{X}$ can be replaced by other letters without changing the length of the word $\hat{X}$, (2) additional letters can be inserted in $\hat{X}$ or letters can be deleted from $\hat{X}$ or both with no spaces but with a possible change in the length of the word $\hat{X}$, and (3) letters in the word can be lost or erased with the spacing preserved so that there is no alteration in length. Suppose $g = 2$ and that $\hat{X} = 1110$ is transmitted. Then the first kind of misspelling might result in the word 0110, the second in the words 101101, 110, or 11011, and the third in the 'word' 1–10 where – denotes a blank for a lost letter which might be 0 or 1. Of course, all three kinds of misspelling may occur in the transmission of a particular $\hat{X}$; in general, what happens depends on many factors but will certainly depend on $\hat{X}$ itself.

Actual transmission devices exhibit behavior which is, at best, only approximately describable in statistical terms. For this reason one resorts to the construction of models of a transmission scheme and our second consideration arises here. Each transmitter accepts all words with letters from our alphabet J and *not just* messages arising from the sentences of A. Hence one might argue that a reasonable model should not depend on any code. This kind of model is usual in Information Theory – one has two probability spaces of doubly infinite 'words' over possibly different alphabets and a family of probability measures on the second space indexed by the first space. The problem of coding for this 'information' model (highly simplified) is to show that, subject to certain restrictions and with a pre-assigned specification of accuracy of transmission, one can always find a natural number n and a set A of words each of n letters such that the messages of the sentences of A can be transmitted within the specified limit of accuracy. So to speak, such a model allows only misspelling of the first kind and describes how these may occur; codes are then chosen to allow satisfactory transmission in the presence of such misspelling on doubly infinite 'words'.

A different kind of model can be devised which depends on the words with letters from J. For example, one could specify such a 'word' model by requiring that for a given natural number n, whenever a word x with length $|x|$ is transmitted the misspellings allowed are determined by the pair of non negative integers m and k for which $|x| = mn + k$; the usual requirement would be that for 'short' words, that is, for which $m = 0$, only few or only special misspellings are permitted and that for 'long words' (with $m \geqslant 1$) more extensive misspellings are allowed. Such models can be referred to as *word per letters* models of transmission. One difficulty with such a model is that long words are (or can be regarded as being) made up of short words and so one has the questions: when we transmit a long word are we really only transmitting a number of short words? Do the misspellings depend on how we regard the words or are they in some sense independent of the words?

An alternative view for a model can be advanced. While it is true that our transmitters accept all words over the alphabet, we only plan to send messages which arise from the sentences from the usable code A.

This means that it is enough to tell what the transmitter does to our messages. From this point of view, we start with a usable code A, look at sentences X over A and their messages $\hat{X}$, and then specify which 'words' $\hat{X}'$ the transmitter will deliver when $\hat{X}$ is sent. If we call this set of 'words' $\beta(X)$, then we can summarize matters in the following diagram:

$$\text{Sentence } X \longrightarrow \text{ message } \hat{X} \longrightarrow \text{ allowable 'words' } \beta(X)$$

Letting $\Sigma(A)$ denote the sentences over A, $\widehat{\Sigma(A)}$ the messages of the sentences of $\Sigma(A)$, and Ω the set of all allowable 'words' from all messages of $\Sigma(A)$, then we have Figure 1.

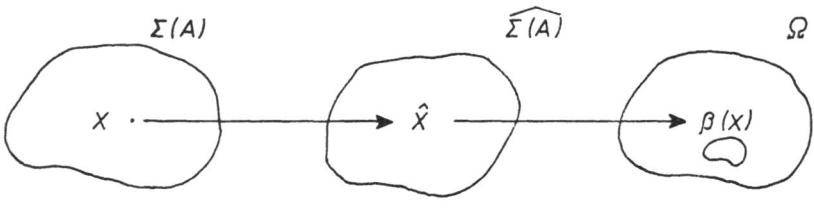

Fig. 1.

Models of transmission like these can be termed *sentence* (or *message*) models. For each sentence X in $\Sigma(A)$ one must describe the set $\beta(X)$ and we now look at various ways to effect such descriptions. There is one rather simple way to do this. Because a sentence X is a sequence $(a_1, a_2, ..., a_k)$ of words of A, one can obtain the set $\beta(X)$ of 'words' by specifying the set $\beta(a_i)$ of allowable 'words' for each of the words a_i in A and then letting $\beta(X)$ be the set of all 'words' $x = x_1 x_2 ... x_k$ each of whose 'subwords' x_i is an allowable 'word' in the corresponding $\beta(a_i)$. Symbolically, we write $\beta(X) = \beta(a_1, a_2, ..., a_k) = \beta(a_1)\beta(a_2) ... \beta(a_k)$. Because $\beta(X)$ for a sentence X in this kind of model is completely determined by $\beta(a)$ for each word a in A, we speak of it as a *sentence per word* model. Such a model regards all sentences as made up of short, that is, one word, sentences.

Other ways to specify sentence models which are not per word word models are more elaborate. One class of such models can be described rather simply. For a positive integer $t > 1$, and $r < t$ define $\beta(X)$ for all sentences X with fewer than t words by specifying which misspellings are allowed; for sentences X with at least t words, let $\beta(X)$ be all 'words' which can be obtained from X by making certain misspellings in each of no more than r of each t consecutive words of X. The explicit models are obtained by spelling out which kinds of and how many misspellings are to be considered allowable. Clearly, substantial variation in such models can be achieved.

All of our discussion above leads to the conclusion that we have to consider two basic interrelated problems: the type of model and the kinds of allowable misspellings. After these are decided, we still have the task of giving adequate definitions for the code properties of interest.

3. THE SETTING FOR THE DEFINITIONS

We would like to consider all possible types of misspellings, now re-named *errors*, and so we shall not consider the 'information' models. The 'word' models have been considered in the literature but usually only in the case in which no 'loss or gain' errors (our type (2) misspellings) can occur. If all words in A have length n and we have a word per n letters model, then the word and the sentence model are the same; this is not the case if the word lengths in A differ. The sentence models seem to permit the greatest freedom with regard to types of allowable errors and, as we shall claim later, cover many of the codes studied in the literature. For those reasons we assume that our present setting is a sentence model for a set A of words. Because the model requires that, for each sentence X over A, we specify $\beta(X)$, we could represent the model by the pair $(\Sigma(A), \beta)$ where, as before, $\Sigma(A)$ denotes the set of sentences over A. Because each word a of A can be regarded as a one-word sentence, the set $\beta(a)$ is specified by $(\Sigma(A), \beta)$; this is another way to say that the behavior of β on the words of A is determined by the behavior of β on the sentences over A. Symbolically, $(\Sigma(A), \beta) \rightarrow (A, \beta)$ and this implication holds in all sentence models. As we mentioned before, in a sentence per word model the behavior of β on the words of A determines the behavior of β on the sentences in $\Sigma(A)$ and so, for this case, we have $(A, \beta) \rightarrow (\Sigma(A), \beta)$ and the pairs may be used interchangeably.

For the sake of being explicit we shall call $(\Sigma(A), \beta)$ a *code* (or an *abstract code*), with *base set* A, and *error pattern* β and define *Abstract Coding Theory* as the study of abstract codes. Each code $(\Sigma(A), \beta)$ yields the pair (A, β) which could be regarded as a code for a sentence per word model; in general, we reserve the word 'code' to mean the pair $(\Sigma(A), \beta)$.

4. DEFINITIONS

With this notion of a code we now turn to the desirable properties that a code may have. If X is a sentence with message $\hat{X}$, then $\hat{X}$ should be one of the allowable 'words' in $\beta(X)$ because we should permit the possibility of unimpaired transmission. We should also make the allowable 'words' in $\beta(X)$ real words in the following way: given our original alphabet J, let us construct another alphabet J^* by adjoining a new letter to J, namely, a blank '–'. Then, as above, 1–10 is a 'word' over J but is an actual word over J^*. Should it happen that β does not allow blanks, then we use only the letters of J as before.

Because we want to use the code to transmit information we want to be able to recover the sentences (that is, the information) transmitted, in spite of the allowable errors described by β. This means that if X is a sentence, $\hat{X}$ is sent, and $\hat{X}'$ is received, then we want to be able to recover X uniquely from $\hat{X}'$. Phrased differently, we want to preserve X throughout the transmission, which is to say that we want to correct any errors that may have occurred. Whenever we can do this for a given code we shall say that the code is *error correcting* (*for the error pattern β*).

In practice, of course, we are in the situation of having a received allowable word x and of trying to decide which sentence had been sent. For error correction we must have x determine a unique sentence. Because x is an allowable word, x is in $\beta(X)$ for some sentence X; error correction demands that this be true for exactly one sentence. If we call $\beta(X)$ *the range of X in the code* $(\Sigma(A), \beta)$, then it is easy to formulate a definition covering error correction:

(I)   A code has the property of *error correction* whenever the ranges of different sentences have no words in common.

It should be observed that if a code is error correcting and X and Y are different sentences, then the messages $\hat{X}$ and $\hat{Y}$ are different because $\hat{X}$ is in the range of X, $\hat{Y}$ is in the range of Y and the ranges have no words in common. This means that our notion of error correction here includes the concept of usable code that we informally talked about in Section 2.

Before we remarked that we needed usable codes. Now it is clear that we need error correcting codes for transmission.

Actually we need something more. Suppose, for example, that very long messages are being transmitted and that very long allowable words are being received; such situations are common in practice. Suppose further that, for some reason, we lose part of our allowable word and then begin to receive successive letters from some point on. If we number the successive letters as $x_1 x_2 x_3 \ldots$, we then have the following problem: without knowing what happened before the letter x_1 can we find a letter numbered x_i such that $x_i x_{i+1} x_{i+2} \ldots$ is in the range of a sentence X and know that the sentence sent contained X? If we cannot, then if we once 'lose our place', we cannot find it again. Another possibility is that we can find our place but that we must look at too many letters before we can do so. What we want, of course, is the ability to limit the number of letters we need to look at before we can be *sure* of finding a 'place'. The letters $x_1 x_2 \ldots x_{i-1}$, from our point of view, might as well be 'blanks' because we are not able to use them to reconstruct any part of the sentence transmitted. Hence they become 'blank' errors which are not specified by β. So to speak, β gives the error pattern only when we know where we are; other extraneous errors can be superimposed on β when we lose our place. More precisely, the letters lost are simply lost. What β 'did' to the transmitted sentence to give the lost letters is completely immaterial because the lost letters are not available to us for interpretation. What we want to guarantee is that we can limit the extraneous errors and the kind of limitation we need can be described in terms of number of letters.

Let us say that a word $x_1 x_2 \ldots x_m$ is a *code infix* if there are words y and z such that $y x_1 x_2 \ldots x_m z$ is in the range of some sentence; informally, a code infix is part of an allowable word. The property we want our codes to have (in addition to error correction) is that whenever we have any sufficiently long code infix, then we can always find *the* 'place' and not just *a* 'place'. The distinction here is if $x = x_1 x_2 \ldots x_m$ is a code infix so that yxz is in the range of a sentence W, then it may happen that, for some i, $x_i x_{i+1} \ldots x_m z$ is in the range of a sentence U: the letter x_i provides *a* 'place'. On the other hand, it could be that the sentence W is made up of two other sentences W_1 and W_2 and that for some $j < i$, $x_1 x_2 \ldots x_{j-1}$ is in the range of W_1 and $x_j x_{j+1} \ldots x_m z$ is in the range of W_2: that is, x_j

provides *the* 'place' in the sentence W. A more precise formulation of this notion is given in our second definition:

(II)   A code has the property of *error limitation* if there exists a positive integer t such that whenever a code infix $x = x_1x_2...x_m$ has length at least t, then $x_ix_{i+1}...x_{i+k} = x'$ is in the range of X for some i, k and some sentence X and moreover whenever x' is a code infix of a word in the range of a sentence W, then W is of the form: a sentence U, followed by X, followed by a sentence V.

It goes without saying that codes which are error correcting and error limiting are pleasant codes, at least in theory. In practice, of course, there may be considerable difficulty about implementing both of these properties. The actual finding of the 'place' or of the sentence transmitted present separate difficulties which cannot be explored here. Our present concern is only with the formulation of adequate definitions.

5. A GUIDE TO THE BOOK

There are two main parts of the book. Part II on Theoretical Studies deals with problems of description, definition, and characterization. Part III on Tests and Constructions also deals with characterization but concentrates on tests characterizing code properties because of their possible use in constructing codes. It also provides families of codes with specified properties.

Because the kinds of ideas needed for Abstract Coding Theory are not in general familiar to many workers in the field, it becomes desirable to provide a somewhat leisurely approach to the subject. This is the reason for the introductory Part I. A first brief attempt at presenting the problems of the theory has already been made in the earlier sections of this chapter but a better treatment is available and appears here as Chapter 2. Originally written early in the study, it presents motivation for and demonstrates the utility of a unified and abstract approach to the problems of Coding Theory. It does so by furnishing numerous examples and proving a number of significant theorems. In terms of Abstract Coding Theory the paper is a restriction to a very special case: a sentence per word model permitting variable length words but allowing only substitution errors. However, it is sufficiently general as an introduction and has the virtue of being expository in character. It also indicates what has to be done in studying that particular model.

The first four chapters of Part II report on the working out of the program sketched. All of them deal with our standard model: the variable length, sentence per word, substitution errors model in Chapter 2 and provide an exhaustive treatment of basic code properties. The properties of irredundance and correcting and the corresponding pre properties are defined, studied, and characterized in Chapter 3. The notion of an expanded code is meaningful and useful because of the nature of the model and is introduced explicitly here; it had been implicitly used in Chapter 2. (The special character of the model is dramatized later in Chapter 9. The tests presented there hold only for such models.) The properties of promptness and decodability with bounded delay are treated in an analogous fashion in Chapter 4. The code properties of synchronizability ($=$ error-limitability) and comma freedom are characterized in Chapter 5. In the next chapter, the properties of correcting, decodability, and synchronizability are studied and characterized from a different point of view.

The material of Chapter 7 was written as the last paper in the study. At that time we had moved to the study of code properties for a completely general model. Substitution and synchronization errors were allowed and our only requirement was that $\hat{X}$ belong to $\beta(X)$ for each sentence X with words from A. This meant, in particular, that most of our carefully constructed tools for the study of the standard model could not be applied to the newer, more general model. It became necessary to look carefully at exactly what was involved in the various code properties. As frequently happens, it turned out that the property of correcting for codes was actually a special case of a property involving mappings and certain binary relations. We were able to prove a pleasant characterization theorem for the general case which, when specialized, gave a neat set of necessary and sufficient conditions in order that an abstract code be correcting. The formulation of the theorem isolates what appears to the essentials of the notion of correcting and provides valuable information about what is needed in order to study and characterize the other code properties.

We dealt with the question of decodability for a general model and gave a characterization theorem which holds only in a restricted setting. The property of error-limitation was treated only briefly. For the standard model, error-limiting codes are always decodable. This is not so for the general model but we did provide a restricted version of the theorem in Chapter 7. We then went on to apply some of the results to particular classes of codes. In order to deal with synchronization errors we introduced the Levenshtein distance and proved a number of theorems about the somewhat difficult task of actually computing the Levenshtein distance between two sequences. We then proved the analogue of the Hamming theorem about the correcting ability of block codes. Finally, we extended a theorem of Chapter 11 which chronologically had appeared before Chapter 7 was written. From the point of view of Abstract Coding Theory, the level of this work represents the most general possible setting in which one can deal or hope to deal with the problems of Coding Theory. It also indicates precisely the difficulties associated with this level of activity.

There are four chapters in Part III, the section of the book devoted to tests and constructions. Chapter 8, at the time it was written, furnished the first proofs in English of known theorems characterizing three code properties for the variable word noiseless model. The methods of proof identified and isolated a number of notions of considerable importance both in themselves and for generalizations. In Chapter 9, the results on Chapter 8 were applied to expanded codes to yield generalizations of the tests for the three code properties for the case of our standard model. It also provides a stock of examples illustrating the kinds of variation which one can encounter dealing only with the standard model.

The last two chapters construct families of codes with desirable properties. Chapter 10 provides a family of error-correcting and error-limiting codes for our standard model. In the last chapter the model allows both substitution and synchronization errors and is a sentence model. A restriction to block codes, however, is made; this condition was imposed because of the presence of synchronization errors. The codes constructed satisfy a decodability condition whose formulation was determined by the generality of the model. Indeed, the necessity for extending the definitions originally set up for the standard model to cover adequately the more general model induced us to deal with the most general model described in Chapter 7.

We have provided fairly complete details of everything we have done; for some readers we have probably included far too much. As a working procedure for the reader, one might suggest starting with Chapter 2 and ignoring the proofs of theorems. Depending on interest, the reader should then go to Part II or Part III, following the main development of the theory and again omitting the proofs. Eventually the diligent and patient reader should come to Chapter 7. When he does, he should probably spend some time on the theorems. If matters still seem a bit too abstract, perhaps a detailed trek through Part I will tie things down somewhat more concretely. Despite the formidable appearance of the theorems, it should be noted that they represent substantial simplifications of earlier versions of the same results.

CHAPTER 2

BASIC PROPERTIES OF ERROR-CORRECTING CODES

L. CALABI AND L. K. ARQUETTE

EDITORIAL NOTE

Among the allegedly determinable traits of the modern mathematician are his passions for generality and precision. Such traits go unnoticed among the fraternity but they sometimes provide cultural shocks for those outside the fold. In this paper both traits are explicitly exhibited.

The authors have observed two features of the literature of Coding Theory; (1) historically separate aspects of coding studies can be treated as special cases of a general theory and (2) there exists a wide diversity of vaguely described code properties and hence there exists a need for precisely formulated definitions of the important code properties. Reacting to these observations, the authors display *a* unified theory, give precisely stated definitions of the presumably major code properties for such a theory, and begin to investigate implications among the properties. Throughout numerous examples serve to motivate the formulation of the theory and the definitions. In terms of models, theirs was a per word model wich allowed only substitution errors. At the time it was written (November 1965), the paper presented a conceptual framework adequate to accommodate all of the known literature on per word models. The style of the paper was expository and the level of presentation was fairly elementary: the aim of the paper was to popularize and, indeed, advertise the conceptual approach of the authors to the problems of Coding Theory. In retrospect, its major drawback was the usual drawback of first formulations: it tended to dominate our thinking on these matters to the exclusion of alternative and more general approaches. Its ongoing virtue was that it provided a strikingly clear outline for characterization studies. Indeed, such studies were promised in the paper and do appear here as later chapters.

1. INTRODUCTION

The Theory of Coding has so far been developed in two different directions. The first emphasizes the improvement of communication over noisy channels, that is the study of error-correcting codes, which are always assumed to be block codes. The second deals with more basic aspects of communication, like unique decipherability or synchroniza-

W. E. Hartnett (ed.), Foundations of Coding Theory, 17–36. All Rights Reserved.
Copyright © 1974 by D. Reidel Publishing Company, Dordrecht-Holland.

bility, allowing the consideration of variable-length codes but assuming noiseless channels.

We present here the beginning of a unified treatment by defining and correlating some fundamental notions at a uniform level of generality. Thus all our definitions apply to variable-length as well as to block codes, over arbitrary alphabets, and to communication in the presence of noise. Moreover the effects of that noise (that is, the error patterns) that the codes are to correct can be chosen with great freedom.

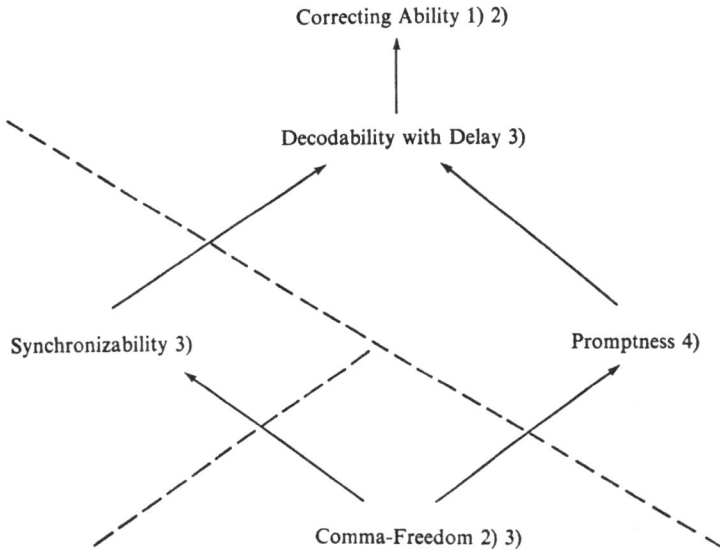

1) Includes 'unique decipherability' as a particular case.
2) Normally defined only for block codes.
3) Normally defined only for noiseless channels.
4) Includes the 'prefix property' of variable length codes and the 'distance property' of block codes as particular cases.

Fig. 1. The basic concepts and their relations.

The concepts discussed are listed in the diagram of Figure 1, in which the arrows indicate all the logical implications which exist among them. For block codes the five notions reduce to three, which are separated in the diagram by dotted lines. There are several equivalent definitions for each of these concepts; we present only those which seem to parallel most closely the corresponding intuitive ideas. In particular we give three definitions of 'promptness' because there are three intuitive ideas involved: 'prompt decodability', an extension of the 'prefix property', and an extension of the 'distance property'.

Observe that, in our context, 'unique decipherability' is a particular case of 'correcting ability'. Notice also that each of the other four properties includes correcting ability; for instance, we call a code 'synchronizable' if it is error-correcting *and* if it is also capable of combating ambiguities due to loss of synchronization even in the presence of (correctable) errors.

Future papers will present a more comprehensive and more formal study; in particular they will show that the tests of Sardinas-Patterson [25] and Levenshtein [14] may be modified and used for the properties discussed here. Under some restrictive assumptions, some of that material is already in circulation (see [PML25] and [PML39]).

Several simple examples are given below to illustrate the exposition and to demonstrate the difference between the various concepts. Many more examples may be found in [PML32] and [PML33].

2. DESCRIPTION OF THE ERROR PATTERNS

We consider sequences $a, b, \ldots, u, v, \ldots x, y, \ldots$ of various lengths, whose terms are elements ('letters') of a set (the 'alphabet'), which is normally but not necessarily assumed finite. We call *code* (the 'vocabulary') a finite set A of such sequences, called *words*. Sequences of words are called *sentences* and denoted $U, V, \ldots, X, Y, \ldots$. Thus, if $a_1, a_2, \ldots, a_r$ are words, $X = (a_1, a_2, \ldots, a_r)$ is a sentence; the sequence $a_1 a_2 \ldots a_r$ obtained by juxtaposing $a_1, a_2, \ldots, a_r$ is denoted $\hat{X}$. In many situations it is essential to distinguish between X (a sequence of words) and $\hat{X}$ (a sequence of letters). Following the custom, we normally write sequences without enclosing parentheses and separating commas; in particular then, when no confusion is possible, we write $a_1 a_2 \ldots a_r$ rather than $(a_1, a_2, \ldots, a_r)$.

In practical communication it often occurs that the received sequence y differs from that sequence x which has been sent. We then say that 'errors' have occurred; when x is a word, we say that these errors form an 'error pattern'. It is important to be able to describe families of error patterns: for instance, the family of those patterns that a code should be able to correct to insure sufficiently reliable communication. To this end, we consider a correspondence α, called an *admissibility mapping*, which associates to each word a of a code A the finite set $\alpha(a)$ of those sequences which, when received, are to be decoded as a. The set $\alpha(a)$ we call the *α-admissibility range of a* (or simply the *range of a*); we call *α-admissible* (or simply *admissible*) any sequence which is an element of the range $\alpha(a)$ of some word a. If then y is an admissible sequence in $\alpha(a)$, the difference between a and y is one of the error patterns described by the mapping α. Observe that each code word is not only admissible but in fact is always contained in its own range.

The manner in which admissibility ranges are constructed should reflect the effect of the transmission noise which we propose to combat. For instance, given the code A and a transmission channel with its noise probability distribution, we could, for each a in A, construct $\alpha(a)$ to satisfy the requirement that the probability of receiving a sequence not in $\alpha(a)$, when a is sent, is smaller than some preassigned number. Other examples are described in Figure 2.

For *block codes*, that is codes whose words all have the same length, (i.e., number of terms), many authors have already considered various kinds of admissibility ranges. For example, in Slepian's theory [29] the range of a given code word is the column of the 'standard array' headed by that word. This choice of ranges for group codes corresponds to the assumption that the 'coset leaders' represent the most likely error patterns. These are, for Slepian, those having the smallest possible number of errors (maximum likelihood principle); but other patterns have also been considered, for example by Banerji [4] and Chien [7]. Ranges have been at least implicitly considered also for non-group, block codes, usually as the sets of those sequences which may be obtained by changing in any one word a number of terms not exceeding some given integer e (the maximum number of errors to be corrected).

We do this also for variable-length codes and for any non-negative integer e, we denote by α_e the corresponding admissibility mapping. Thus $\alpha_e(a)$ is the set of those sequences which may be obtained by changing in the word a, in any possible fashion, a number of terms not exceeding e. In particular then $\alpha_0(a)$ is the set containing only the sequence a itself. More generally, to every word a of a code we associate, instead of the fixed number e, a non-negative integer $v(a)$, called its *index* (see [PLM25]). We may then take for the range of the word a the set of those sequences

$\alpha(a)$	$\alpha(b)$	Remarks
00001	0011011	The admissible sequences are the words themselves
00000	0001011	and those sequences obtained from the words by
	0010011	changing a single 1 into 0.
	0011001	
	0011010	
00001	0011011	The allowable error patterns are those with no
10001	1011011	errors, one error, or two consecutive errors.
01001	0111011	
00101	0001011	
00011	0010011	
00000	0011111	
11001	0011001	
01101	0011010	
00111	1111011	
00010	0101011	
	0000011	
	0010111	
	0011101	
	0011000	
00001	0011011	If v is the index function defined by $v(a) = 2$ and
10001	1011011	$v(b) = 1$, we have here the ranges of the mapping
01001	0111011	α_v. That is, the range of a contains those sequences
00101	0001011	differing from a in at most 2 terms; and the range of
00011	0010011	b contains those sequences differing from b in at
00000	0011111	most 1 term.
11001	0011001	
10101	0011010	
10011		
10000		
01101		
01011		
01000		
00111		
00100		
00010		
00001	0011011	This is α_0, that is, α_v when $v(a) = v(b) = 0$.
00001	0011011	The allowable error patterns are those with at most
–0001	–011011	one *erasure*, denoted –. Here the 'alphabet' has
0–001	0–11011	three elements: 0, 1, –, though only two are used in
00–01	00–1011	the code.
000–1	001–011	
0000–	0011–11	
	00110–1	
	001101–	

Fig. 2. Examples of five admissibility mappings and the corresponding ranges for the code consisting of the two words $a = 00001$, $b = 0011011$.

which may be obtained by changing in a any number of terms not exceeding $v(a)$. The corresponding admissibility mapping is denoted α_v (see Figure 2). In general there seems to be no reason to keep $v(a)$ constant: indeed we may wish to correct in each word a number of errors which is, for example, dependent on the length of the word or on its probability of being sent.

Notice that the length of every sequence x of $\alpha_v(a)$ is, by definition, equal to that of a. This is not necessarily true for more general types of admissibility mappings. For simplicity, and without any apparent loss in scope, we consider in this paper only mappings α for which the length of a word a is also the length of every sequence in the range of a. In other words, we consider here codes that may correct erroneous terms of the sequences, but not errors in the number of such terms.

As indicated by the last example of Figure 2, not every 'letter' of the 'alphabet' needs to appear as a term in some code word. This enables us to consider 'erasures' as a type of error, and more generally to include in our treatment the distinction between 'input alphabet' and 'output alphabet' often made in Information Theory (cf. [33]).

3. CORRECTING ABILITY AND DECODABILITY

If a code A is to combat successfully the noise effects expressed by an admissibility mapping α, then it must have the property that distinct code words possess disjoint admissibility ranges:

(I)   If a and b are distinct words, then $\alpha(a) \cap \alpha(b) = \emptyset$.

Indeed, if there exists a sequence x belonging to both $\alpha(a)$ and $\alpha(b)$, then x is decodable as either a or b and consequently decoding cannot be accomplished unambiguously. Observe that if $\alpha = \alpha_0$ then (I) requires only that any two words be different sequences; in this case then, (I) expresses the condition for the code A to be what Abramson [1] has called 'nonsingular'. If A is a block code and $\alpha = \alpha_e$, then (I) requires that every sequence differing from any word in at most e terms differ from every other word in more than e terms; that is, in this case, (I) expresses the condition for A to be able to correct up to e errors. For variable-length codes, however, (I) is too weak to characterize correcting ability, as indicated by the following simple example.

Example 1. Let $A = \{a, b\}$ be the ternary code consisting of the words $a = 0$ and $b = 02$. Since a is shorter than b, every sequence in $\alpha(a)$ is shorter than any sequence in $\alpha(b)$, whatever mapping α we may consider. Thus (I) always holds for the code A. Let us in particular consider that mapping α which allows as error patterns those in which any number of 0's become 1's, any number of 1's become either 0's or 2's, and any number of 2's become 1's (errors of 'absolute magnitude' equal to 1). The ranges are then

$$\alpha(a) = \{0, 1\}$$
$$\alpha(b) = \{02, 12, 01, 11\}.$$

If we receive the sequence 01, we cannot decide whether aa was sent (an allowable error pattern having occurred in the second word) or whether b was sent (with another allowable error pattern having occurred). This ambiguity prevents us from saying that our code A is capable of correcting the error patterns represented by the ranges $\alpha(a)$ and $\alpha(b)$ and hence by the admissibility mapping α. We must therefore postulate a property stronger than (I).

It is first necessary to extend the notion of admissibility range. If X is a sentence, that is a string of words, we denote by $\alpha(X)$ the set of all those sequences which, when received, are to be decoded as X. Extending the terminology introduced above, we call $\alpha(X)$ the *α-admissibility range* (or simply *range*) *of the sentence X*; we call a sequence x *α-admissible* (or *admissible*) if there is a sentence X such that x belongs to the range $\alpha(X)$. If $a_1, a_2, ..., a_r$ are the words of X, and if x is to be decoded as X, then x is necessarily the juxtaposition $x_1 x_2 ... x_r$ of sequences x_i belonging to the ranges of the individual words a_i. Conversely if x_i belongs to $\alpha(a_i)$, then $x = x_1 x_2 ... x_r$ belong to $\alpha(X)$. Thus $\alpha(X) = \alpha(a_1)\alpha(a_2)...\alpha(a_r)$, where we use the convenient notation for set juxtaposition, defined as follows: if A and B are sets of sequences, then AB is the set of all those sequences which are obtained by juxtaposing a sequence in B after a sequence in A.

For example, letting the code A and the mapping α be those of Example 1 above, and letting the sentence X consist of the words a, b, a, then $\alpha(X) = \{0020, 0021, 0120, 0121, 0010, 0011, 0110, 0111, 1020, 1021, 1120, 1121, 1010, 1011, 1110, 1111\}$. If Y is the sentence aa, we similarly have $\alpha(Y) = \{00, 01, 10, 11\}$; hence both $\alpha(b)$ and $\alpha(Y)$ contain, in particular, the sequence 01. This indeed is the cause of our trouble, since 01 may be decoded in two different ways.

We are thus led to the following definition. Given a code A and an admissibility mapping α, we call A α-*correcting* if and only if the following statement holds:

(II) $\alpha(X) \cap \alpha(Y) = \emptyset$ for any two different sentences X and Y.

Observe in fact that if this property holds, any admissible sequence x may be obtained from only one sentence X with allowable error pattern and thus can be decoded unambiguously. Where no error patterns are allowed ($\alpha = \alpha_0$), statement (II) reduces to the usual definition of unique decipherability: different sentences X, Y do not yield the same received sequence; that is, $\hat{X} \neq \hat{Y}$. If we allow any pattern of up to e errors per word ($\alpha = \alpha_e$), we obtain a logical extension of the standard definition given for block codes. Indeed we have:

THEOREM 1. *If all code words have equal length, then statement* (I) *implies statement* (II); *that is, a block code is* α-*correcting if and only if* (I) *holds.*

For the proof, assume $\alpha(X) \cap \alpha(Y) \neq \emptyset$ and $a_1, a_2, ..., a_r$ and $b_1, b_2, ..., b_s$ to be the words of X and Y respectively; we then have $r = s$, $\alpha(a_1) \cap \alpha(b_1) \neq \emptyset$ and $\alpha(a_2 a_3 ... a_r) \cap \alpha(b_2 b_3 ... b_r) \neq \emptyset$, since all words have the same length. By (I) then $a_1 = b_1$. Repeating this reasoning r times, we obtain $a_2 = b_2$, $a_3 = b_3$, ..., $a_r = b_r$; that is, $X = Y$, establishing (II).

Observe that (II) always implies (I), since a single word is also as entence. Example 1 above shows, however, that Theorem 1 cannot be extended to variable length codes. The next example shows that α-correcting codes may be difficult to decode.

Example 2. Let $A = \{a, b\}$ be the binary code for which $a = 000$ and $b = 00011111$. It is easy to show that A is not α_2-correcting. However, let the index function v be given by $v(a) = 1$ and $v(b) = 2$, and consider the corresponding admissibility mapping α_v. By applying the Sardinas-Patterson test for unique decipherability [15] to the code $\alpha_v(a) \cup \alpha_v(b)$, we can prove that A satisfies (II) (see [PML25]). That is, A corrects up to one error in the word a and up to two in the word b (in spite of the fact that a is a prefix of b). But this code has arbitrarily long sentences whose first word cannot be decoded before the last word is received, if we allow all the error patterns represented by α_y. Indeed suppose we receive an α_y-admissible sequence which begins

000001110111111 $\underline{11011111}$...,

with the underlined portion repeating. If we start decoding before this periodicity stops, we cannot decide whether *aabb*... or *bbb*... was sent.

To avoid this situation, it is necessary to consider codes for which there exists a fixed positive integer r such that the first r terms of any admissible sequence uniquely determine the first word of the sentence sent. Clearly, no such integer exists for the code of Example 2. We then call a code α-*decodable with delay at most r* (or simply α-*decodable*) if and only if it has the following property (formulated by Levenshtein [14] for the case $\alpha = \alpha_0$):

(III)   There exists a positive integer r such that for all sequences x of length at least r and for all sentences Y, Z, if $xy \in \alpha(Y)$ and $xz \in \alpha(Z)$ for some sequences y, z then Y and Z have the same first word.

Obviously, if a code is α-decodable with delay at most r, it is also α-decodable with delay at most s, for any integer $s \geqslant r$. Of importance is the smallest integer r for which (III) holds: we call it the α-*decodability delay* of the code. If A has α-decodability delay r, then the decoder has to wait for at most r terms to arrive in order to decode the first word. Hence, if n is its length, then at most n further terms have to be received before the second word may be decoded, and so forth.

Observe that statement (III) concerns α-admissible sequences, not only sentences. This implies that an α-decodable code may be decoded as just described even in the presence of allowable error patterns. We further have:

THEOREM 2. If A is α-decodable with delay at most r, then it is also α-correcting.

For the proof, assume that there exists a sequence u and that $u \in \alpha(X) \cap \alpha(Y)$ for some sentences X, Y; further let V be a sentence such that $v = \hat{V}$ has length at least r. Setting $x = uv$ we then have $x \in \alpha(XV)$

and $x \in \alpha(YV)$. Since v, and hence x, is long enough, our assumption implies that the first words of XV and of YV, and thus those of X and Y, are equal: say $X = aX_1$ and $Y = aY_1$. Since u, $\hat{X}$ and $\hat{Y}$ are equally long, either $X = a = Y$ as required, or else neither X_1 nor Y_1 is empty. In this second case, u has a suffix u_1 such that $u_1 \in \alpha(X_1) \cap \alpha(Y_1)$; setting $x_1 = u_1 v$, we may repeat the reasoning above to prove that X_1 and Y_1 have the same first word. Repeating this process we obtain $X = Y$; hence statement (II) holds and the code is α-correcting.

The concepts of decodability and of decodability delay are illustrated in the next example.

Example 3. Let $A = \{a, b\}$ be the binary code in which $a = 010110$ and $b = 01001101$. It can be shown that A satisfies property (III) with $\alpha = \alpha_1$ and $r = 27$. We prove now that the α_1-decodability delay is itself 27. Indeed, if we examine the first 26 terms of the sequence

$$x = 01001001010001010001101110110110$$

which belongs to $\alpha_1 (bbaa)$ we cannot decide whether the first word sent was a or b.

The question naturally arises of determining 'instantaneous' codes (Abramson [1]), i.e., codes which possess the stronger property of 'word by word' decodability. Such a property can be formulated as follows:

(IV)   For every sentence X, if a sequence of $\alpha(a)$ is a prefix of some sequence in $\alpha(X)$, then a is the first word of X.

We call a code α-*prompt* if and only if it satisfies this statement for a given mapping α, since, at the receiving end, every word sent is recognizable as soon as it has been received with an allowable error pattern. Notice that, in Example 3, $x \in \alpha_1(X)$ if $X = bbaa$; but x has $y = 010010$ as prefix and $y \in \alpha_1 (a)$ though a is not the first word of X.

The two kinds of decodability are related by the following result, the proof of which is immediate.

THEOREM 3. If a code, with largest word length n, is α-prompt, then it is also α-decodable with delay at most n.

The following example shows that the converse does not hold.

Example 4. Let A be the two-word binary code with $a = 01$ and $b = 0110100$. Clearly A is not α_0-prompt since a is a prefix of b; *a fortiori A* will not be α_1-prompt. It is, however, easy to recognize by inspection that A is α_1-decodable with delay at most $6 < n = 7$.

As shown by Abramson [1] when $\alpha = \alpha_0$, a code is 'instantaneous' if and only if it has the 'prefix property'. We have more generally:

THEOREM 4. A code is α-prompt if and only if it satisfies the following statement:

(V)   For any two distinct code words a, b no sequence in $\alpha(a)$ is a prefix of (or has as prefix) a sequence in $\alpha(b)$.

The proof is immediate and is omitted.

Theorem 4 could justify the terminology 'α-prefix code'; we prefer the name α-prompt because it expresses a behavioral rather than a structural property.

Example 5. Let A be the quaternary code consisting of the words $a = 0000$, $b = 01230$, and $c = 10232$, and consider again the admissibility mapping α_1. Clearly A satisfies property (V).

We observe that, in Example 5, b and c have Hamming distance 3. In a natural sense, we could also say that a and b have 'distance' 3 if we compare a with that prefix of b which has the same number of terms as a. This suggests extending the notion of Hamming *distance* by defining it for any pair of sequences to be the number of terms of the shorter sequence which differ from the corresponding terms of the longer sequence. If we denote the distance between x and y by $\rho(x, y)$, we observe that $\rho(x, y) = \rho(y, x)$ and that if x is shorter than y, $\rho(x, y) = \rho(x, y')$ if y' is that prefix of y whose length is equal to the length of x. (See [PML25] for a discussion of the triangle inequality.)

With this notation, any two words of a prefix code satisfy the inequality $\rho(a, b) > 0$. Indeed we have more generally:

THEOREM 5. Given a code A and an admissibility mapping α_v, A is α_v-prompt if and only if the following statement holds:

(VI) $\rho(a, b) > v(a) + v(b)$ for any two distinct words a, b.

An elementary proof consists in showing that (VI) is equivalent to (V) with $\alpha = \alpha_v$. In the particular case in which $v(a) = e$ for every word a, codes verifying (VI) have been said to have distance $d = 2e + 1$ (cf. [PML25]), in conformity with the standard terminology for block codes.

The distinctions between the three notions defined in this section vanish when we restrict our attention to block codes. We have in fact:

THEOREM 6. For a block code, statements I, II, III, IV, and V are equivalent.

Thanks to the equivalences and implications already established, to prove this theorem it is enough to recognize that (II) implies (V) when all words have the same length.

Corollary 7. A block code is α-prompt if and only if it is α-correcting.

Observe that, when $\alpha = \alpha_e$, this corollary reduces, in view of Theorem 5, to the well known statement that a block code corrects up to e errors if and only if it has distance $d = 2e + 1$.

4. SYNCHRONIZABILITY AND COMMA-FREEDOM

For actual communication purposes α-decodable codes, and in particular α-prompt codes, are satisfactory as long as the decoder knows exactly where the sentences start, and also as long as the occurrence of error patterns not corresponding to α-admissible sequences has a negligible effect. The following three examples show that even α-prompt codes are not capable of limiting the influence of unallowable error patterns or of 'synchronization loss'.

Example 6. Let A be the α_0-prompt code whose words are

$$
\begin{array}{ll}
a = 00 & d = 101 \\
b = 010 & e = 111 \\
c = 011 & f = 1001
\end{array}
$$

Space	0000000
E	1000110
T	0100101
A	0010011
O	0001111
I	1100011
N	1010101
S	1001001
R	0110110
H	0101010
L	0011100
D	1110000
U	1101100
C	1011010000
F	1011010111
M	0111001000
W	0111001111
Y	111111111100
G	111111100111
P	1111111100011
B	1111111010101
V	11111110000000
K	11111111101100
X	1111111001001000
J	1111111001001111
Q	11111110100101000
Z	11111110100101111

Fig. 3. This code for the English alphabet is α_1-prompt; that is, every two words have distance at least $3 = 2 \cdot 1 + 1$.

and suppose that we send the sentence $X = ccfbcfbcfb\ldots$. If the first c is received in error as 110, we receive

$$x = 110011100101\underline{0011100101}\ldots$$

with the underlined portion repeating. Since no admissible sequence (in this case: no word, since $\alpha = \alpha_0$) is a prefix of x, we immediately recognize that something is amiss. We can choose between two hypotheses: either x is not the prefix of a received sentence (some previous terms having been lost), or an unallowable error pattern occurred in the first word. Since the lengths of the code words are 2, 3, and 4, there are four trials that we can attempt. First we assume that the first term of x is the last term of a word otherwise lost. Trying then to decode $10011100101\underline{0011100101}\ldots$ we obtain the word f and then exactly the same difficulty arises again. In the second trial, we disregard the first two terms, considered as the end of a word (c or e), or else as the word a incorrectly received. The sequence 0011100101<u>0011100101</u>... is then decoded as $Y = aeadaead$... We cannot accept this as the solution, however, since the third and fourth trials also lead to possible decodings. Indeed 0111001010011100101... yields $X_1 = cf\underline{bcfb}$... (that is, X without the first word) and 11100101<u>0011100101</u>... yields $Y_1 = ea\underline{daead}$... (that is Y without the first word). To decide which of X_1 or Y_1 leads to the correct decoding, we must wait until the end of the transmission.

Example 7. Using again the α_0-prompt code of Example 6, assume now that we send $Z = be\underline{be}$... and receive, because of errors in the first word, $z = 000111\underline{010111}...$. The decoder cannot detect any trouble and starts decoding $U = acd\underline{cd}...$. It is only at the end of the transmission that a discrepancy is discovered.

Example 8. Consider the α_1-prompt, block code A whose words are $a = 0101$ and $b = 1010$. It is capable of correcting up to one error in each word, as long as synchronization is maintained. However, if we send aaa... we may be in trouble if we lose an odd number of terms, even if no error occurs in transmission. Indeed we then receive 10101<u>0</u>... and decode $b\underline{b}b$...

   In all three examples a localized disturbance causes wrong or impossible decoding for arbitrarily long sentences. This happens because arbitrarily long sequences can be decoded as either of two sentences without common 'commas' or 'spaces': no word of one sentence starts where a word of the other begins. Hence we are led to consider codes for which such a situation is impossible. We thus require the ability to determine the beginning of at least one word in any sufficiently long portion of an admissible sequence. We accordingly ask that every such sequence x have a fixed decomposition $x = x_1x_2$ such that whenever a sequence yxz in the range of some sentence X is received, then a word of X starts where x_2 starts. More formally, calling *infix* of a sequence x' any sequence x such that $x' = uxv$ for some (possibily empty) sequences u and v, we consider the following statement:

(VII)   There exists a positive integer t such that every sequence x of
          length at least t, which is an infix of an α-admissible sequence,

has at least one decomposition $x = x_1 x_2$ with the following property: for every pair of sequences y, z such that yxz is α-admissible, each of yx_1 and $x_2 z$ is either α-admissible or empty.

In other words, if we lose synchronization (that is, if we lose the first part y of an admissible sequence yxz), we need only consider the next t terms in order to determine where a word ends and the next begins, without waiting until the whole message is received. This results in the loss of x_1 (besides that of y) and in the resumption of normal decoding with the beginning of x_2. If in addition the code is α correcting, then the decoding of $x_2 z$ is unambiguous.

Given a code A and a mapping α, we then call A *α-synchronizable with delay at most t* (or simply *α-synchronizable*) if and only if it is α-correcting and satisfies statement (VII). When $\alpha = \alpha_0$ this definition is equivalent to that of Levenshtein [14] and probably also to that of Even [10]. Neumann's 'n-definite' codes [23] are all α_0-synchronizable; an example is given in Figure 4. The smallest integer t for which a code satisfies (VII) is called the *α-synchronizability delay* of that code.

Extending a result of [14] we have:

THEOREM 8. *If a code A is α-synchronizable with delay at most t, then it is also α-decodable with delay at most $t+1$.*

For the proof, let x have length at least $t+1$ and assume $xz \in \alpha(Z)$, $xz' \in \alpha(Z')$: we have to prove that Z and Z' have the same first word. Set $x = yx'$ with x' of length t and hence $y \neq \emptyset$; then by synchronizability $x' = x_1 x_2$ with yx_1, $x_2 z$ and $x_2 z'$ admissible. If $yx_1 \in \alpha(Y)$ we have $Y \neq \emptyset$ and (II) then insures that Y is unique and is a prefix of both Z and Z'. Hence the first word of Z and that of Z' are equal, since they are the first word of Y. The theorem is thus established.

Observe that a synchronizable block code has a property much stronger than (VII). Indeed, when all the words are equally long, the knowledge of where one word starts is enough to determine where any other word starts. Of the next two examples, the first shows that this stronger property is not equivalent to (VII); and the second proves that it is not peculiar to block codes.

Space	10
E	010
T	110
A	0010
O	0110
I	1110
N	00010
S	00110
R	01110
H	11110
L	000010
D	000110
U	001110
C	011110
F	111110
M	0000010
W	0000110
Y	0001110
G	0011110
P	0111110
B	1111110
V	00000010
K	00000110
X	00001110
J	00011110
Q	00111110
Z	01111110

Fig. 4.   This code for the English alphabet, due to Neumann [23], is α_0-synchronizable
with delay at most 9.

Example 9. Consider the binary code A whose words are $a = 10$, $b = 101$,
$c = 11101$; Levenshtein's test [14] shows that A is α_0-synchronizable with
delay at most 6. If we consider the sequence $x = 1101101011$, which is
an infix of an α_0-admissible sequence, we observe not only that a word
has to start after the fourth term, but also that that word is a:

$$x = 1101 \mid a \mid 1011.$$

That is, we know even more than is required by the definition of α-syn-
chronizability. However, we still do not have a complete decomposition
into words, since x is an infix of many different sentences, for instance:

    bbaac, with separation after the 1st, 4th, and 6th term of x,

or

    caba, with separation after the 4th, 6th, and 9th term of x.

Example 10. We consider now the code A whose words are $a = 0001011$, $b = 00111001$. By applying Levenshtein's test to $\alpha_1(a) \cup \alpha_1(b)$ we establish that A is α_1-synchronizable with delay at most $t = 23$. Since a differs in three terms from both the prefix and the suffix of b of length 7, whenever we know where one word begins in an admissible sequence, we can determine also where every other word begins, though A is not a block code. To see that no value of t smaller than 23 will do, consider the following 22-term sequence:

$$x = 0000011000100110111001.$$

Then if $y = 00111$ and $z = 011$, we have

$$yxz = 00111000 \vdots 00110001 \vdots 0011011 \vdots 1001011$$

which is in $\alpha(bbaa)$. Now take y' and z' empty to obtain

$$y'xz' = x = 0000011 \vdots 0001001 \vdots 10111001$$

which is in $\alpha(aab)$. Clearly, no decomposition x_1x_2 for x exists which yields admissible sequences yx_1 and x_2z and which is independent of y and z.

One of the interesting features of the last example is the synchronizability delay $t = 23$, suggesting that codes with many words may have quite large values of t. Remember that t not only measures here a waiting period, but also gives an indication of the number of terms (of x_1) to be discarded before achieving synchronization. It is thus important, in parallel to what has been done for decodability, to consider a property of 'prompt synchronizability'. To do so, we could require the decomposition of statement (VII) to be unique for every sequence x for which it exists. This is, however, a very strong requirement. Indeed, if a binary code with such a property has a word ending with a '0' and another starting with a '1', then the sequence $x = 01$ cannot be the infix of any word. Thus every code word has to have the form $11...100...0$. We shall hence weaken our requirement and ask that the decomposition of statement (VII) be unique for every sequence which is 'not too short'. We shall call *proper infix* of a sequence x' any non-empty sequence x such that $x' = uxv$ for some u, v not both empty. We then consider the following statement:

(VIII)   Every sequence x which is an infix of an α-admissible sequence, but not a proper infix of a sequence in the α-range of a code word, has at least one decomposition $x = x_1 x_2$ with the following property: for every pair of sequences y, z such that yxz is α-admissible, each of yx_1 and $x_2 z$ is either α-admissible or empty.

A code satisfying this statement and illustrating the exceptional role of the proper infixes of, say, code words is given in the next example.

Example 11. Let A be the binary code whose words are $a = 01$, $b = 0011$ and $c = 0111$. Using Theorem 9 below it is easy to verify that A satisfies statement (VIII) with $\alpha = \alpha_0$. However, consider the proper infix $x = 01$ of b; it is also a proper infix of c and even $x = a$. Thus x has no decomposition as infix of b, may be decomposed into $x_1 = \emptyset$, $x_2 = 01$ as infix of c, and into $x_1' = 01$, $x_2' = \emptyset$ as (improper) infix of a.

We could now define 'prompt α-synchronizability' as the conjunction of statements (II) and (VIII), and observe that it implies α-synchronizability with delay at most n (the length of the longest word). It seems natural, instead, to consider (VIII) together with the requirement that no sequence $x \in \alpha(a)$, which is to be decoded as a word, should be a proper infix of another sequence $y \in \alpha(b)$ with the same property. Joining this to statement (I) we obtain

(IX)   For any two distinct code words a, b no sequence in $\alpha(a)$ is an infix of a sequence in $\alpha(b)$.

Since this statement immediately implies (V), and hence α-correcting, the conjunction of (VIII) and (IX) is stronger than 'prompt α-synchronizability'. We have also:

THEOREM 9. The conjunction of Statements (VIII) and (IX) is equivalent to the following statement:

(X)   For any three code words a, b, c if a sequence in $\alpha(a)$ is an infix of a sequence x in $\alpha(bc)$, then it is a prefix of x and $a = b$, or else it is a suffix of x and $a = c$.

Let us first show that (VIII) and (IX) imply (X). Assuming $y \in \alpha(a)$ and $x = uyv \in \alpha(bc)$ we know by (IX) that y cannot be a proper infix of a word and hence by (VIII) that u and yv [or uy and v] are admissible or empty. If $u \neq \emptyset$ [or $v \neq \emptyset$] the length of $u[v]$ has to be equal to that of $b[c]$ otherwise we violate (IX): thus $u \in \alpha(b)$ [$v \in \alpha(c)$] and consequently $yv \in \alpha(\iota)$ [$uy \in \alpha(b)$]. But (IX) implies now $v = \emptyset[u = \emptyset]$ and $a = c[a = b]$. If $u = \emptyset$ [$v = \emptyset$] the proof is similar. Thus (VIII) and (IX) imply (X). To prove the converse we first show that (X) implies (IX). Let $x \in \alpha(a)$ and $uxv \in \alpha(b)$, whence also $ux(vx) \in \alpha(ba)$. Since $vx \neq \emptyset$, (X) implies $u \neq \emptyset$ and $a = b$. Thus indeed (IX) holds. To prove (VIII) we assume (X) true but (VIII) false to arrive at a contradiction. If (VIII) is false there are admissible sequences yxz and $y'xz'$ such that however we decompose x into x_1x_2 with yx_1 and x_2z empty or admissible, then $y'x_1$ or x_2z' is neither empty nor admissible. But, since x is not a proper infix of a word, there are decompositions x_1', x_2' such that $y'x_1'$ and $x_2'z'$ are either empty or admissible. For two given decompositions x_1x_2 and $x_1'x_2'$, we may assume without loss of generality that x_1 is longer than x_1' and then $x_1 = x_1'x_1''$ with x_1'' a prefix of x_2'. Now let (see Figure 5) $y'xz' \in \alpha(U'aV')$ with $y'x_1' \in \alpha(U')$ and $yxz \in \alpha(UbcV)$ with $yx_1 \in \alpha(Ub)$; also let $x_0 = x_1''x_2''$ be that prefix of x_2' which belongs to $\alpha(a)$. Because of our assumptions on x_1x_2 and $x_1'x_2'$, x_2'' is not empty; and, because of (IX), x_2'' is strictly shorter than c; hence $x_0 \in \alpha(a)$ is a proper infix of a sequence in $\alpha(bc)$ in violation of (X). The proof is thus completed.

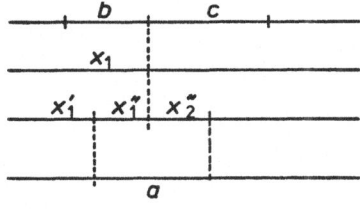

Fig. 5.

Statement (X) becomes very simple when $\alpha = \alpha_0$: if a is an infix of bc: $uav = bc$, then either $a = b$ and $v = c$ or else $u = b$ and $a = c$. That is, no code word is an 'overlap' [13]. Hence, for block codes (X) reduces to the usual definition of comma-freedom [13]. We accordingly call a code α-comma-free if and only if it satisfies statement (X). Summarizing the implications observed in the discussion above, Theorem 9 yields the weaker result:

Corollary 10. If a code, with largest word length n, is α-comma-free, then it is α-synchronizable with delay at most n and is α-prompt.

Since, for a block code, (I) implies (IX), we have also:

Corollary 11. An α-correcting block code is α-comma-free if and only if it satisfies statement (VIII).

If $a = 00001$, $b = 0011011$ and $A = \{a, b\}$, let

α' : admissibility mapping that allows up to two consecutive errors in each word (second example in Figure 2).

α'' : admissibility mapping that allows up to one error in a and up to two consecutive errors in b.

Then A is

not α_2-correcting, but α'-correcting;

not α'-decodable, but α''-decodable with delay at most $r, r \geqslant 11$;

not α''-prompt, but α_1-prompt;

not α_1-synchronizable, but α_0-comma-free.

Fig. 6. Some properties of the binary code consisting of the two words
$a = 00001$, $b = 0011011$.

PART II

THEORETICAL STUDIES

OVERVIEW

Free semigroups are of importance in Coding Theory and Chapter 3 opens with a characterization theorem for free semigroups (Theorem 2.3). Next, certain mappings associated with codes are introduced and studied; all of them occur later in characterization theorems. The two code properties of irredundance and precorrecting are defined and characterized; irredundance in Theorem 4.1 and precorrecting in Theorem 4.2. Another characterization of free semigroups is presented in Theorem 4.3. The code property of correcting is defined and characterized in Theorem 5.1 which gives nine statements equivalent to correcting. Finally, Theorem 5.4 characterizes correcting in terms of correcting for 'short' sentences, a theorem important for algorithms.

Chapter 4 begins with a resumé of work already completed: in the present version, this work encompasses the results given in Chapters 2, 3, 8, and 9. It then passes on to a discussion of the mappings used in Chapter 3 and provides some elementary information about mappings designed to clarify the significance of the particular mappings used in Coding Theory. The notion of an expandable code property, which runs through much of the study, is formally defined and discussed. Then a new theorem (Theorem 3.4) extending the characterization of correcting to seventeen equivalent statements is given. The code properties of pre-decodability and decodability with bounded delay are introduced: the intent being to show that predecodability plus some other property is equivalent to decodability. Theorem 4.7 provides nine statements equivalent to the assertion of decodability one of which involves the expected statement about predecodability. Finally, immediate decodability or promptness is defined and studied together with the notion of preprompt. Theorem 5.1 provides five statements equivalent to the statement that a code is prompt.

The code properties of synchronizability and comma-freedom are treated in Chapter 5. The special character of these properties makes the details more involved and the formulation of the definitions less direct than in the two preceding chapters. The property of presynchronizability is defined and then characterized in Lemma 2.2 and that of synchronizability in Theorem 2.3. This latter theorem gives six equivalent statements. The properties of precomma-freedom and comma-freedom are defined and Theorem 3.1 gives five necessary and sufficient conditions that a code be comma-free.

The characterization of code properties continues in Chapter 6. A generalization of the notion of scansion is used to introduce the concept of an unambiguous set. This latter notion permits a characterization of the code-related properties of irredundance, correctability, decodability, and synchronizability. The approach used is somewhat different from that of Chapters 2, 3, 4, and 5.

Chapter 7 deals with a general rather than a standard model. New definitions for the code properties of decodability and error-limitation are formulated and additional code properties are identified and isolated. The transition from a standard to a general model is discussed first. The idea of a mapping being separating for a binary relation is introduced; Theorem 1.1 and Corollary 1.2 completely characterize this notion. Specialization of these results to codes yields Theorem 2.1, which characterizes correcting in terms of three new code properties. After formulation of the appropriate notions, theorems and corollaries are given which relate the properties of correctability and decodability. The generality of the setting requires the introduction of a number of new concepts.

A detailed study of Levenshtein distance and seven Lemmas about computing such distances are presented. Theorem 6.1 presents the analogue of the Hamming theorem for the case of block codes and the Levenshtein metric. Finally, Theorem 7.1 gives a theorem which generalizes the theorem given in Chapter 11 and provides a sufficient condition for decodability.

CHAPTER 3

A STUDY OF ERROR-CORRECTING CODES, I

L. CALABI AND L. K. ARQUETTE

EDITORIAL NOTE

In his admirably succinct fashion, Russell once defined mathematics as the study of implications and this paper is an example of what he had in mind. The authors, making good on an earlier promise, began a lengthy and detailed investigation of code properties, their characterizations, and implications for a per word model allowing only substitution errors. In this their first report (August 1966), they concentrate on just two properties. Their formal exposition requires the introduction of a variety of new notions, auxiliary results, and technical tools in order to forge the theory. As frequently happens in such activity some of their results can be carried over and applied to one of the fields of pure mathematics, the theory of free semigroups.

1. INTRODUCTION

Several basic properties of variable-length error-correcting codes, along with their interrelationships, have been discussed in [PLM35]. These properties include those of irredundance (which was not given a specific name in [PLM35]), correcting ability, decodability with delay, promptness, synchronizability, and comma freedom. In this report, we begin a more formal and detailed study of these properties and others related to them.

Our results are partly new and partly extensions of known ones. Some are of direct practical interest: e.g., Theorem 5.4, which shows how to determine whether a variable-length code is error-correcting by examining only an appropriate finite set of sequences.

Some of the auxiliary notions introduced and discussed in Section 3 merit mention here: they formalize some essential steps involved in the communication process and provide tools for the development of the theory.

In Section 2 we present background material on sequences in general, and delineate the notation to be employed thereafter. In Section 3, we

W. E. Hartnett (ed.), Foundations of Coding Theory, 41–59. All Rights Reserved.
Copyright © 1974 by D. Reidel Publishing Company, Dordrecht-Holland.

introduce the notions of 'code' and 'admissibility mapping' to provide a formal exposition of error-correcting capability; also introduced are the associated notions of 'scanning mapping', 'correcting mapping', and 'decoding mapping'. In Section 4, we introduce the concept of 'pre-correcting codes', logically prior to that of 'correcting codes'; new results are also obtained in the theory of free semigroups. The notion of 'correcting code' is studied in Section 5.

In a later report, similar detailed studies will be made of the properties of decodability with delay, promptness, synchronizability, and comma-freedom.

2. PRELIMINARIES

We consider a fixed arbitrary set J which we call the *alphabet*, and the elements of which we call *letters*. We denote by $\Sigma(J)$, or simply by Σ, the free semigroup over J. That is, $\Sigma(J)$ is the set of all finite sequences the terms of which are elements of J. The number of terms of a sequence x in Σ is called its *length* and is denoted by $|x|$. If $|x| = 0$, then we call x the *empty sequence* and denote it by $\emptyset$. We denote the set $\Sigma - \{\emptyset\}$ of nonempty sequences by Σ^+.

We employ the notation AB to denote the set of all sequences ab such that $a \in A$ and $b \in B$.

Given a sequence $w = xyz$, we call x a *prefix*, y an *infix*, and z a *suffix* of w. A prefix [resp. suffix] of w which is nonempty and different from w we call a *proper prefix* [resp. *proper suffix*] of w. An infix of w which is neither a prefix nor a suffix, we call a *proper infix* of w.

Given $A \subset \Sigma^+$, we denote by P [resp. S] the set of those sequences in Σ which are prefixes [resp. suffixes] of elements of A. Further, we denote $P \cap S$ by Q; observe that $\emptyset \in Q$. When necessary, we shall write $P(A)$, $S(A)$ and $Q(A)$ instead of P, S and Q respectively.

Any equality

$$sa_1a_2...a_hp = s'b_1b_2...b_kp'$$

in which $s, s' \in S$, $p, p' \in P$, a_i, $b_j \in A$, we call a *relation over A of length* $l = |sa_1a_2...a_hp|$. Moreover we say that the relation is *irreducible* if $s \neq s'$ (except when they are both empty) and $sa_1a_2...a_i \neq s'b_1b_2...b_j$, for every i and j (except when $i = h$, $j = k$ and $p = p' = \emptyset$).

The illustrations of Figure 1 may help visualize these definitions. In Figure 1(a) and Figure 1(b) are represented a reducible and an irreducible relation, respectively. If the relation is irreducible then each a_i is a proper infix of some b_j (Figure 1(c)), or else there is a sequence u which is a proper suffix of a_i and a proper prefix of some b_j which 'partially overlaps' a_i; similarly there is a sequence v which is a prefix of a_i and a suffix of some b_j which 'partially overlaps' a_i (Figure 1(d)).

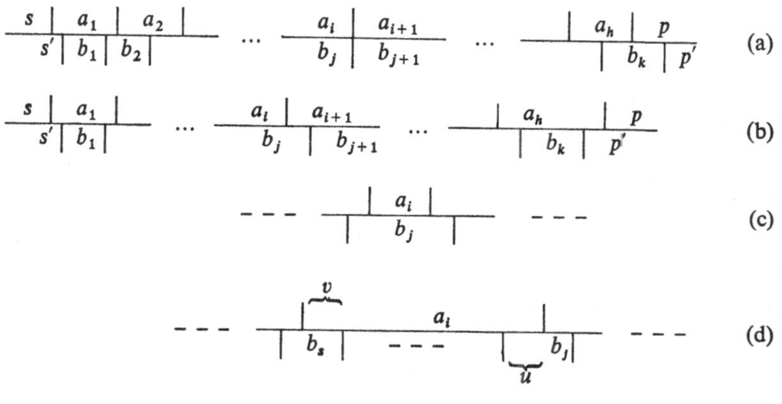

Fig. 1.

Such sequences u, v we call 'links' of the relation. More precisely, assume that, for some sequence $u \in Q$, we have

$$sa_1...a_i \neq s'b_1...b_{j-1}u, \qquad ua_{i+1}...a_hp = b_j...b_kp'$$

[respectively $sa_1...a_{i-1}u = s'b_1...b_j$, $a_i...a_hp = ub_{j+1}...b_kp'$] with $1 \leqslant i \leqslant h$, $1 \leqslant j \leqslant k$; then the triplet (u, a_i, b_j) [resp. (u, b_j, a_i)] is called an *a-link* [resp. *b-link*] of the relation

$$sa_1...a_hp = s'b_1...b_kp';$$

either triplet will be simply called a *link*. Notice that, if the relation is irreducible, the sequence u of an *a*-link (u, a_i, b_j) is a proper suffix of a_i and a proper prefix of b_j; and similarly for *b*-links.

Lemma 2.1. If an irreducible relation has exactly m links, then it has exactly m' *a*-links [resp. *b*-links] where $[\frac{1}{2}m] \leqslant m' \leqslant [\frac{1}{2}(m+1)]$.

Proof. For every b-link (u, b_j, a_i), but possibly for the one having the largest subscript j, there is an a-link (v, a_i, b_j) with the same subscript i. Thus if m'' is the number of b-links, we have $m'' - 1 \leqslant m'$, that is $m - 1 \leqslant 2m'$, establishing the first inequality. By symmetry we then have also, $m - 1 \leqslant 2m''$, or $2m' = 2m - 2m'' \leqslant m + 1$.

Lemma 2.2. Assume that each element of A has length at most n; then an irreducible relation $sa_1...a_h p = s'b_1...b_k p'$ of length $l \geqslant (m+1)(n-1) + \min(|s|, |s'|) + \min(|p|, |p'|) + 1$ has at least m links.

Proof. Let r be the number of links in the given relation and let $u_1, u_2, ..., u_r$ be the sequences of Q appearing in them, in the order of their occurrence (see Figure 2). As already observed, for each $i < r$, u_i and u_{i+1} belong to the same sequence a or b, that is, they are contained within an interval of length n. And since $|u_{i+1}| \geqslant 1$, we have $l \leqslant (r-1)(n-1) + n_0 + n_1$ where the numbers n_0, n_1 are defined as follows: n_0 is the length of the prefix preceding u_1, and n_1 is the sum of $|u_r|$ and of the length of the suffix following u_r. It is easy to see that $n_1 \leqslant n + \min(|p|, |p'|)$, and similaily $n_0 \leqslant n + \min(|s|, |s'|) - |u_1| \leqslant n + \min(|s|, |s'|) - 1$. Consequently

$$(m+1)(n-1) + \min(|s|, |s'|) + \min(|p|, |p'|) + 1$$
$$\leqslant l \leqslant (r-1)(n-1) + n + \min(|s|, |s'|) - 1 + n + \min(|p|, |p'|).$$

Simplifying, we obtain $m \leqslant r$, as desired.

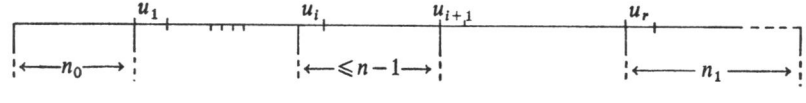

Fig. 2.

THEOREM 2.3. Assume that every element of A has length at most n and that the set Q has q elements. Then the subsemigroup Γ of Σ generated by A is free if and only if there are no irreducible relations over A

$$a_1 a_2 ... a_h = b_1 b_2 ... b_k$$

of length $l \leqslant (q+1)(n-1)$.

Proof. Clearly if Γ is free, then no such relations exist. If Γ is not free, then there are irreducible relations. If one of them, say

$$a_1 a_2 \ldots a_h = b_1 b_2 \ldots b_k$$

is of length $l \geqslant (q+1)(n-1)+1$, then we apply Lemma 2.2 with $m = q$. But there are only $q-1$ non-void elements in Q. Thus, the same sequence u appears in two links and we have, say, either (Figure 3(a))

$$a_1 a_2 \ldots a_{i-1} u v a_{i+1} \ldots a_{r-1} u v' a_{r+1} \ldots a_h = b_1 \ldots b_j b_{j+1} \ldots b_s b_{s+1} \ldots b_k$$
$$a_1 \ldots a_{i-1} u = b_1 \ldots b_j$$
$$v a_{i+1} \ldots a_r u = b_{j+1} \ldots b_s$$

or else (Figure 3(b))

$$a_1 a_2 \ldots a_{i-1} u v a_{i+1} \ldots a_r a_{r+1} \ldots a_h = b_1 \ldots b_j b_{j+1} \ldots b_{s-1} u v' b_{s+1} \ldots b_k$$
$$a_1 \ldots a_{i-1} u = b_1 \ldots b_j$$
$$v a_{i+1} \ldots a_r = b_{j+1} \ldots b_{s-1} u.$$

In the first case we obtain

$$a_1 a_2 \ldots a_{i-1} u v' a_{r+1} \ldots a_h = b_1 \ldots b_j b_{s+1} \ldots b_k$$

and in the second

$$a_1 \ldots a_{i-1} u v' b_{s+1} \ldots b_k = b_1 \ldots b_j a_{r+1} \ldots a_h;$$

in either case, a shorter relation that is easily shown irreducible. Thus, if Γ is not free, we have irreducible relations of length $l \leqslant (q+1)(n-1)$ and the theorem is established.

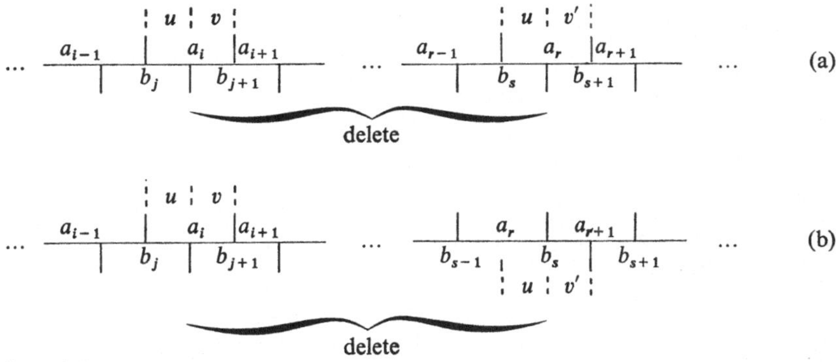

Fig. 3.

A similar result has been stated by A. A. Markov [20] but his proof is incomplete. Another proof of our theorem, with a different bound, may be easily obtained from the work of Levenshtein [15] (see also [PLM34]). The aim of these theorems, as well as of Theorems 3.5 and 5.4 below, is to determine a property of an infinite set (in our case, Γ) by the examination of a finite subset (in our case, the subset of those sequences of Γ of length not more than $(q+1)(n-1)$). In a later report, Lemmas 2.1 and 2.2 will provide the key for other important results.

Beside the subsemigroup $\Gamma = \Gamma(A)$ of Theorem 2.3, to every subset A of Σ^+ we can associate also the free semigroup $\Sigma(A)$ it generates. The elements of $\Sigma(A)$ we call *sentences over A*; they are sequences $X = (a_1, a_2, ..., a_k)$ of *words* $a_i \in A$. To each such sentence X we associate an element $\hat{X}$ of Γ, called the *train* of the sentence and defined by $\hat{X} = a_1 a_2 ... a_k$. Note that the mapping $X \to \hat{X}$ is that homomorphism of $\Sigma(A)$ onto $\Gamma(A)$ determined by $(a) \to a$ for each $a \in A$. Henceforth we identify $(a) \in \Sigma(A)$ with $a \in A \subset \Gamma(A)$. The *length* $|X|$ of a sentence is the number of its terms (i.e., words); its *span* is defined to be the length $|\hat{X}|$ of X.

We remark that definitions and results concerning sequences of Σ hold for sequences of any free semigroup; in particular, they hold for sentences in $\Sigma(A)$. We have also:

Lemma 2.4. Given a set $A \subset \Sigma^+$ and sentences $W, X, Y, Z \in \Sigma(A)$, assume $XY = ZW$ and $|\hat{X}| \leqslant |\hat{Z}|$; then X is a prefix of Z.
Proof. Assuming $XY = ZW$ and $|\hat{X}| \leqslant |\hat{Z}|$, suppose $|Z| < |X|$. Then by the cancellation law of free semigroups, Z is a prefix of X whence every word in Z is a word in X so that $|\hat{Z}| \leqslant |\hat{X}|$. But if $|\hat{Z}| = |\hat{X}|$, then also $|Z| = |X|$. Thus $|\hat{Z}| < |\hat{X}|$, contradicting the hypothesis. Therefore $|X| \leqslant |Z|$ whence X is a prefix of Z.

In comparing sentences it is very important to have ways of comparing the 'positions of their commas', that is, to compare the lengths of their words. Formally, given sets A, B and sentences $X \in \Sigma(A)$, $Y \in \Sigma(B)$, we say that X *prematches* Y iff for each $X_1, X_2 \in \Sigma(A)$ with $X = X_1 X_2$, there exist $Y_1, Y_2 \in \Sigma(B)$ with $Y = Y_1 Y_2$ such that $|\hat{X}_1| = |\hat{Y}_1|$, $|\hat{X}_2| = |\hat{Y}_2|$.

To illustrate let $A = \{a_1, a_2\}$ and $B = \{b_1, b_2, b_3\}$ satisfy $|a_1| = 4$, $|a_2| = 6$, $|b_1| = 2$, $|b_2| = 3$ and $|b_3| = 4$. Then $X = (a_1, a_2, a_2, a_1)$ prematches $Y = (b_1, b_1, b_2, b_1, b_2, b_2, b_2)$. We have:

Lemma 2.5. Let $X = (a_1, ..., a_r) \in \Sigma(A)$ and $Y \in \Sigma(B)$; then X prematches Y iff there exist $Y_1, Y_2, ..., Y_r \in \Sigma(B)$ such that $Y = Y_1 Y_2 ... Y_r$ and $|a_i| = |\hat{Y}_i|$, $i = 1, ..., r$.

The proof, by induction on $|X|$, is straightforward and is omitted. The proofs of the following two corollaries are immediate.

Corollary 2.6. If $X \in \Sigma(A)$ prematches $Y \in \Sigma(B)$, then $|X| \leqslant |Y|$.

Corollary 2.7. Given sets $A, B \subset \Sigma^+$ and sentences $X_1, X_2 \in \Sigma(A)$, $Y \in \Sigma(B)$; if $X_1 X_2$ prematches Y, then there exist $Y_1, Y_2 \in \Sigma(B)$ with $Y = Y_1 Y_2$ such that X_1 prematches Y_1 and X_2 prematches Y_2.

Given sets $A, B \subset \Sigma^+$ and sentences $X \in \Sigma(A)$, $Y \in \Sigma(B)$, we say that X *matches* Y iff X prematches Y and Y prematches X. By Lemma 2.5, it immediately follows that $X = (a_1, ..., a_r)$ matches $Y = (b_1, ..., b_s)$ iff $r = s$ and $|a_i| = |b_i|$ for $i = 1, ..., r$.

It is convenient to call *uniform* a set $A \subset \Sigma$ iff $|a| = |b|$ for every $a, b \in A$. We then have:

Lemma 2.8. Let $A_i, B_i \subset \Sigma^+, i = 1, 2, ..., r$, with $A_1 A_2 ... A_r \cap B_1 B_2 ... B_r \neq \emptyset$. If $A_i \cup B_i$ is uniform, then $A_i \cap B_i \neq \emptyset$, for each i.

Proof. Assuming the hypotheses, there exists $z \in \Sigma^+$ such that $z \in A_1 A_2 ... A_r$, $z \in B_1 B_2 ... B_r$, whence $z = a_1 a_2 ... a_r = b_1 b_2 ... b_r$ with $a_i \in A_i$, $b_i \in B_i$ for $i = 1, 2, ..., r$. By the uniformity of $A_1 \cup B_1$, $|a_1| = |b_1|$ when $a_1 = b_1$ so that $A_1 \cap B_1 \neq \emptyset$; moreover, $a_2 a_3 ... a_r = b_2 b_3 ... b_r$ by the cancellation property of the free semigroup Σ. Repeating this reasoning, we find $a_2 = b_2$ when $A_2 \cap B_2 \neq \emptyset$; continuing in this manner, we find $A_i \cap B_i \neq \emptyset$ for $i = 1, 2, ..., r$.

3. MAPPINGS ASSOCIATED WITH A CODE

We now turn our attention to Coding Theory proper. First, we define the notion of 'admissibility mapping'; recall from [PML35] that this mapping associates to each sentence X all those sequences which, when received, are to be interpreted, or decoded, as X.

Given a set $A \subset \Sigma^+$, a (set-valued) mapping α of $\Sigma(A)$ into 2^Σ is called an *admissibility mapping* (*on* $\Sigma(A)$) iff the following properties hold for arbitrary $x \in \Sigma$, a, $b \in A$ and X, $Y \in \Sigma(A)$:

(A1) $\hat{X} \in \alpha(X)$.

(A2)   If $x \in \alpha(X)$, then $|x| = |\hat{X}|$; i.e., $\alpha(X)$ is uniform.

(A3)   If $\alpha(a) \cap \alpha(b) \neq \emptyset$, then $a = b$.

(A4) $\alpha(XY) = \alpha(X)\alpha(Y)$.

Since 2^{Σ} is itself a semigroup (with the operation $(A, B) \to AB$) (A4) states that α is a homomorphism of $\Sigma(A)$ into 2^{Σ}. Hence it is uniquely determined by its values on the generating set A. Observe that, for any $A \subset \Sigma^{+}$, the mapping $\iota: \Sigma(A) \to 2^{\Sigma}$ defined by $\iota(X) = \{\hat{X}\}$ is an admissibility mapping.

Slightly modifying the terminology of our previous report [PML35], we call *code* a pair (A, α) where $A \subset \Sigma^{+}$ and α is an admissibility mapping on $\Sigma(A)$. If $\alpha = \iota$, the code is called *simple* and we often identify (A, ι) with A and $\iota(X) = \{\hat{X}\}$ with $\hat{X}$. The set $\alpha(X)$ we call the α-*range* (or simply *range*) of the sentence X. The set $E = \bigcup \{\alpha(a) \,|\, a \in A\}$ (or the pair (E, ι)) we call the *expanded code* of (A, α) and the elements of $\Omega = \bigcup \{\alpha(X) \,|\, X \in \Sigma(A)\}$ we call *admissible sequences* for (A, α) (when necessary we write $E(A, \alpha)$ and $\Omega(A, \alpha)$ instead of E and Ω, respectively).

Lemma 3.1. $\Omega(A, \alpha) = \Gamma(E)$.
Proof. Let $z \in \Omega$; that is, $z \in \alpha(a_1)\alpha(a_2)...\alpha(a_r)$ for some $(a_1, ..., a_r) \in \Sigma(A)$. Thus $z = z_1 z_2 ... z_r$ with $z_i \in \alpha(a_i) \subset E$ and $z = \hat{U}$ if $U = (z_1, z_2, ..., z_r)$. But $\hat{U} \in \Gamma(E)$, so that $z \in \Gamma(E)$ whence $\Omega \subset \Gamma(E)$. Conversely, let $z \in \Gamma(E)$. Then $z = \hat{U}$ for some $U \in \Sigma(E)$; that is, $z = z_1 z_2 ... z_r$ with $z_i \in \alpha(a_i)$ for some $a_i \in A$. If $X = (a_1, ..., a_r) \in \Sigma(A)$, then $z \in \alpha(X)$ and $\alpha(X) \subset \Omega$. Therefore $z \in \Omega$ whence $\Gamma(E) \subset \Omega$. It follows that $\Omega = \Gamma(E)$.

This result will be used often without explicit mention.

We denote by E_0 the maximal subset of E the elements of which are not products of two or more elements of Ω: it is the only minimal generating set for the subsemigroup Ω of Σ (cf. [18]). By the definition, for each $c \in E$ there exists a unique $a \in A$ with $c \in \alpha(a)$. (Note that if $c \notin E_0$, then there also exists $X \in \Sigma(A)$ with $X \notin A$, such that $c \in \alpha(X)$.) This mapping of E onto A can be extended to a unique homomorphism γ of $\Sigma(E)$ into $\Sigma(A)$ called the *correcting homomorphism for* (A, α). Then by construction, for any $U \in \Sigma(E)$, we have $\hat{U} \in \alpha\gamma(U)$ and U matches $\gamma(U)$. Moreover:

Lemma 3.2. Given $X \in \Sigma(A)$ and $z \in \alpha(X)$, there exists $U \in \Sigma(E)$ such that $z = \hat{U}$ and $\gamma(\bar{U}) = X$.

Proof. Let $X = (a_1, a_2, ..., a_r)$, and let $z \in \alpha(X)$. Then $z \in \alpha(a_1)\alpha(a_2)...\alpha(a_r)$ whence $z = z_1 z_2 ... z_r$, $z_i \in \alpha(a_i)$. Consequently, $z_i \in E$, and $\gamma(z_i) = a_i$. Therefore $(z_1, z_2, ..., z_r) \in \Sigma(E)$; call it U. By construction, $z = \hat{U}$, and $\gamma(U) = X$.

A mapping [resp. homomorphism] $\delta: \Omega \to \Sigma(A)$ is called a *decoding mapping* [resp. *homomorphism*] *for* (A, α) iff $x \in \alpha(\delta(x))$ for each $x \in \Omega$. A decoding mapping σ for (E, ι) is called a *scanning mapping* for (A, α). We observe that the notions of scanning and decoding mappings coincide for simple codes.

The overall decoding procedure is explainable in terms of the mappings just introduced. Suppose a received sequence z is admissible (i.e., $z \in \Omega$). The scanning mapping σ then assigns separations ('commas') among the letters of z thereby breaking it up into words of E; that is, $\sigma(z)$ is a sentence of $\Sigma(E)$. Next, the correcting homomorphism γ associates to $\sigma(z)$ a sentence in $\Sigma(A)$ which contains z in its α-range. The decoding mapping δ is the composition $\gamma\sigma$ (see Lemma 3.3 below): thus $\delta(z) = \gamma\sigma(z)$ is the 'decoded version' of z, obtained by first dividing z into words of E (that is words possibly with errors), then by correcting these into words of A.

The relations between the various mappings are given in Figure 4.

Lemma 3.3. To every decoding [resp. scanning] mapping δ [resp. σ] for (A, α) there corresponds a scanning [resp. decoding] mapping σ [resp. δ] such that $\delta = \gamma\sigma$.

Proof. Given δ, we define σ using Lemma 3.2. That is, for $z \in \Omega$, we let $\sigma(z) = U$, if $\hat{U} = z$ and $\gamma(U) = \delta(z)$. For the other statement, given σ we let $\delta = \gamma\sigma$: then $z = \widehat{\sigma(z)} \in \alpha\gamma\sigma(z) = \alpha\delta(z)$, showing that δ is a decoding mapping.

Corollary 3.4. Let δ, δ' be any two decoding mappings for (A, α). Then the following statements hold:

(a) $\delta(E_0) \subset A$.

(b)   For each $x \in E_0$, $\delta(x) = \delta'(x)$.

Proof. These statements are immediate for scanning mappings (or decoding mappings for E); for decoding mappings for (A, α), they follow then from Lemma 3.3.

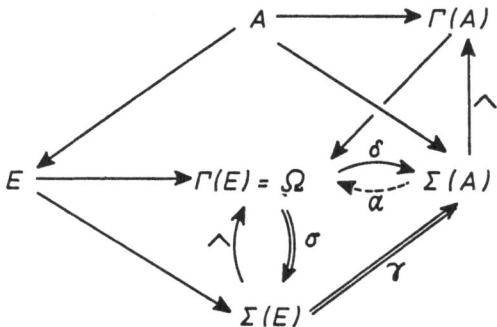

unlabelled arrows: inclusion mappings
$- - - \rightarrow$: multivalued correspondence
$\Longrightarrow$: the two decoding steps

Fig. 4. Diagram of mappings.

We observe that if $x \in E \backslash E_0$, then there exist decoding mappings δ, δ' such that $\delta(x) \neq \delta'(x)$. Therefore E_0 is the maximal subset of E on which all decoding mappings for (A, α) agree.

THEOREM 3.5. Given the code (A, α), assume that every element of A has length at most n and that the set $Q(E)$ has q elements. Then the following statements are equivalent:

(1)   There exists only one decoding mapping for (A, α).

(2)   There exists only one scanning mapping for (A, α).

(3)   All decoding mappings for (A, α) agree on every $x \in \Omega$ with $|x| \leqslant (q+1)(n-1)$.

(4)   All scanning mappings for (A, α) agree on every $x \in \Omega$ with $|x| \leqslant (q+1)(n-1)$.

Proof. The equivalences $(1) \Leftrightarrow (2)$ and $(3) \Leftrightarrow (4)$ follow from Lemma 3.3. To prove the equivalence $(2) \Leftrightarrow (4)$, observe that it σ, σ' are two scanning mappings and $U = \sigma(z) \neq \sigma'(z) = V$, then $\hat{U} = z = \hat{V}$ is a relation over E. Theorem 2.3 then completes the proof.

The importance of the preceding theorem becomes evident when we remember that a (simple) code may be used over a noiseless channel only if it is 'uniquely decipherable', that is if it admits only one decoding mapping. This remains true for codes (A, α) on noisy channels (cf. Theorem 5.1 below). As we shall see, the existence of a decoding, or scanning, homomorphism is a weaker requirement. Note also that if δ, or σ, is a homomorphism, then it is enough to know its values for the elements of E_0 (since these elements generate Ω); otherwise, it is in general necessary to have a decoding book of infinite size.

Lemma 3.6. Let δ be a decoding homomorphism for (A, α) and let $Y \in \Sigma(A)$. If $x \in \alpha(Y)$, then Y prematches $X = \delta(x)$.
Proof. Let $Y = (b_1, b_2, ..., b_r)$. Then $x = x_1 x_2 ... x_r$, $x_i \in \alpha(b_i)$, $i \in N_r$. Denoting $\delta(x_i)$ by X_i, we have $\delta(x) = X = X_1 X_2 ... X_r$, since δ is a homomorphism. Since $x_i \in \alpha(b_i)$, $|b_i| = |x_i| = |\hat{X}_i|$ by (A2); it follows that Y prematches X.

Lemma 3.7. For every $X, Y \in \Sigma(A)$, if X matches Y and $\alpha(X) \cap \alpha(Y) \neq \emptyset$ then $X = Y$.
Proof. If X matches Y, then $X = (a_1, a_2, ..., a_r)$, $Y = (b_1, b_2, ..., b_r)$ with $|a_i| = |b_i|$; thus $\alpha(a_i) \cup \alpha(b_i)$ is uniform for each i. Hence if $\alpha(a_1)\alpha(a_2)...\alpha(a_r) \cap \alpha(b_1)\alpha(b_2)...\alpha(b_r) \neq \emptyset$, then $\alpha(a_i) \cap \alpha(b_i) \neq \emptyset$ by Lemma 2.8, whence $a_i = b_i$ by (A3); therefore $X = Y$.

These two lemmas yield immediately:

THEOREM 3.8. There exists at most one decoding homomorphism δ for (A, α). If it exists, then $\delta(x)$ is the unique sentence in $\Sigma(A)$ which is prematched by every $Y \in \Sigma(A)$ for which $x \in \alpha(Y)$.

In Theorem 4.1 below we shall see that the existence of a decoding homomorphism is equivalent to that of a scanning homomorphism; and that both exist if and only if Ω is a free semigroup.

4. IRREDUNDANT AND PRECORRECTING CODES

We turn now to a detailed study of some properties of codes which have been introduced in [PML35], to which we refer for interpretative discussions.

We call a code (A, α) *irredundant* iff the following statement holds:

(IR1)   For each $z \in E$ there exists a unique $X \in \Sigma(A)$ such that $z \in \alpha(X)$.

If $\alpha = \iota$, and then $E = A$, this statement may be formulated as follows: no word a in A is the product of other words of A.

THEOREM 4.1. Given a code (A, α), the following statements are equivalent:

(IR1) (A, α) is irredundant.
(IR2) E (i.e., (E, ι)) is irredundant.
(IR3) $E = E_0$.
(IR4)   All decoding mappings for (A, α) agree on E.
(IR5)   All scanning mappings for (A, α) agree on E.
(IR6)   If $a \in A$, $X \in \Sigma(A)$, and $\alpha(a) \cap \alpha(X) \neq \emptyset$, then $X = a$.

Proof. Suppose (IR2) false. Then there exist $U \in \Sigma(E)$ and $z \in E$ such that $U \notin E$ but $\hat{U} = z$. It follows that $z \in \alpha \gamma(U) \cap \alpha \gamma(z)$. Since $\gamma(U)$ matches U, and $\gamma(z)$ matches z, but U does not match z so $\gamma(U) \neq \gamma(z)$ and (IR1) is false, proving (IR1) $\Rightarrow$ (IR2).

If E is irredundant, then every $z \in E$ is the train of a unique $U \in \Sigma(E)$; this U must equal z. Therefore no word in E is the train of a sentence in $\Sigma(E)$ of length greater than one so that $E = E_0$ proving (IR2) $\Rightarrow$ (IR3).

That (IR3) $\Rightarrow$ (IR4) is an immediate consequence of Corollary 3.4.

To prove the implication (IR4) $\Rightarrow$ (IR6), let $z \in \alpha(a) \cap \alpha(X)$; then there exists a decoding mapping δ for which $\delta(z) = a$ and another δ' for which $\delta'(z) = X$. But $z \in E$ and thus by (IR4), $X = a$; this proves (IR4) $\Rightarrow$ (IR6).

To prove (IR6) $\Rightarrow$ (IR1), assume $z \in E$ and $z \in \alpha(X)$. Then there is also $a \in A$ with $z \in \alpha(a)$. By (IR6), then $X = a$. That is, from (IR6) and $z \in E$, follows that there is but one $X \in \Sigma(A)$ (namely $a \in A$) with $z \in \alpha(X)$, proving (IR6) $\Rightarrow$ (IR1).

So far, we have proved all statements equivalent excepting (IR5). In particular, (IR1) $\Leftrightarrow$ (IR4); applying this result to (IR2) and (IR5), we see that (IR2) $\Leftrightarrow$ (IR5) since every decoding mapping on a simple code such as E is also a scanning mapping, and conversely.

The equivalence of statements (IR1) and (IR2) is of especial significance: it asserts that the property of irredundance of a code (A, α), which is designed to combat errors in a noisy communications channel, can be studied in terms of the property of irredundance of a code (viz., (E, ι)) which is used for a noiseless channel. It will be seen below that analogous equivalences hold for the properties of precorrecting and correcting.

We call a code (A, α) *precorrecting* iff the following statement holds:

(PC1)   For each $z \in \Omega$ there exists $X \in \Sigma(A)$ with $z \in \alpha(X)$, such that if $Y \in \Sigma(A)$ with $z \in \alpha(Y)$, then Y prematches X.

We observe that the sentence X in the above statement is unique, due to Lemma 3.7.

THEOREM 4.2. Given a code (A, α), the following statements are equivalent:

(PC1) (A, α) is precorrecting.
(PC2) E is precorrecting.
(PC3)   There exists a scanning homomorphism for (A, α).
(PC4)   There exists a decoding homomorphism for (A, α).
(PC5)   If $x \in \Sigma$, $x\Omega \cap \Omega \neq \emptyset$, and $\Omega x \cap \Omega \neq \emptyset$, then $x \in \Omega$.
(PC6)   If $x \in \Sigma$, $X \in \Sigma(A)$, $x\alpha(X) \cap \Omega \neq \emptyset$, and $\alpha(X)x \cap \Omega \neq \emptyset$, then $x \in \Omega$.
(PC7)   If $x \in \Sigma$, $y \in \Omega$, $xy \in \Omega$, and $yx \in \Omega$, then $x \in \Omega$.
(PC8)   If $x \in \Sigma$ and $x\Omega \cap \Omega x \cap \Omega \neq \emptyset$, then $x \in \Omega$.
(PC9)   If $x \in \Sigma$, $y \in \Sigma$, $xy \in \Omega$, $yx \in \Omega$, and $(xy)^r x \in \Omega$ for some non-negative integer r, then $x \in \Omega$.
(PC10) Ω is a free semigroup.
(PC11)   If $X \in \Sigma(A)$, $Y \in \Sigma(A)$ and $\alpha(X) \cap \alpha(Y) \neq \emptyset$, then there exists $Z \in \Sigma(A)$ such that X and Y each prematch Z, and $\alpha(X) \cap \alpha(Y) \cap \alpha(Z) \neq 0$.

Proof. We prove the theorem by establishing the following implications:

$$(PC1) \Rightarrow (PC2) \Rightarrow (PC3) \Rightarrow (PC4) \Rightarrow (PC5) \Rightarrow (PC6) \Rightarrow (PC7) \Rightarrow (PC8) \Leftrightarrow (PC9)$$

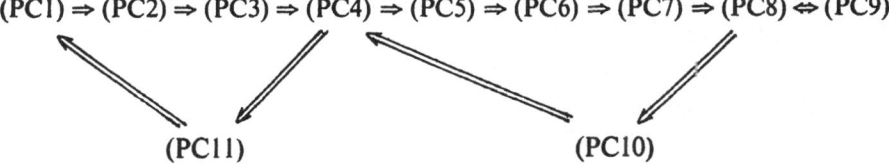

(PC11)   (PC10)

To prove the first implication, let $z \in \Omega$ and $X \in \Sigma(A)$ with $z \in \alpha(X)$ be that sentence which is prematched by all those Y having z in their ranges.

By Lemma 3.2 there exists $U \in \Sigma(E)$, matching X, with $\hat{U} = z$; if $V \in \Sigma(E)$ is such that $\hat{V} = z$, then $Y = \gamma(V)$ has z in its range and hence prematches X. But V matches Y and consequently it will prematch U, establishing (PC2).

Assuming (PC2), for $z \in \Omega$ let $\sigma(z)$ be that sentence $U \in \Sigma(E)$ which satisfies $z = \hat{U}$ and which is prematched by every $V \in \Sigma(E)$ for which $z = \hat{V}$. Clearly, σ is a scanning mapping; we wish to show that it is also a homomorphism. For $x, y \in \Omega$ we let $\sigma(x) = X$, $\sigma(y) = Y$, and $\sigma(xy) = Z$. But $xy = \widehat{XY}$ so that XY prematches Z. Then $Z = Z_1 Z_2$ and X, Y prematch Z_1, Z_2 respectively by Corollary 2.7. Further $\hat{X} = \hat{Z}_1$, $\hat{Y} = \hat{Z}_2$ and then Z_1, Z_2 prematch X, Y; by Lemma 3.7, then, $X = Z_1$, $Y = Z_2$, proving (PC2) $\Rightarrow$ (PC3).

That (PC3) $\Rightarrow$ (PC4) follows directly from Lemma 3.3.

Assuming (PC4), let $xy \in \alpha(U)$, $zx \in \alpha(V)$, with $y \in \alpha(Y)$, $z \in \alpha(Z)$. To show $x \in \Omega$, we can assume $Y = \delta(y)$, $Z = \delta(z)$, $U = \delta(xy)$, $V = \delta(zx)$, where δ is a decoding homomorphism. Then $ZU = \delta(z) \delta(xy) = \delta(zxy) = \delta(zx) \delta(y) = VY$. Since $|\hat{Z}| < |\hat{V}|$, by Lemma 2.4 $V = ZX$ for some $X \in \Sigma(A)$; therefore $x \in \alpha(X) \subset \Omega$ (and in fact, $X = \delta(x)$), proving (PC4) $\Rightarrow$ (PC5).

The implications (PC5) $\Rightarrow$ (PC6) $\Rightarrow$ (PC7) are immediate; and the equivalence of (PC7), (PC8) and (PC10) are well known (cf. [26], [24], [8]).

Let xy, yx, $(xy)^r x \in \Omega$ whence $(xy)^r$, $(yx)^r \in \Omega$ for r a nonnegative integer. Now $(xy)^r x = x(yx)^r$ so that $\Omega \cap x\Omega \cap \Omega x \neq \emptyset$; by (PC8), $x \in \Omega$; proving (PC8) $\Rightarrow$ (PC9).

To prove (PC9) $\Rightarrow$ (PC8), we let $x\Omega \cap \Omega x \cap \Omega \neq \emptyset$, so that $xu = vx \in \Omega$ with $u, v \in \Omega$. Then, using Lemma 2 of [19], $x = (yz)^r y$ with $v = yz$, $u = zy$ for some $y, z \in \Sigma$ and nonnegative integer r. By (PC9), $y \in \Omega$ so that $v^r y = x \in \Omega$; this proves (PC9) $\Rightarrow$ (PC8).

Assuming (PC10) we now establish (PC4): we have that Ω is a free semigroup over E_0. Let then δ be the unique homomorphism which extends to Ω the mapping of E_0 into $\Sigma(A)$ which is the common restriction of all decoding mappings. If $z = z_1 z_2 ... z_r$, $z_i \in E_0$, then $\delta(z) = \delta(z_1) \delta(z_2) ... \delta(z_r)$ and $z_i \in \alpha \delta(z_i)$ so that $z \in \alpha \delta(z)$ whence δ is a decoding homomorphism. This proves (PC10) $\Rightarrow$ (PC4).

Assuming (PC4), let $z \in \alpha(X) \cap \alpha(Y)$ and let $Z = \delta(z)$, where δ is the homomorphism of (PC4). Then, by Lemma 3.6, X, Y each prematch Z and $z \in \alpha(Z) \cap \alpha(X) \cap \alpha(Y)$ This proves (PC4) $\Rightarrow$ (PC11).

Finally, we assume (PC11). Let $z \in \Omega$ and let $X_1, X_2, ..., X_r$ be those sentences for which $z \in \alpha(X_i)$, ordered so that $|X_i| \leqslant |X_{i+1}|$. By (PC11), for each i, there exists $X_{\varphi(i)}$ prematched by X_i and X_r. By Corollary 2.6, $|X_{\varphi(i)}| \geqslant |X_r|$ so that $X_{\varphi(i)} = X_r$, whence X_r is prematched by X_i for all $i = 1, 2, ..., r-1$. This proves (PC11) $\Rightarrow$ (PC1).

The equivalence between (PC9) and (PC10) is a new characterization of free subsemigroups of a free semigroup. The equivalence between (PC3), or (PC4), and (PC10) is a consequence also of the next theorem in which we prove that a semigroup is free if and only if it is projective.

THEOREM 4.3. Given a semigroup S, the following three statements are equivalent:

(1) S is free.
(2)   To every semigroup T and homomorphism f of T onto S there corresponds a homomorphism g of S into T such that fg is the identity mapping on S.
(3)   To some free semigroup T and homomorphism f of T onto S there corresponds a homomorphism g of S into T such that fg is the identity mapping on S.

Proof. The implication $(1) \Rightarrow (2)$ is a particular case of a well-known general result. To prove it in our context, define g' on the minimal generating set G of S so as to satisfy $fg' =$ identity mapping on G; by freedom, extend g' to a homomorphism g of S into T. Such g satisfies then the requirement of (2).

The implication $(2) \Rightarrow (3)$ is immediate. To complete the proof of the theorem, we assume (3) and observe that S is then isomorphic to the subsemigroup $g(S)$ of T. Statement (1) is then established by showing that from $ab = cd$ in S it follows that, in S, a is a left divisor of c or c is a left divisor of a (see e.g. [8]). Since $g(a)g(b) = g(c)g(d)$ in T and T is free, then, say, $g(a) = g(c)x$ with $x \in T$ and thus $a = cf(x)$ in S.

If (A, α) is precorrecting, it does not necessarily follow that the simple code (A, ι) is precorrecting. In fact, suppose $A = \{a, b, c, d\}$ where

$a = 01$	$\alpha(a) = \{01, 11\}$
$b = 10$	$\alpha(b) = \{10\}$
$c = 0111$	$\alpha(c) = \{0111\}$
$d = 1110;$	$\alpha(d) = \{1110, 0000\}.$

Then (A, ι) is not precorrecting: consider the ι-admissible sequence $011110 = ad = cb$; neither of the sentences $(a, d), (c, b)$ prematches the other. Nevertheless, (A, α) is precorrecting, since Ω is free over $E_0 = \{01, 10, 11, 0000\}$. This result may also be formulated by saying that the freedom of Ω does not imply that of Γ.

Examples in which Γ is free but Ω is not are easily come by; the case in which both are free, over A and over $E_0 = E$ respectively, is studied in the next section. Intermediate situations, in which Γ and Ω are free over subsets of A and E, respectively, may be of interest in a study of 'dictionaries with compound words'.

5. CORRECTING CODES

We call a code (A, α) *correcting* iff the following statement holds:

(C1)   For each $z \in \Omega$ there exists a unique $X \in \Sigma(A)$ such that $z \in \alpha(X)$.

Notice that, if $\alpha = \iota$, this statement reduces to the usual definition of *unique decipherability*. In our notation: for each $z \in \Omega$ there is one and only one sentence X such that $z = \hat{X}$.

THEOREM 5.1. Given a code (A, α), the following statements are equivalent:

(C1) (A, α) is correcting.
(C2) E is uniquely decipherable.
(C3)   There exists only one scanning mapping for (A, α).
(C4)   There exists only one decoding mapping for (A, α).
(C5)   There exists a decoding homomorphism δ for (A, α) such that if $X \in \Sigma(A)$ and $x \in \alpha(X)$, then $\delta(x) = X$.
(C6)   There exists a scanning homomorphism σ for (A, α) such that if $U \in \Sigma(E)$ and $z = \hat{U}$, then $\sigma(z) = U$.
(C7)   The semigroup Ω is free over E.
(C8)   If $X \in \Sigma(A)$, $Y \in \Sigma(A)$, and $\alpha(X) \cap \alpha(Y) \neq \emptyset$, then $X = Y$.
(C9)   If $X, Y \in \Sigma(A)$, $\alpha(X)\Omega \cap \alpha(Y)\Omega \neq \emptyset$, and $|\hat{X}| \leqslant |\hat{Y}|$, then X is a prefix of Y.
(C10)   If $a, b \in A$ and $\alpha(a)\Omega \cap \alpha(b)\Omega \neq \emptyset$, then $a = b$.

Proof. We prove the theorem by establishing the following implications:

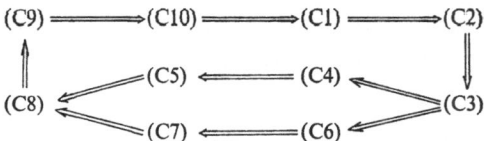

Assuming (C2) false, there exist $z \in \Omega$; $U, V \in \Sigma(E)$ such that $z = \hat{U} = \hat{V}$ with $U \neq V$. Then U, V are not matching, and $z \in \alpha\gamma(U) \cap \alpha\gamma(V)$. But $\gamma(U) \neq \gamma(V)$ since U matches $\gamma(U)$ and V matches $\gamma(V)$. Therefore (C1) is also false, proving (C1) $\Rightarrow$ (C2).

The implication (C2) $\Rightarrow$ (C3) is immediate, and (C3) $\Rightarrow$ (C4) follows from Lemma 3.3.

Assuming (C4), we observe that the unique decoding mapping δ associated thereto is a homomorphism. Indeed, since $x \in \alpha\delta(x)$ and $y \in \alpha\delta(y)$, we have $xy \in \alpha\delta(x)\alpha\delta(y) = \alpha(\delta(x)\delta(y))$; moreover, $xy \in \alpha\delta(xy)$ whence $\delta(xy) = \delta(x)\delta(y)$. Now if $x \in \alpha(X)$ with $x = x_1 x_2 \ldots x_r$, $x_i \in E_0$, then $\delta(x_i) = a_i \in A$ and $x_i \in \alpha(a_i)$, $i = 1, 2, \ldots, r$; therefore $X = (a_1, a_2, \ldots a_r) = \delta(x)$. This proves (C4) $\Rightarrow$ (C5). The implication (C3) $\Rightarrow$ (C6) is proved similarly.

Assuming (C6), we observe that $\sigma: \Omega \to \Sigma(E)$ is one-to-one and onto whence it is an isomorphism. Since $\Sigma(E)$ is the free semigroup generated by E, it follows that Ω is free over E. This proves (C6) $\Rightarrow$ (C7).

Assuming (C7), suppose

$$z \in \alpha(X) \cap \alpha(Y) = \alpha(a_1) \ldots \alpha(a_r) \cap \alpha(b_1) \ldots \alpha(b_s).$$

Then $z = u_1 u_2 \ldots u_r = v_1 v_2 \ldots v_s$, $u_i \in \alpha(a_i)$, $v_j \in \alpha(b_j)$. By (C7), $r = s$ and $u_i = v_i$ whence $\alpha(a_i) \cap \alpha(b_i) \neq \emptyset$ so that $a_i = b_i$ for each i; therefore $X = Y$, proving (C7) $\Rightarrow$ (C8).

Assuming (C8) and the hypothesis of (C9), we have $\alpha(X)\alpha(Z) \cap \alpha(Y)$ $\alpha(W) \neq \emptyset$ with $|\hat{X}| \leqslant |\hat{Y}|$ for $W, X, Y, Z \in \Sigma(A)$. By (C8), $XZ = YW$; applying Lemma 2.4, we have that X is a prefix of Y, proving (C8) $\Rightarrow$ (C9). Note that (C9) with $\alpha = \iota$ is but condition II of [8].

The implication (C9) $\Rightarrow$ (C10) is immediate.

Assuming (C10), let $z \in \alpha(X) \cap \alpha(Y) = \alpha(a_1, a_2, \ldots, a_r) \cap \alpha(b_1, b_2, \ldots, b_s)$ by (C10), $a_1 = b_1$ whence $\alpha(a_2, a_3, \ldots, a_r) \cap \alpha(b_2, b_3, \ldots, b_s) = \emptyset$. Again by (C10), $a_2 = b_2$; repeating this process, we obtain $a_i = b_i$ for $i = 1, 2, \ldots$, $r = s$ whence $X = Y$, proving (C10) $\Rightarrow$ (C1).

We prove now (C5) $\Rightarrow$ (C8): if $z \in \alpha(X) \cap \alpha(Y)$, by (C5) we have $\delta(z) = X$ and $\delta(z) = Y$, hence $X = Y$.

The three properties of codes which we have discussed in this and the previous section are related as follows:

Corollary 5.2. The following statements are equivalent:

(a) (A, α) is correcting.

(b) (A, α) is precorrecting and irredundant.

Proof. Statement (a) is equivalent to (C7) which is the conjunction of (IR3) and (PC10).

Parallel relations are described in the comparative table at the bottom of this page. Theorem 5.1 has also the following consequence:

Corollary 5.3. Let (A, α), (B, β) be codes such that $E(B, \beta) \subset E(A, \alpha)$. Then (B, β) is correcting whenever (A, α) is correcting.
Proof. Assuming the hypotheses, we have that $E(A, \alpha)$ is uniquely decipherable by (C2). Therefore $E(B, \beta)$ is also uniquely decipherable whence (B, β) is correcting, again by (C2).

A particular case is obtained by letting $B \subset A$ and taking for β any admissibility mapping such that $\beta(a) \subset \alpha(a)$ for $a \in B$.

TABLE I

Comparisons among some of the statements given for code properties

Irredundance	Precorrecting	Correcting
(IR4) All decoding mappings agree on E.	(PC4) There exists a decoding homomorphism.	(C4) There exists only one decoding mapping
(IR3) $E_0 = E$.	(PC10) Ω is free.	(C7) Ω is free over E.
(IR6) If $\alpha(a) \cap \alpha(X) \neq \emptyset$, then $a = X$.	(PC11) If $\alpha(X) \cap \alpha(Y) \neq \emptyset$, then there exists Z, prematched by both X and Y, such that $\alpha(X) \cap \alpha(Y) \cap \alpha(Z) \neq \emptyset$.	(C8) If $\alpha(X) \cap \alpha(Y) \neq \emptyset$, then $X = Y$.

Theorem 3.5 gives a practical test for the validity of statement (C3) or (C4); similarly, Theorem 2.3 for statement (C2). We may obtain similar finite tests also for the other statements. In particular we have:

THEOREM 5.4. Given the code (A, α) assume every element of A to have length at most n, and let $Q(E)$ have q elements. Then (A, α) is correcting if and only if $\alpha(X) \cap \alpha(Y) \neq \emptyset$ implies $X = Y$ for every X, Y in $\Sigma(A)$ for which $|\hat{X}| \leqslant (q+1)(n-1)$.

Proof. This follows at once from Theorem 2.3 by observing that every nonempty intersection $\alpha(X) \cap \alpha(Y)$ yields a relation over E.

CHAPTER 4

A STUDY OF ERROR-CORRECTING CODES, II:
DECODABILITY PROPERTIES

L. K. ARQUETTE AND W. E. HARTNETT

EDITORIAL NOTE

Rarely will a mathematician contend that a particular piece of work (even his own) cannot be improved and/or extended. The authors run true to form in this paper (November 1966): the ink had scarcely dried on the material just presented before they took up the challenge to improve and extend it. The first part of the paper records the outcome of these efforts.

Continuing with the same class of models, the authors then proceeded to treat two more code properties in an analogous fashion. They provide a view of the whole program intended to comfort any misgivings of the reader about the formidable character of the presentation.

At the time the paper was written, it was felt that the code mappings would prove to be extremely useful and the authors lavished a good bit of care on an exposition of the basic ideas involved. As it turned out, the mappings failed to live up to our expectations.

The paper referred to as [PML 42] had already been written at this time. In our arrangement of the papers, it appears as Chapter 9 in this book.

1. INTRODUCTION

This report is the fifth in a projected series of papers on codes and their properties. The first paper [PML34] dealt with special codes called simple codes and established results involving certain code properties which had been known for some time but for which proofs had not previously been available. The second paper [PML35] was expository in character and sketched out motivation for and examples of the principal code properties; in addition, it showed some of the relationships between the properties. The third paper in the series [PML42] generalized the results of [PML34]; it also gave a historical motivation for the more general codes introduced in [PML35]. The first and third papers were primarily concerned with the construction of tests for certain code properties and were more involved

W. E. Hartnett (ed.), Foundations of Coding Theory, 61–82. All Rights Reserved.
Copyright © 1974 by D. Reidel Publishing Company, Dordrecht-Holland.

with the details of the tests than with the broader aspects of study of code properties.

The fourth paper [PML43], this paper, and a paper to follow deal with particular code properties and it might be well to explain the program involved. Following [PML35] and the definitions given there, we say that a code (A, α) may have the property of being correcting, decodable, prompt, synchronizable, or comma-free. The basic results in [PML34] and [PML42] were tests for the properties of correctability, decodability, and synchronizability; [PML34] treated simple codes and [PML42] the general codes (A, α) of [PML35]. The fourth paper of the series dealt with correcting codes in rather elaborate detail; the main result was a lengthy theorem which gave a variety of statements each of which was equivalent to the assertion that a code is correcting. The theorem could be regarded as an 'equivalence' theorem for correctability.

This paper concentrates on the properties of decodability and promptness for a code. It provides the expected 'equivalence' theorems for both of these properties and extends the length of the 'equivalence' theorem for correctability of [PML43] by adding new statements.

One of the results of [PML35] is the statement: 'prompt codes are decodable codes and decodable codes are correcting codes.' When we finish this paper we will have given 6 different ways to assert that a code is prompt, 11 different ways to say that a code is decodable, and 17 different ways to express the fact that a code is correcting. It follows as a simple exercise in arithmetic that we shall then know 1122 different ways to say the same thing!

At this point a somewhat natural question may have arisen in the mind of the reader and courtesy demands that we furnish an answer. The reasons we want so many ways to say the same thing are essentially two. As we mention below, many of the ways to say that a code is correcting, decodable, or prompt have appeared in the literature in one guise or another and so should be recorded here. Hence one reason is historical completeness. The second reason is freedom. Our present context for codes is broad enough to include almost all of the codes encountered in the literature and within this broad context we are free to choose any of the equivalent ways to make assertions. If we are dealing with applications to particular codes as in constructability studies, we use one set of ways to say things and if we are interested in more theoretical aspects, we use another and different set of ways. We enjoy a freedom that simply is not available in a narrower and more restrictive framework of operation.

The next paper will give the 'equivalence' theorems for synchronizability and comma-freedom of a code and will follow the pattern of the present paper. Clearly that paper will depend upon this one which, in turn, depends on [PML43]. Needless to say, we plan to extend our freedom in the next paper.

We now turn to an explanation of the structure of this paper. The last three sections are technical treatments of correcting, decodable, and prompt codes. As such, they are completely straightforward presentations which tend to be rather dull and dry. In those sections we do not attempt to motivate the particular (or perhaps peculiar) form of the statements of the theorems. Suffice to say that many of these formulations were suggested by statements found in the literature of Coding Theory as cited for example in [PML42] and [PML43].

The second section does a number of things which are intended to lessen the starkness of the last sections. It introduces the usual notations and conventions for codes and summarizes some of the results [PML43]. It recognizes the frequent utility of mappings associated with codes or sets derived from codes and introduces enough elementary information about mappings so that the reader can keep track of what we are doing and feel reasonably at ease while doing so. If a first reading of the material on mappings fails to ease the mind of the reader, then he should go on to the later sections and refer back to this material only when he thinks it might help. This will almost certainly occur when we treat the expandability of codes and expandable code properties in detail.

The problem of notation is always bothersome and we have made substantial efforts to achieve simplicity. The end result may not be impressive but it does represent a decided improvement over previous formulations. The conventions at the end of Section 2 should be noted with particular care because for the most part they will be used in the later sections without comment. Finally, it should be confessed that some of our choices have been influenced by the fact that substantial work on codes and their properties still remains to be done.

It is a pleasure to acknowledge with gratitude the aid and guidance of L. Calabi in this work. Despite the fact that he is not one of the authors of the paper, he has contributed greatly to its preparation.

2. CODES AND MAPPINGS

In this section we recall a few notions about functions, set down notation, and review some results of [PML43] which will be needed later. We shall be working with a number of sets and functions throughout and so it seems helpful to furnish a housekeeping scheme for the reader. This is provided by diagrams which indicate most of the pertinent sets and functions that appear in our study of codes. In order to draw the diagrams in question we first have to look at a few ideas about functions.

We suppose that M and N are nonempty sets and define a *function* (or *mapping*) *from M into N* to be a set of rules f with the property that f associates with each $m \in M$ one and only one $n \in N$, written $f(m)$. We write $f: M \to N$ to indicate that f is a function from M into N and set $f(M) = \{f(m): m \in M\}$. The set M is called *the domain $\mathscr{D}_f$ of f*, the set $f(M)$ is called *the range $\mathscr{R}_f$ of f*, and because $f(M) \subset N$ the set N is simply a set that contains the range of f.

If $f: M \to N$, then f may enjoy two properties of importance. We say that f is *onto N* iff $f(M) = N$; informally, f is onto N if for each $n \in N$, there exists some $m \in M$ such that $f(m) = n$. We say that f is *one-to-one* iff whenever $m_1 \neq m_2$ in $\mathscr{D}_f$, then $f(m_1) \neq f(m_2)$ in $\mathscr{R}_f$; informally, if f is one-to-one, then f is distinctness-preserving.

Given a nonempty set M there exists a unique function $j: M \to M$ with the property that $j(m) = m$ for each $m \in M$. We call j the *identity mapping on M* and observe that j is obviously both one-to-one and onto. Notice that $j: M \to M^*$ whenever $M \subset M^*$.

If N is a nonempty set, we let 2^N denote the set of all subsets of N. Now if $f: M \to 2^N$, then for each $m \in M$, $f(m)$ is a subset of N and so is a member of 2^N. The usual concepts of one-to-one and onto still apply but we may now introduce still another notion. We shall say that f is *separating* iff whenever $m_1 \neq m_2$ in $\mathscr{D}_f$, then $f(m_1) \cap f(m_2) = \emptyset$; the requirement of being separating is stronger than the requirement of being one-to-one. Clearly, a separating function is one-to-one but not conversely.

Two more notions about functions are convenient. If $f: M \to N$ and $m \in M$, we let $[m] = \{m': m' \in M, f(m') = f(m)\}$ and call $[m]$ *the f-relation class of m*. Notice that if $f(m_1) = f(m_2)$, then $m_1 \in [m_2]$ and $m_2 \in [m_1]$. Indeed, $[m_1] = [m_2]$. It turns out, and one can easily check, that for $m_1, m_2 \in \mathscr{D}_f$ either $[m_1] = [m_2]$ or $[m_1] \cap [m_2] = \emptyset$; we say that f splits $\mathscr{D}_f$

into a family of subsets which are pairwise disjoint in that each distinct pair has an empty intersection. For the second notion we observe that if $M_0 \subset M$ and $f : M \to N$, then f defines a function f_0 from M_0 into N called *the restriction of f to M_0*. On the other hand, if $g_0 : M_0 \to N$ and there exists a function g defined from M into N whose restriction to M_0 is g_0, then g is said to be *an extension of g_0*. These notions are important for two reasons. We shall be concerned whether the restriction of a function has a property that the function did not have and whether the extension of a function has the same property that the function had. When no confusion can result we use the same notation for a function, its restrictions, and its extensions.

To begin to deal with codes themselves we let J denote a finite non-empty set called *the alphabet*, let $\Sigma(J) = \Sigma$ denote *the set of all finite sequences over J*, and let Σ^+ denote all nonempty members of Σ. If $x \in \Sigma^+$, then the domain of x is a finite set, say $\{1, 2, ..., n\}$ and the range consists of $\{x_1, x_2, ..., x_n\}$ with $x_i \in J$ for each i. As usual we identify the sequence x with the ordered n-tuple $(x_1, x_2, ..., x_n)$. For $x \in \Sigma^+$ *the length $|x|$ of x* is the number of occurrences of members of J in x; phrased differently, $|x|$ is the number of elements in $\mathscr{D}_x$. If $x, y \in \Sigma^+$, then *the juxtaposition product of x and y* is given by $xy = (x_1, ..., x_n, y_1, ..., y_k)$ if $x = (x_1, x_2, ..., x_n)$ and $y = (y_1, y_2, ..., y_k)$. As is well known, Σ^+ together with the juxtaposition product is a cancellation semigroup in which $|xy| = |x| + |y|$. The cancellation property means that whenever $xyw = xzw$, then $xy = xz$, $yw = zw$, and $y = z$. If C and D are subsets of Σ^+, then the juxtaposition product CD of the sets is given by $\{cd : c \in C, d \in D\}$.

We now let $\Sigma(\Sigma(J)) = \Sigma(\Sigma)$ denote the set of all finite sequences over $\Sigma(J)$. If $X \in \Sigma(\Sigma)$, then X is a finite sequence $(x_1, x_2, ..., x_m)$ where each $x_i \in \Sigma$, that is, each x_i is a sequence of members of J. So X is a sequence of sequences. The mapping $\wedge : \Sigma(\Sigma) \to \Sigma$ defined by $\hat{X} = x_1 x_2 ... x_m$ when $X = (x_1, x_2, ..., x_m)$ is called *the train mapping* and has the property that $\widehat{XY} = \hat{X} \hat{Y}$ for $X, Y \in \Sigma(\Sigma)$; we say that $\wedge$ is *a homomorphism on $\Sigma(\Sigma)$* because it preserves the juxtaposition product.

Suppose now that $A \subset \Sigma^+$ is finite and nonempty. Then A is a set of finite nonempty sequences over J and we let $\Sigma(A)$ denote the set of all finite sequences over A. If $X \in \Sigma(A)$, then we say that X is *a sentence over A* and that $\Sigma(A)$ is *the set of all sentences over A*. With the juxtaposition product of sentences $\Sigma(A)$ is a cancellation semigroup. Notice that $\Sigma(A) \subset \Sigma(\Sigma)$ and hence that $\wedge$ is defined on $\Sigma(A)$ by restriction. We say that a function $\alpha : \Sigma(A) \to 2^\Sigma$ is *an admissibility mapping* (*on* $\Sigma(A)$) iff α has the following properties:

(A1) $\hat{X} \in \alpha(X)$.

(A2) If $x \in \alpha(X)$, then $|x| = |\hat{X}|$.

(A3) If $\alpha(a) \cap \alpha(b) \neq \emptyset$ for a, $b \in A$, then $a = b$; that is, the restriction of α to A is separating.

(A4) $\alpha(XY) = \alpha(X)\alpha(Y)$, that is, α is a homomorphism on $\Sigma(A)$.

If α is an admissibility mapping for $\Sigma(A)$, then we call the pair (A, α) *a code* (*over* J); each $a \in A$ is *a code word* and, as usual, we identify a code word a with the sentence (a) consisting of a alone. We let $\Sigma^+(A)$ denote the set of all nonempty members of $\Sigma(A)$ and for $Z \in \Sigma(A)$ we let $Z(1)$, $Z(2)$, ..., $Z(*)$ respectively denote the first, second, ..., last word of Z. We then define the suffix Z_t and the prefix Z_h of Z by requiring that $Z = Z(1)Z_t = Z_h Z(*)$. Notice that if Z consists of a single word then $Z(1) = Z(*)$ and both Z_t and Z_h are empty. If $Z \in \Sigma^+(A)$, then *a decomposition of Z* is an ordered n-tuple $(Z_1, Z_2, ..., Z_n)$ of members of $\Sigma^+(A)$ such that $Z = Z_1 Z_2 ... Z_n$. If Z has more than one word, then $(Z(1), Z_t)$, $(Z_h, Z(*))$, and $(Z(1), Z(2), ..., Z(*))$ are decompositions of Z.

If (A, α) is a code and $\alpha(a) = \{a\}$ for each $a \in A$, then A is called *a simple code*. We shall always write ι for the admissibility mapping of a simple code. Hence for each finite nonempty subset F of Σ^+ we may form the simple code (F, ι).

We now let $\alpha(\Sigma(A)) = \bigcup\{\alpha(Z) : Z \in \Sigma(A)\}$ and denote $\alpha(\Sigma(A))$ by Ω. Then α, restricted to A, gives $\alpha(A) = \bigcup\{\alpha(a) : a \in A\}$ and we have $A \subset \alpha(A)$ and $\alpha(A) \subset \Omega$. As in [PML43], Ω is termed *the set of admissible sequences for (A, α)*, Ω^+ denotes the set of nonempty members of Ω, and the simple code $(\alpha(A), \iota)$ is called *the expanded code for* (A, α) where the admissibility mapping ι is defined by $\iota(U) = \{\hat{U}\}$ for $U \in \Sigma(\alpha(A))$, the set of sentences over $\alpha(A)$. It should be noticed that we are making use of the trivial observation that whenever $F \subset \Sigma^+$ we may always define the admissibility mapping ι on the sentences $\Sigma(F)$ over F by setting $\iota(V) = \{\hat{V}\}$. If we identify $\{\hat{V}\}$ with $\hat{V}$, then ι is essentially the mapping $\wedge$. It should be explicitly pointed out that we could well have two different codes (A, α) and (B, β) such that $\alpha(A) = \beta(B)$. But then the simple codes $(\alpha(A), \iota)$ and

$(\beta(B), \iota)$ are the same and so the codes (A, α) and (B, β), while different, have the same expanded code. Phrased differently, the obvious expansion mapping E, which maps a code onto its expanded code and is formally defined by $E(A, \alpha) = (\alpha(A), \iota)$, is not one-to-one.

To look at this from still one other point of view notice that each code (over J) has an E-relation class. Observe that if $[(A, \alpha)]$ is the E-relation class of the code (A, α), then $(A, \alpha) \in [(A, \alpha)]$ and $(\alpha(A), \iota) \in [(A, \alpha)]$. Notice further that for each simple code (F, ι), $E(F, \iota) = (\iota(F), \iota) = (F, \iota)$. Hence E is a mapping from the class of all codes over J onto the class of simple codes over J whose restriction to the class of simple codes is the identity mapping. In particular, for each code (A, α), $[(A, \alpha)] = [(\alpha(A), \iota)]$.

We now say that a code property P is an *expandable property* iff, for each E-relation class, either all members of the class have the property or no member has the property. In detail this means that whenever (A, α) has the property, then the expanded code $(\alpha(A), \iota) = E(A, \alpha)$ has the property and that whenever a simple code (F, ι) has the property then each code in $[(F, \iota)]$ has the property. With a slight difference in notation, [PML43] showed that the code properties of irredundance, precorrecting, and correcting were expandable properties. Later we shall prove that two other code properties of interest, namely, decodability and promptness, are expandable; the paper to follow will demonstrate expandability for two other code properties, synchronizability and comma-freedom.

When we recall that $\alpha(A) = \bigcup \{\alpha(a): a \in A\}$ and that (A3) holds for α, we see that there exists a natural mapping $\gamma: \alpha(A) \to A$ defined by $\gamma(x) = a \in A$ iff $x \in \alpha(a)$. We may extend γ to obtain a mapping $\gamma: \Sigma(\alpha(A)) \to \Sigma(A)$ in the following way. If $U \in \Sigma(\alpha(A))$, then $U = (u_1, u_2, ..., u_k)$ for $u_i \in \alpha(A)$ for each i and so we may set $\gamma(U) = (\gamma(u_1), \gamma(u_2), ..., \gamma(u_k)) \in \Sigma(A)$ in a unique way. Notice that γ is now a homomorphism as a mapping from $\Sigma(\alpha(A))$ into $\Sigma(A)$; the mapping γ is the *correcting homomorphism* of [PML43]. We can relate γ to $\wedge$ and α by considering the diagram of Figure 1 in which sets are denoted by regions, subsets by subregions, functions by labelled arrows, and members of sets by dots in the appropriate regions. In the figure we indicate the fact that

$$\alpha(\Sigma(A)) = \widehat{\Sigma(\alpha(A))} = \{\hat{U}: U \in \Sigma(\alpha(A))\} = \Omega.$$

Several items of interest about the diagram should be noted. First, we have given two copies of Ω to emphasize the fact that we have two mappings $\wedge$ and α to deal with. Actually, α is not a mapping from $\Sigma(A)$ into Ω, but into 2^{Ω}, the class of all subsets of Ω; in the diagram we simply indicate the fact that $\alpha(X)$ for $X \in \Sigma(A)$ is a subset of Ω. Second, γ is onto $\Sigma(A)$; this is clear when we recall that $\Sigma(A) \subset \Sigma(\alpha(A))$. Third, if $U \in \Sigma(\alpha(A))$, then $\gamma(U) \in \Sigma(A)$, $\alpha(\gamma(U)) \subset \Omega$, $\hat{U} \in \Omega$, $j(\hat{U}) \in \Omega$ and finally $\hat{U} \in \alpha(\gamma(U))$; these facts follow from our definitions. Fourth, $\wedge$ is onto Ω because $\widehat{\Sigma(\alpha(A))} = \Omega$. In particular, these observations imply that, given $z \in \Omega$, then $z \in \alpha(X)$ for some $X \in \Sigma(A)$ and there exists $U \in \Sigma(\alpha(A))$ such that $\hat{U} = z \in \alpha(X)$ with $\gamma(U) = X$. This result is Lemma 3.2 of [PML43].

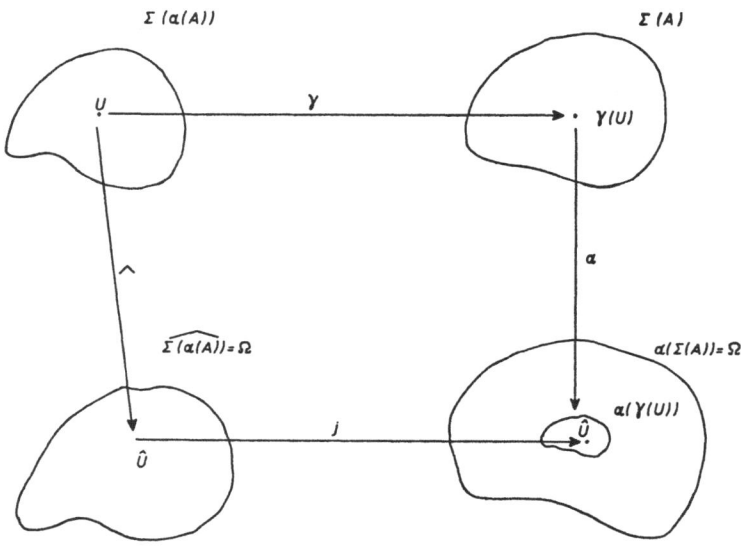

Fig. 1.

The diagram also allows us to describe other mappings of importance that were defined in [PML43]. A mapping $\delta : \Omega \to \Sigma(A)$ is called a *decoding mapping for* (A, α) iff $z \in \alpha(\delta(z))$ for each $z \in \Omega$. A mapping $\sigma : \Omega \to \Sigma(\alpha(A))$ is called a *scanning mapping for* (A, α) iff $z = \widehat{\sigma(z)}$ for each $z \in \Omega$. Notice that a scanning mapping for (A, α) is just a decoding mapping for $(\alpha(A), \iota)$ because $\iota(\sigma(z)) = \{\widehat{\sigma(z)}\}$; hence $z \in \iota(\sigma(z))$ iff $z = \widehat{\sigma(z)}$. It may happen that a decoding mapping preserves the operation of juxtaposition, that is, $\delta(z_1 z_2) = \delta(z_1) \delta(z_2)$; if it does it is termed a *decoding homomorphism*.

In general, a number of decoding mappings may exist but for each scanning mapping the diagram of Figure 2 holds. In this case, the decoding mapping acts as the 'diagonal' mapping and we write $\delta = \gamma \circ \sigma$ as *the composition of σ followed by γ*. Lemma 3.3 of [PML43] says that given δ, there exists some σ such that $\delta = \gamma \circ \sigma$ and given σ, there exists some δ such that $\delta = \gamma \circ \sigma$. Hence there may be many valid 'triangular' diagrams for a given code (A, α).

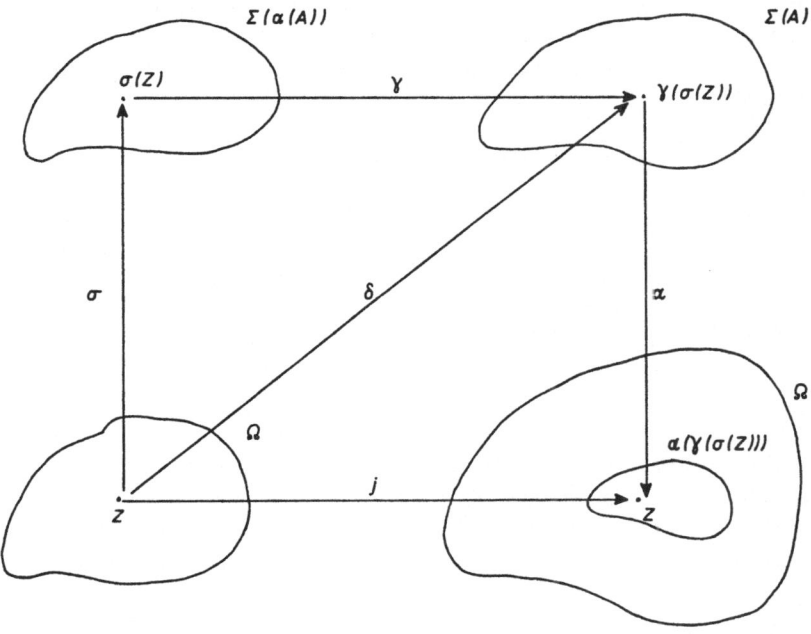

Fig. 2.

Because γ is onto $\Sigma(A)$ there are exactly as many distinct γ-relation classes of members of $\Sigma(\alpha(A))$ as there are members of $\Sigma(A)$. Indeed, because $\Sigma(A) \subset \Sigma(\alpha(A))$ we see that each $X \in \Sigma(A)$ determines a γ-relation class $[X]$ and that if $Y \in \Sigma(A)$ is a different sentence from X, then $[X] \cap [Y] = \emptyset$. Hence $\{[X] : X \in \Sigma(A)\}$ is the family of all distinct γ-relation classes in $\Sigma(\alpha(A))$. It is easy to check that for each $X \in \Sigma(A)$, $\alpha(X) = [\hat{X}] = \{\hat{U} : U \in [X]\}$, and that $\wedge$ is one-to-one when restricted to the set $[X]$.

We can then think of $\wedge$ as defined on $\Sigma(\alpha(A))$ and defined also on $\{[X]:X\in\Sigma(A)\}$. It turns out (and one can check) that $\wedge$ is one-to-one on $\Sigma(\alpha(A))$ iff $\wedge$ is separating on the classes $[X]$. But clearly $\wedge$ is separating on the classes $[X]$ iff α is separating on $\Sigma(A)$. In the formulation of [PML43] expressed in these terms, $(\alpha(A), \iota)$ is correcting iff $\wedge$ is one-to-one on $\Sigma(\alpha(A))$ and (A, α) is correcting iff α is separating. Our statements just above then really furnish the argument that correcting is an expandable property.

With all this discussion out of the way we may now go on to talk about properties of codes. Whenever convenient we shall utilize the results of this section. In order to simplify matters somewhat we agree to use the following notation throughout the rest of the paper (with subscripts if needed):

$$a, b, c \in A \qquad a', b', c' \in \alpha(A)$$
$$t, u, v, w, x, y, z \in \Sigma(J)$$
$$T, U, V, W, X, Y, Z \in \Sigma(A)$$
$$T', U', V', W', X', Y', Z' \in \Sigma(\alpha(A))$$

$\emptyset$ for empty sequence or empty set.

3. CORRECTING CODES

In this section we obtain new statements equivalent to the statement that a code (A, α) is correcting. These will be combined with Theorem 5.1 of [PML43] to provide a long list of diverse equivalent statements. Some of them are useful in dealing with output strings of alphabet symbols; others are helpful in more theoretical studies.

We begin by specifying three sets which will be needed in the sequel. We let $L(\Omega^+)$ or L denote $\{x:x\in\Sigma, x\Omega^+\cap\Omega^+\neq\emptyset\}$, let $R(\Omega^+)$ or R denote $\{x:x\in\Sigma, \Omega^+x\cap\Omega^+\neq\emptyset\}$, and let $D(\Omega^+)$ or D denote $\{x:x\in\Sigma, x\Omega^+\cap\Omega^+x\neq\emptyset\}$. Notice that if $x\in L$, then there exist X and Y such that $x\alpha(X)\cap\alpha(Y)\neq\emptyset$. Similarly, if $x\in R$, then $\alpha(Z)x\cap\alpha(W)\neq\emptyset$ for some Z and W and if $x\in D$, then $x\alpha(V)\cap\alpha(U)x\neq\emptyset$ for certain V and U. It is clear that $L\cap R\subset D$ because if $x\in L\cap R$, then with the notation above $x\alpha(XW)\cap\alpha(YZ)x\neq\emptyset$ and hence $x\in D$. It is also clear that $\Omega\subset L\cap R$ and hence that $\Omega\subset D$.

In [PML43] a code (A, α) was said to be correcting iff the following statement holds: (C1) For each $z \in \Omega$ there exists a unique $X \in \Sigma(A)$ such that $z \in \alpha(X)$. In this paper we shall use Statement (C8) of Theorem 5.1 of [PML43] for our definition of correcting because of its technical convenience. We shall say that (A, α) is *correcting* iff $\alpha(X) \cap \alpha(Y) \neq \emptyset$ implies $X = Y$, that is, iff α is separating. In a similar way we shall use Statement (PC6) of Theorem 4.2 of [PML43] for our definition of pre-correcting. With the terminology above we say that (A, α) is *precorrecting* iff $L \cap R \subset \Omega$, that is, iff $L \cap R = \Omega$.

We also use condition (IR6) of Theorem 4.1 of [PML43] for our definition of irredundance. The code (A, α) is said to be *irredundant* iff $\alpha(a) \cap \alpha(X) \neq \emptyset$ implies $X = a$.

Two Lemmas and a Corollary will be exhibited before we state and prove the theorem on correcting.

Lemma 3.1. The following statements are equivalent:

(1) $\alpha(X) \cap \alpha(Y) \neq \emptyset$ implies $X = Y$.

(2)   If $\alpha(Y)x \cap \alpha(Z) \neq \emptyset$ and $x\alpha(V) \cap \alpha(U) \neq \emptyset$, then $YXV = YU = ZV$ with $x \in \alpha(X)$.

(3)   If $\alpha(Y)x \cap \alpha(Z) \neq \emptyset$, $x\alpha(V) \cap \alpha(U) \neq \emptyset$,   and $x\alpha(T) \cap \alpha(W)x \neq \emptyset$,   then $YXTV = YWU = YWXV =$ $= ZTV$ with $x \in \alpha(X)$.

Proof. Assume (1). The hypotheses of (2) yield the fact that $\alpha(YU) \cap \alpha(ZV) \neq \emptyset$. We may then apply (1) to conclude that $YU = ZV$. Because $|\hat{Y}| \leqslant |\hat{Z}|$ we see that Y is a prefix of Z and so there exists an X such that $x \in \alpha(X)$ and $YX = Z$. But then X is unique because if $YX_1 = Z = YX_2$, we may left cancel in our cancellation semigroup to obtain $X_1 = X_2$. Because $x \in \alpha(X)$, $XV = U$. Hence $YXV = YU = ZV$. So (1) implies (2).

Now assume (2). The first two statements of the hypotheses of (3) together with (2) show that $YXV = YU = ZV$ with $x \in \alpha(X)$ with X unique. The complete hypotheses of (3) imply that $\alpha(Y)x \cap \alpha(Z) \neq \emptyset$ and that $x\alpha(TV) \cap \alpha(WU) \neq \emptyset$ so we may again apply (2) with V replaced by TV and U replaced by WU to conclude that $YXTV = YWU = ZTV$. However, $U = XV$ and hence $YXTV = YWU = YWXV = ZTV$. Therefore (2) implies (3).

Clearly, (3) implies that $L \cap R = \Omega$ so (A, α) is precorrecting. But (A, α) is also irredundant because $\alpha(Y)a \cap \alpha(a) \neq \emptyset$, $a\alpha(V) \cap \alpha(a) \neq \emptyset$ where $Y = V = \emptyset$, the empty sentence. By (3) there exists a unique X such that $YX = \emptyset X = a$. Hence $X = a$. Using Corollary 5.2 and statements (C1) and (C8) of Theorem 5.1 of [PML43] we conclude that (1) holds. Therefore (3) implies (1).

Corollary 3.2. Suppose that (A, α) is correcting, $x \in \Sigma^+$, $\Omega^+ x \cap \alpha(Z) \neq \emptyset$, $x\Omega^+ \cap \alpha(U) \neq \emptyset$, and $x\alpha(T) \cap \alpha(W)x \neq \emptyset$. Then $x \in \Omega^+$ and $|x| \geqslant \max$ $\{|Z(*)|, |U(1)|, |T(*)|, |W(1)|\}$.

Proof. Part (1) and (3) of Lemma 3.1 show that $x \in \Omega^+$ and that $YXTV = YWU = YWXV = ZTV$ for certain Y and V with $YX = Z$, $XV = U$. Clearly, $|x| = |\hat{X}|$ by property (A2) and so $|x| \geqslant \max\{|Z(*)|, |U(1)|\}$. Cancelling in $YXTV = YWXV$ we conclude that $XT = WX$. Hence $|x| \geqslant \max\{|T(*)|, |W(1)|\}$.

Our next lemma involves certain constructions which can be carried out if (A, α) is not correcting.

Lemma 3.3. Suppose that (A, α) is not correcting. Then for each of the following statements there exists some $x \in \Omega^+$ such that the statement holds.

(1)	$x\Omega^+ \cap \alpha(U) \neq \emptyset$	and	$|x| < |U(1)|$.
(2)	$x\Omega^+ \cap \alpha(W)x \neq \emptyset$	and	$|x| < |W(1)|$.
(3)	$\Omega^+ x \cap \alpha(Z) \neq \emptyset$	and	$|x| < |Z(*)|$.
(4)	$x\alpha(V) \cap \Omega^+ x \neq \emptyset$	and	$|x| < |V(*)|$.

Proof. We give the proof of (1) and (2); the proof for (3) and (4) is similar. If (A, α) is not correcting, then there exist X and Y such that $X \neq Y$ but $\alpha(X) \cap \alpha(Y) \neq \emptyset$. To prove (1) and (2) we assume, as we may, that $|X(1)| < |Y(1)|$. (For (3) and (4) we would assume that $|X(*)| < |Y(*)|$.)

Let $U = YX(1)$ and notice that the assumptions imply that $\alpha(XX(1)) \cap \alpha(YX(1)) = \alpha(X(1)X_tX(1)) \cap \alpha(U) \neq \emptyset$. Hence $\alpha(X(1))\alpha(X_tX(1)) \cap \alpha(U) \neq \emptyset$ and so there exists some $x \in \alpha(X(1))$ such that $x\alpha(X_tX(1)) \cap \alpha(U) \neq \emptyset$. Clearly $x \in \Omega^+$ and by (A2) $|x| = |X(1)| < |Y(1)| = |U(1)|$. Therefore statement (1) holds.

Now observe that $x\alpha(X_tX(1))\alpha(X(1)) \cap \alpha(U)x \neq \emptyset$ because $x \in \alpha(X(1))$.

Hence $x\Omega^+ \cap \alpha(U)x \neq \emptyset$ and $|x| < |U(1)|$. So statement (2) holds with $W = U$.

The proof of (3) and (4) follows the obvious pattern of construction.

We may now state our theorem giving propositions equivalent to the fact that (A, α) is a correcting code. Recall that for a simple code (F, ι) to say that $\iota(U) \cap \iota(V) \neq \emptyset$ for $U, V \in \Sigma(F)$ is to say that $\{\hat{U}\} \cap \{\hat{V}\} \neq \emptyset$. Hence $\iota(U) \cap \iota(V) \neq \emptyset$ means that $\hat{U} = \hat{V}$. Recall also that we use X, Y, and Z to denote members of $\Sigma(A)$ and X', Y', and Z' to denote members of $\Sigma(\alpha(A))$.

THEOREM 3.4. The following statements are equivalent for a code (A, α):

(C1)   For each $x \in \Omega$ there exists a unique X such that $x \in \alpha(X)$.

(C2)   For each $x \in \Omega$ there exists a unique X' such that $x = \hat{X}'$.

(C3)   There exists only one scanning mapping for (A, α).

(C4)   There exists only one decoding mapping for (A, α).

(C5)   There exists a decoding homomorphism δ for (A, α) such that $\delta(x) = X$ whenever $x \in \alpha(X)$.

(C6)   There exists a scanning homomorphism σ for (A, α) such that $\sigma(x) = X'$ whenever $x = X'$.

(C7)   The semigroup Ω is free over $\alpha(A)$.

(C8)   If $\alpha(X) \cap \alpha(Y) \neq \emptyset$, then $X = Y$; that is, α is separating.

(C9)   If $\alpha(X)\Omega \cap \alpha(Y)\Omega \neq \emptyset$, $|\hat{X}| \leqslant |\hat{Y}|$, then X is a prefix of Y.

(C10)   If $\alpha(a)\Omega \cap \alpha(b)\Omega \neq \emptyset$, then $a = b$.

(C11) $L \cap R = \Omega$ and if $\alpha(a) \cap \alpha(X) \neq \emptyset$, then $a = X$.

(C12)   If $x \neq \emptyset$, $x \in L \cap R$ and $x\Omega^+ \cap \alpha(W)x \neq \emptyset$, then $|x| \geqslant |W(1)|$.

(C13)   If $x \neq \emptyset$, $x \in L \cap R$, and $x\alpha(V) \cap \Omega^+x \neq \emptyset$, then $|x| \geqslant |V(*)|$.

(C14)   If $x \neq \emptyset$, $x \in R$, and $x\Omega^+ \cap \alpha(U) \neq \emptyset$, then $|x| \geqslant |U(1)|$.

(C15)   If $x \neq \emptyset$, $x \in L$, and $\Omega^+x \cap \alpha(Z) \neq \emptyset$, then $|x| \geqslant |Z(*)|$.

(C16)   If $\alpha(Y)x \cap \alpha(Z) \neq \emptyset$ and $x \in L$, then $Y(1) = Z(1)$.

(C17)   If $\alpha(Y)x \cap \alpha(Z) \neq \emptyset$ and $x \in L$, then Y is a prefix of Z.

Proof. The equivalence of (C1) through (C10) is Theorem 5.1 and the equivalence of (C1) and (C11) is Corollary 5.2 of [PML43].

Lemma 3.1 and Corollary 3.2 show that (C8) implies (C12), (C13), (C14), and (C15). Conversely, each of the latter implies (C3) by virtue of

Lemma 3.1 because a denial of (C8) contradicts (C12), (C13), (C14), and (C15).

Lemma 3.1 shows that (C8) implies (C16). On the other hand, (C16) implies (C17) because if $\alpha(Y)x \cap \alpha(Z) \neq \emptyset$ and $Y(1) = Z(1)$, then $\alpha(Y_t)x \cap \alpha(Z_t) \neq \emptyset$ and so by repeated applications of (C16) we may obtain (C17) in view of the fact that $|\hat{Y}| \leqslant |\hat{Z}|$.

Finally, (C17) implies statement (2) of Lemma 3.1 for certain V and U. But in the lemma, (2) is equivalent to (1) which is (C8). Hence (C17) implies (C8) and the theorem is established.

4. Decodable codes

The aim of this section is to provide a theorem which lists a number of conditions equivalent to the fact that a code (A, α) is decodable. One definition of decodability was given in [PML35] but for this paper we find that another definition is more convenient. We first give a lemma which shows the equivalence of the two. Next we give the expected lemma that decodability is an expandable property. This is followed by the definition of predecodability and then lemmas similar to those of Section 3 are given. In order to establish Lemma 4.6, it becomes necessary to prove another lemma of independent interest. Finally we give our theorem on decodability which incorporates our first two lemmas. Because the statements will appear later in the theorem we number them with that in mind.

We consider the following conditions for a code (A, α):

(D1)   There exists an integer $n > 0$ such that if $|\hat{X}| \geqslant n$ and
        $\alpha(X)\Sigma \cap \alpha(Y) \neq \emptyset$, then $X(1) = Y(1)$.

(D2)   There exists an integer $m > 0$ such that if $|x| \geqslant m$, $xy \in \alpha(Y)$,
        and $xz \in \alpha(Z)$, then $Y(1) = Z(1)$.

In the terminology of [PML35], a code was decodable iff (D2) held. We shall call (A, α) a *decodable code* iff (D1) holds. This means, of course, that we must show the equivalence.

Lemma 4.1. Let (A, α) be a code. Then (D1) holds iff (D2) holds.
Proof. (D1) implies (D2). Suppose that (D1) holds and $xy \in \alpha(Y)$ and $xz \in \alpha(Z)$. We shall then show how to choose m so that (D2) holds. We

may certainly assume that $|x|$ is larger than k, the length of the longest word of A. Then let Y_1 be the longest prefix of Y and Z_1 the longest prefix of Z such that $|\hat{Y}_1| \leqslant |x|$ and $|\hat{Z}_1| \leqslant |x|$. We see that $x \in \alpha(Y_1)u$ and $x \in \alpha(Z_1)v$ for certain $u, v \in \Sigma$. Suppose that $|u| \leqslant |v|$. Then $v = wu$ for some $w \in \Sigma$. Hence $\alpha(Y_1)u \cap \alpha(Z_1)wu \neq \emptyset$ and so $\alpha(Y_1) \cap \alpha(Z_1)w \neq \emptyset$. If we now set $m = nk$, then when $|x| \geqslant m, |\hat{Z}_1| \geqslant n$ and so by (D1), $Y_1(1) = Z_1(1)$. But $Y_1(1) = Y(1)$, $Z_1(1) = Z(1)$, and hence when $|x| \geqslant m$, $xy \in \alpha(Y)$ and $xz \in \alpha(Z)$, then $Y(1) = Z(1)$. Therefore (D1) does imply (D2).

To go the other way assume (D2) and let $n = m$. If $\alpha(X)\Sigma \cap \alpha(Y) \neq \emptyset$, then there exists some $x \in \alpha(X)$, $u \in \Sigma$, and $y \in \alpha(Y)$ such that $xu = y$. Clearly, $x\emptyset \in \alpha(X)$, $xu \in \alpha(Y)$, and $|\hat{X}| = |x|$. Therefore, when $|x| \geqslant m$, $X(1) = Y(1)$. Hence if $|\hat{X}| \geqslant n$, $X(1) = Y(1)$, and so (D2) implies (D1).

We next show that decodability is an expandable property. Again we use a convenient numbering. However before we begin we use some of the results of Section 2. Recall that whenever $X' \in [X]$, then X' and X have the same number K of words, $|X'(i)| = |X(i)|$ for $i = 1, 2, \ldots, K$, $\iota(X') \subset [\hat{X}] = \alpha(X)$ and $\hat{X}' \in \alpha(X)$. Also recall that for each X', there exists a unique X, namely $\gamma(X')$, such that $X' \in [X]$ and that for each X there exists some $X' \in [X]$. We need these facts in the next lemma.

Lemma 4.2. The following statements are equivalent for a code (A, α):

(D1) There exists an integer $n > 0$ such that if $|\hat{X}| \geqslant n$ and $\alpha(X)\Sigma \cap \alpha(Y) \neq \emptyset$, then $X(1) = Y(1)$.

(D3) There exists an integer $n > 0$ such that if $|\hat{X}'| \geqslant n$ and $\iota(X')\Sigma \cap \iota(Y') \neq \emptyset$, then $X'(1) = Y'(1)$.

Proof. The proof is routine. Assume (D1) and suppose that $|\hat{X}'| \geqslant n$ and $\iota(X')\Sigma \cap \iota(Y') \neq \emptyset$. By our comments just before the lemma, we have $\gamma(X') = X$, $\gamma(Y') = Y$ and $\alpha(X)\Sigma \cap \alpha(Y) \neq \emptyset$. Because $|\hat{X}| = |\hat{X}'| \geqslant n$, (D1) tells us that $X(1) = Y(1)$. However $|X'(1)| = |X(1)|$, $|Y'(1)| = |Y(1)|$, and, because $\hat{X}'u = \hat{Y}'$ for some $u \in \Sigma$, $X'(1) = Y'(1)$ and so (D1) implies (D3).

Now assume (D3) and suppose $|\hat{X}| \geqslant n$, and $\alpha(X)\Sigma \cap \alpha(Y) \neq \emptyset$. Then there exists some $X' \in [X]$ and $Y' \in [Y]$ such that $\iota(X')\Sigma \cap \iota(Y') \neq \emptyset$. By (D3), $X'(1) = Y'(1)$. But $|X'(1)| = |X(1)|$, $|Y'(1)| = |Y(1)|$, and hence $\alpha(X(1)) \cap \alpha(Y(1)) \neq \emptyset$; by (A3) $X(1) = Y(1)$ and so (D3) implies (D1).

We shall say that a code (A, α) is *predecodable* iff $L \cap D = \Omega$. Clearly predecodable codes are always precorrecting because $L \cap R \subset D$. It should also be observed that decodable codes are correcting codes, a known result of [PML35]. To see this observe that if (A, α) is decodable with integer n and $\alpha(X) \cap \alpha(Y) \neq \emptyset$, then for some integer m we have $\alpha(XX^m) \cap \alpha(YY^m) \neq \emptyset$ with $|\hat{X}^m| \geqslant n$. Repeated applications of the decodability of (A, α) shows that X is a prefix of Y and, by symmetry, that Y is a prefix of X. Hence $X = Y$ and (A, α) is indeed correcting.

Lemma 4.3. Suppose that (A, α) is decodable with integer n. If $\alpha(Y)x \cap \alpha(Z) \neq \emptyset$ and $x\alpha(U) \cap \alpha(W)x \neq \emptyset$, then $YXU = ZU = YWX$ with $x \in \alpha(X)$.

Proof. We first observe that $\alpha(Y)x\alpha(U) \cap \alpha(Y)\alpha(W)x \neq \emptyset$ and so conclude that $\alpha(Z)\alpha(U) \cap \alpha(Y)\alpha(W)x \neq \emptyset$. Hence $\alpha(ZU) \cap \alpha(YW)x \neq \emptyset$. A routine argument now shows that $\alpha(ZU^m) \cap \alpha(YW^m)x \neq \emptyset$ for each integer $m > 0$. Hence we may choose m so that $|\widehat{W^m}| \geqslant n$. Using the decodability of (A, α) we may conclude that $YW^m(1) = ZU^m(1)$ and hence that $Y(1) = Z(1)$. It follows that $\alpha(Z_tU^m) \cap \alpha(Y_tW^m)x \neq \emptyset$ with $|\hat{Y}_t\widehat{W^m}| \geqslant n$; by decodability of (A, α) we see that $Z_tU^m(1) = Y_tW^m(1)$. But $Z_tU^m(1) = Z_t(1) = Z(2)$ and $Y_tW^m(1) = Y_t(1) = Y(2)$ and so $Z(2) = Y(2)$. Now $|\hat{Y}| \leqslant |\hat{Z}|$ and continuing the argument we conclude that Y is a prefix of Z. Hence there exists a unique X such that $YX = Z$ and $x \in \alpha(X)$. We then have $\alpha(XU) \cap \alpha(WX) \neq \emptyset$ and so $XU = WX$ because (A, α) is correcting. Hence $YXU = ZU = YWX$.

Corollary 4.4. Suppose that (A, α) is decodable, $x \in \Sigma^+$, $\alpha(Y)x \cap \alpha(Z) \neq \emptyset$, and $x\alpha(U) \cap \alpha(W)x \neq \emptyset$. Then

$$|x| \geqslant \max\{|Z(*)|, |U(*)|, |W(1)|\}.$$

Proof. By Lemma 3.1 $YXU = ZU = YWX$ with $x \in \alpha(X)$. Then $YX = Z$, $XU = WX$, and $|x| = |\hat{X}|$. Hence the lemma follows.

Before we prove our next lemma we make several formal definitions. If F is a nonempty subset of Σ, then $P(F) = \{u : uv \in F\}$ is called *the set of prefixes of F*, $S(F) = \{v : uv \in F\}$ is called *the set of suffixes of F*, $Q(F) = P(F) \cap S(F)$ is called *the set of affixes of F*.

Suppose now that (A, α) is a code and that $x \in Q(\alpha(A))$. Then the pair $(\alpha(Y)x, \alpha(Z))$ for which $\alpha(Y)x \cap \alpha(Z) \neq \emptyset$ is said to be *irreducible* iff there exists no decomposition (Y_1, Y_2) of Y and (Z_1, Z_2) of Z such that $\alpha(Y_1) \cap \alpha(Z_1) \neq \emptyset$ and $\alpha(Y_2)x \cap \alpha(Z_2) \neq \emptyset$; otherwise the pair is said to be *reducible*. If, for the pair $(\alpha(Y)x, \alpha(Z))$, $\alpha(Y)x \cap \alpha(Z) \neq \emptyset$, then *the length of the pair* is defined to be $|\hat{Z}|$. Observe that if (A, α) is decodable with integer n, then each pair whose length is at least n is reducible because $(Y(1), Y_t)$ is a decomposition for Y, $(Z(1), Z_t)$ a decomposition for Z, and $Y(1) = Z(1)$.

Now suppose that $\alpha(Y)x \cap \alpha(Z) \neq \emptyset$ and that $Y = Y(1)...Y(m_1)$, $Z = Z(1)...Z(m_2)$. Using the terminology of [PML43] with the obvious modifications we say that $u \neq \emptyset$ is *an (i, j) right-link* for the pair $(\alpha(Y)x, \alpha(Z))$ iff for some $1 \leqslant i \leqslant m_1$ and $1 \leqslant j \leqslant m_2$, $\alpha(Y(1)...Y(i)) \cap \alpha(Z(1)...Z(j))u \neq \emptyset$ and $u\alpha(Y(i+1)...Y(m_1))x \cap \alpha(Z(j+1)...Z(m_2)) \neq \emptyset$ with $|u| < |Y(i)|$ and $|u| < |Z(j+1)|$. An (i, j) *left-link* is defined analogously; $u \neq \emptyset$ is a *link* iff it is a left-link and/or a right-link. Notice that when u is a right-link, then $u \in S(\alpha(Y(i)))$ and $u \in P(\alpha(Z(j+1)))$. Hence $u \in Q(\alpha(A))$. Clearly all links are in $Q(\alpha(A))$. Observe further that if u is an (i, j) right-link and an (i', j') right-link for the pair $(\alpha(Y)x, \alpha(Z))$ with $i < i'$ and $j < j'$, then there exist decompositions (Y_1, Y_2, Y_3) of Y and (Z_1, Z_2, Z_3) of Z such that $\alpha(Y_1) \cap \alpha(Z_1)u \neq \emptyset$, $u\alpha(Y_2) \cap \alpha(Z_2)u \neq \emptyset$ and $u\alpha(Y_3)x \cap \alpha(Z_3) \neq \emptyset$. If u is such a 'repeating' right-link we may let $Y_1 = Y(1)...Y(i)$, $Y_2 = Y(i+1)...Y(i')$, $Y_3 = Y(i'+1)...Y(m_1)$ and let $Z_1 = Z(1)Z(2)...Z(j)$, $Z_2 = Z(j+1)...Z(j')$, $Z_3 = Z(j'+1)...Z(m_2)$. Clearly, these decompositions satisfy our requirements. Our lemma will essentially say that sufficiently long irreducible pairs do have a repeating right-link. In the proof we use Lemmas 2.1 and 2.2 of [PML43]. Lemma 2.2 gives information about links; Lemma 2.1 information about right or left-links.

Lemma 4.5. Suppose that $\max\{|a|: a \in A\} = k$ and that $Q(\alpha(A))$ has q members. If the pair $(\alpha(Y)x, \alpha(Z))$ is irreducible and $|\hat{Z}| \geqslant (2q+2)(k+1) \geqslant 2(q+1)(k+1)$, then there exists some $u \in Q(\alpha(A))$ which is an (i, j) right-link and an (i', j') right-link for the pair with $i < i'$ and $j < j'$. Hence there exist decompositions (Y_1, Y_2, Y_3) of Y and (Z_1, Z_2, Z_3) of Z such that $\alpha(Y_1) \cap \alpha(Z_1)u \neq \emptyset$, $u\alpha(Y_2) \cap \alpha(Z_2)u \neq \emptyset$, and $u\alpha(Y_3)x \cap \alpha(Z_3) \neq \emptyset$ with $|u| < \min\{|Y_1(*)|, |Z_2(1)|, |Y_2(*)|\}$.

Proof. In view of our earlier observations we need only exhibit the 'repeating' right-link. Because $\alpha(Y)x \cap \alpha(Z) \neq \emptyset$ there exists $a'_1, a'_2, ...,$

$a'_{m_1}, b'_1, b'_2, \ldots, b'_{m_2}$ in $\alpha(A)$ such that $a'_1 a'_2 \ldots a'_{m_1} x = b'_1 b'_2 \ldots b'_{m_2}$. We now look at Lemma 2.2 of [PML43] with $s = s' = p' = \emptyset$, $p = x$, $h = m_1$ and $k = m_2$. For $m = 2q$, $n = k$, the lower bound of Lemma 2.2 is $(2q+1)(k-1)+0+|x|+1$ and we see that $(2q+1)(k-1)+|x|+1 < (2q+1)(k-1)+k+1 < (2q+2)(k+1)$. Because $|\hat{Z}| \geqslant (2q+2)(k+1)$ the hypotheses of Lemma 2.2 are satisfied and hence there are at least $2q$ links. Lemma 2.1 now tells us that there are at least q right-links. But each right-link is in $Q(\alpha(A))$ and nonempty while $Q(\alpha(A))$ has only $q-1$ nonempty members. Hence some right-link, say u, appears twice and clearly u is an (i, j) right-link and an (i', j') right-link with $i < i'$ and $j < j'$. So the lemma follows.

Lemma 4.6. Suppose that (A, α) is not decodable. Then there exists an $x \in \Sigma^+$ such that $\alpha(Y)x \cap \alpha(Z) \neq \emptyset$, $x\alpha(U) \cap \alpha(W)x \neq \emptyset$, and such that $|x| < \min\{|Z(*)|, |W(1)|, |U(*)|\}$.

Proof. If (A, α) is decodable, then each sufficiently long pair is reducible. Hence if (A, α) is not decodable, then there exist arbitrarily long irreducible pairs $(\alpha(T)v, \alpha(V))$. Hence we may choose a pair with $|\hat{V}| \geqslant (2q+2)(k+1)$ and apply Lemma 4.5 to produce the u, T_1, T_2, T_3, V_1, V_2, V_3 of the lemma. If we let $V_1 = Y$, $T_1 = Z$, $T_2 = U$, $V_2 = W$ and $u = x$, we have the result we want.

After all these preliminaries, we may state and prove our theorem about decodable codes.

THEOREM 4.7. The following statements are equivalent for a code (A, α):

(D1)   There exists an integer $n > 0$ such that if $|\hat{X}| \geqslant n$ and $\alpha(X)\Sigma \cap \alpha(Y) \neq \emptyset$, then $X(1) = Y(1)$.

(D2)   There exists an integer $m > 0$ such that if $|x| \geqslant m$, $xy \in \alpha(Y)$ and $xz \in \alpha(Z)$, then $Y(1) = Z(1)$.

(D3)   There exists an integer $n > 0$ such that if $|\hat{X}'| \geqslant n$ and $\iota(X')\Sigma \cap \iota(Y') \neq \emptyset$, then $X'(1) = Y'(1)$.

(D4)   If $x \neq \emptyset$, $x \in R$, and $x\Omega^+ \cap \alpha(W)x \neq \emptyset$, then $|x| \geqslant |W(1)|$.

(D5)   If $x \neq \emptyset$, $x \in R$, and $x\alpha(U) \cap \Omega^+ x \neq \emptyset$, then $|x| \geqslant |U(*)|$.

(D6)   If $x \neq \emptyset$, $x \in D$, and $\Omega^+ x \cap \alpha(Z) \neq \emptyset$, then $|x| \geqslant |Z(*)|$.

(D7) $L \cap D = \Omega$ and if $\alpha(a) \cap \alpha(X) \neq \emptyset$, then $a = X$.

(D8) There exists an integer $r > 0$ such that if $x \neq \emptyset$, $|x| \geqslant r$, $x \in \alpha(a)\Omega\Sigma \cap \alpha(b)\Omega$, then $a = b$.

(D9) If $\alpha(Y)x \cap \alpha(Z) \neq \emptyset$ and $x \in D$, then $Y(1) = Z(1)$.

(D10) If $\alpha(Y)x \cap \alpha(Z) \neq \emptyset$ and $x \in D$, then Y is a prefix of Z.

(D11) (A, α) is correcting and there exists an integer $h > 0$ such that if $u \in \Omega$, $w \in \Omega$, $|w| \geqslant h$, $v \in \Sigma$ and $uwv \in \Omega$, then $wv \in \Omega$.

Proof. The equivalence of (D1) and (D2) is Lemma 4.1 and the equivalence of (D1) and (D3) is Lemma 4.2. (D1) by Lemma 4.3 and Corollary 4.4 implies (D4), (D5), and (D6). On the other hand, (D4), (D5) and (D6) separately imply (D1) in view of Lemma 4.6 because a denial of (D1) contradicts (D4), (D5), and (D6).

Now (D1) implies (D7) because of Lemma 4.3. If $x \in L \cap D$, then x satisfies the pertinent hypotheses of Lemma 4.3 and hence $x \in \Omega$ and (A, α) is predecodable. On the other hand, with $Y = \emptyset$, $Z = U = W = a$, we have $\alpha(Y)a \cap \alpha(Z) \neq \emptyset$ and $a\alpha(U) \cap \alpha(W)a \neq \emptyset$ as required by Lemma 4.3 and hence there exists a unique X such that $\emptyset X = a$. Therefore (D1) implies (D7).

Recalling that Corollary 4.4 depends essentially on the fact that a certain identity holds, and that the identity implies (D4), (D5) and (D6), we show that (D7) implies (D4), (D5), and (D6) by showing that such an identity does hold. Now (D7) clearly implies (C11) and hence (C8), that is, (A, α) is correcting. For (D4), (D5) and (D6) we may assume that the x's of the statements satisfy the requirement that $\alpha(Y)x \cap \alpha(Z) \neq \emptyset$ and $x\alpha(U) \cap \alpha(W)x \neq \emptyset$ for certain Y, Z, U, W. By (D7) $x \in \Omega^+$ and so there exists X such that $x \in \alpha(X)$ and hence $\alpha(YX) \cap \alpha(Z) \neq \emptyset$ and $\alpha(XU) \cap \alpha(WX) \neq \emptyset$. However (A, α) is correcting and so $YX = Z$, $XU = WX$, and $YXU = ZU = YWX$. But now obviously (D7) implies (D4), (D5), and (D6).

Clearly (D1) implies (D8) and (D8) certainly implies (D2). Because of Lemma 4.3, (D1) implies (D9) and (D10) and certainly (D10) implies (D9). On the other hand repeated applications of (D9) establish (D10) because if $\alpha(Y)x \cap \alpha(Z) \neq \emptyset$ and $x \in D$, and $Y(1) = Z(1)$, then $\alpha(Y_t)x \cap \alpha(Z_t) \neq \emptyset$ and $x \in D$ and so because $|\hat{Y}| \leqslant |\hat{Z}|$, (D9) implies (D10). To complete a loop in the implications we show that (D10) implies (D7). Suppose $x \in L \cap D$, then $x \in D$ and $\alpha(Y)x \cap \alpha(Z) \neq \emptyset$ for certain Y and Z. By (D10), Y is a prefix of Z, hence $YX = Z$ for a unique X with $x \in \alpha(X)$; hence

$x \in \Omega$. With $Y = \emptyset$, $x = a$ and $Z = a$ we have $\alpha(Y)a \cap \alpha(a) \neq \emptyset$ and $a \in D$. But $YX = a$ with $Y = \emptyset$ and so $X = a$. Hence (D10) implies (D7).

Finally we show that (D11) and (D1) are equivalent where we write (D11) as follows: There exists an integer $m > 0$ such that if $\alpha(UW)x \cap \alpha(Z) \neq \emptyset$ and $|\hat{W}| \geqslant m$, then $UX = Z$ for some X and $\alpha(W)x \cap \alpha(X) \neq \emptyset$. To show that (D1) implies (D11) suppose that $\alpha(UW)x \cap \alpha(Z) \neq \emptyset$. Let us further suppose that $t = n$; then when $|\hat{W}| \geqslant t = n$ we have $|\widehat{UW}| \geqslant n$ and so by (D1) $UW(1) = Z(1)$, that is $U(1) = Z(1)$. But then $\alpha(U_tW)x \cap \alpha(Z_t) \neq \emptyset$, $|\widehat{U_tW}| \geqslant n$ and by (D1) again $U_t(1) = Z_t(1)$ and so $U(2) = Z(2)$. Clearly the argument can be continued to conclude that U is a prefix of Z because $|\hat{U}| < |\hat{Z}|$. Hence $UX = Z$ for a unique X. Obviously $\alpha(W)x \cap \alpha(X) \neq \emptyset$. So (D1) implies (D11).

To show that (D11) implies (D1) we assume that $\alpha(X)z \cap \alpha(Y) \neq \emptyset$ and that $|\hat{X}| \geqslant k + t$. Then $\alpha(X(1)X_t)z \cap \alpha(Y) \neq \emptyset$ and $|\hat{X}_t| \geqslant t$. Applying (D11) we conclude that $X(1)Z = Y$ for some Z and hence $X(1) = Y(1)$ and so (D11) implies (D1).

5. PROMPT CODES

We follow the pattern of the previous sections here and begin by adopting a different definition of a prompt code. Next we show that promptness is an expandable property. Finally we give a theorem which lists statements equivalent to the statement that a code is prompt. As before we use a convenient numbering.

We consider the following conditions for a code (A, α):

(P1) $\alpha(Y)x \cap \alpha(Z) \neq \emptyset$ implies $YX = Z$ that is, Y is a prefix of Z.

(P2) $\alpha(a)x \cap \alpha(Z) \neq \emptyset$ implies $a = Z(1)$.

In the language of [PML35] a code (A, α) was prompt iff (P2) held. We shall call (A, α) a *prompt code* iff (P1) holds. This means, of course, that we must show the equivalence.

Lemma 5.1. Let (A, α) be a code. Then (P1) holds iff (P2) holds.
Proof. (P1) clearly implies (P2). To show that (P2) implies (P1) we suppose that $\alpha(Y)x \cap \alpha(Z) \neq \emptyset$. Then $\alpha(Y(1))\alpha(Y_t)x \cap \alpha(Z) \neq \emptyset$. By (P2), $Y(1) = Z(1)$. But $\alpha(Y_t)x \cap \alpha(Z_t) \neq \emptyset$ and repeating the argument we see that $Y_t(1) = Y(2) = Z_t(1) = Z(2)$. Because $|\hat{Y}| \leqslant |\hat{Z}|$ we may conclude that Y is a prefix of Z. Hence $YX = Z$ for some X.

We make the obvious comment that prompt codes are decodable and hence are correcting.

Lemma 5.2. The following statements are equivalent for a code (A, α):

(P1) $\alpha(Y)x \cap \alpha(Z) \neq \emptyset$ implies $YX = Z$.

(P3) $\iota(Y')x \cap \iota(Z') \neq \emptyset$ implies $Y'X' = Z'$.

Proof. (P1) implies (P3). Assume $\iota(Y')x \cap \iota(Z') \neq \emptyset$. Let $\gamma(Y') = Y$, $\gamma(Z') = Z$. Then $\alpha(Y)x \cap \alpha(Z) \neq \emptyset$ and so $YX = Z$. Hence $x \in \alpha(X)$ and so $x = \hat{X}'$ for $X' \in [X]$. Therefore $\iota(Y')\iota(X') \cap \iota(Z') = \iota(Y'X') \cap \iota(Z') \neq \emptyset$. Now (A, α) is prompt, hence (A, α) is correcting and then $(\alpha(A), \iota)$ is correcting because correcting is an expandable property. It follows that $Y'X' = Z'$.

(P3) implies (P1). Assume that $\alpha(Y)x \cap \alpha(Z) \neq \emptyset$. Then there exists $Y' \in [Y]$, $Z' \in [Z]$ such that $\iota(Y')x \cap \iota(Z') \neq \emptyset$. By (P3) $Y'X' = Z'$. But then $\alpha(YX) \cap \alpha(Z) \neq \emptyset$. Now (P3) implies (D3), (D3) implies (C2), and (C2) implies (C8). Hence $YX = Z$ with $\gamma(X') = X$.

A code (A, α) is said to be *preprompt* iff $R = \Omega$. It is obvious that preprompt codes are predecodable and hence are precorrecting.

THEOREM 5.1. The following statements are equivalent for a code (A, α):

(P1) $\alpha(Y)x \cap \alpha(Z) \neq \emptyset$ implies $YX = Z$.

(P2) $\alpha(a)x \cap \alpha(Z) \neq \emptyset$ implies $a = Z(1)$.

(P3) $\iota(Y')x \cap \iota(Z') \neq \emptyset$ implies $Y'X' = Z'$.

(P4)   If $x \neq \emptyset$, $\Omega^+ x \cap \alpha(Z) \neq \emptyset$, then $|x| \geqslant |Z(*)|$.

(P5) $R = \Omega$ and if $\alpha(a) \cap \alpha(X) \neq \emptyset$, then $a = X$.

(P6)   If $\alpha(a)\Sigma \cap \alpha(b)\Omega \neq \emptyset$, then $a = b$.

Proof. The equivalence of (P1) and (P2) is Lemma 5.1 and the equivalence of (P1) and (P3) is Lemma 5.2.

Now (P1) implies (P4) because if $x \neq \emptyset$ and $\Omega^+ x \cap \alpha(Z) \neq \emptyset$, then $\alpha(Y)x \cap \alpha(Z) \neq \emptyset$ for some Y and, by (P1), we have $YX = Z$. Hence $|x| = |\hat{X}| \geqslant |Z(*)|$. Conversely (P4) implies (P1) because suppose (P1) does not hold. Then we claim that we can produce some $x \neq \emptyset$, Y, and Z such that $\alpha(Y)x \cap \alpha(Z) \neq \emptyset$ with $|x| < |Z(*)|$. Because (P1) does not hold there exists some U, V, w such that $\alpha(U)w \cap \alpha(V) \neq \emptyset$ with $U(1) \neq V(1)$.

If $|U(1)| < |V(1)|$, then for some u, $\alpha(U(1))u \cap \alpha(V(1)) \neq \emptyset$ with $|u| < |V(1)|$. Similarly, if $|V(1)| < |U(1)|$, then for some v, $\alpha(V(1))v \cap \alpha(U(1)) \neq \emptyset$ and $|v| < |U(1)|$. With the obvious choices of Y, Z, and x, we have $\alpha(Y)x \cap \alpha(Z) \neq \emptyset$ with $|x| < |Z(*)|$. Hence a denial of (P1) contradicts (P4) and so (P4) implies (P1).

By a now routine argument (P1) implies (P5). But (P5) implies (P1) because if $\alpha(Y)x \cap \alpha(Z) \neq \emptyset$, then, by (P5), $x \in \Omega$ and so $x \in \alpha(X)$ for some X and hence $\alpha(YX) \cap \alpha(Z) \neq \emptyset$. Now (P5) clearly implies that (A, α) is correcting and hence $YX = Z$ and so (P5) implies (P1).

Finally, it is evident that (P1) implies (P6). But (P6) implies (P2) because if $\alpha(a)x \cap \alpha(Z) \neq \emptyset$, then $\alpha(a)x \cap \alpha(Z(1))\alpha(Z_t) \neq \emptyset$ and, by (P6), $a = Z(1)$. Therefore, (P6) implies (P2) and, of course, (P2) implies (P1). Hence (P6) implies (P1) and we are finished.

CHAPTER 5

A STUDY OF ERROR-CORRECTING CODES, III: SYNCHRONIZABILITY AND COMMA-FREEDOM

L. ARQUETTE, L. CALABI, AND W. E. HARTNETT

EDITORIAL NOTE

The two remaining code properties of synchronizability and comma freedom for the per word substitution error models are given the now standard treatment which was developed in the preceding chapters. The attendant profusion of implication chains suggests the desirability of a graphical or tabular summarization of results. These are provided by the diligent authors at the end of the chapter, written in December 1966.

1. INTRODUCTION

This report is the sixth in a series devoted to the study of codes and their properties. The general program was outlined in [PML44] and will not be repeated here. We recall only that irredundant codes and correcting codes are studied in [PML43], decodable codes and prompt codes are discussed in [PML44]. Presented here are synchronizable codes and comma-free codes.

We assume that the reader is familiar with both [PML43] and [PML44]; a knowledge of [PML35] is not required but helpful. The general assumptions, basic definitions and notations are not reintroduced here.

Following the plan set down in [PML44] we shall operate with the original definitions of synchronizability and comma-freedom as given in [PML35]. They had been chosen as particularly appropriate to describe properties of the communication process. We shall introduce here many equivalent formulations, some of which are particularly pleasant for an axiomatic theory; they are easily stated, compared and used.

The various implications between code properties, already established in [PML35], may now be proven in many ways, because of the many equivalent statements obtained. For the record: 13090 ways! These implications are summarized at the end of this report in a diagram and three tables listing particularly interesting chains of statements (or axioms).

2. SYNCHRONIZABLE CODES

In [PML35] a code was said to be synchronizable iff it was correcting and satisfied a certain statement involving lengths of sequences. We shall exhibit five such 'length' statements and show that they are all equivalent. We shall then prove that each of these statements together with the property of precorrecting is equivalent to each of two other statements still to be formulated. After these preliminaries we state and prove the characterization or 'equivalence' theorem for synchronizable codes. Throughout we assume a detailed knowledge of [PML44]. In particular we recall that k is the maximum word length in A.

As usual we assign statement numbers with an eye to our lemmas which follow. For a code (A, α) consider the property expressed by the statement:

(L1)   There exists an integer $t > 0$ such that if $x \in \Sigma$, $|x| \geqslant t$, and $uxv \in \Omega$, then x has at least one decomposition $x = x_1 x_2$ such that whenever $yxz \in \Omega$, then $yx_1 \in \Omega$ and $x_2 z \in \Omega$.

Notice two things about (L1): first, yx_1 or $x_2 z$ but not both can be the void sequence, and second, the condition involves only Ω and does not mention (A, α) explicitly. This last fact means that if (L1) holds for a particular code (A, α), then it holds for each other code (B, β) for which $\beta(\Sigma(B)) = \alpha(\Sigma(A))$. In the obvious sense (L1) is a property only of Ω or is an Ω-property.

We state our first lemma about the equivalence of (L1) and other similar length statements. The notation used reflects the fact that statement (L2) was first used by Levenshtein [15].

Lemma 2.1. Each of the following statements is equivalent to (L1):

(L2)   There exists an integer $r > 0$ such that if $|x| \geqslant r$, $x\Sigma \cap \Omega \neq \emptyset$, $\Sigma x \cap \Omega \neq \emptyset$, then $x \in \Omega$.

(L3)   There exists an integer $r > 0$ such that if $|x| \geqslant r$, $x\Sigma \cap \alpha(Y) \neq \emptyset$, $\Sigma x \cap \alpha(Y) \neq \emptyset$, then $x \in \Omega$.

(L4)   There exists an integer $r>0$ such that if $|x| \geqslant r$, $x\Sigma x \cap \Omega \neq \emptyset$, then $x \in \Omega$.

(L5)   There exists an integer $s>0$ such that if $|x| \geqslant s$, $yxz \in \Omega$, then $yx \in \Omega$ whenever $\Sigma x \cap \Omega \neq \emptyset$ and $xz \in \Omega$ whenever $x\Sigma \cap \Omega \neq \emptyset$.

Proof. Our scheme of proof is circular.

(L1) $\Rightarrow$ (L2): Let $r = t$ in (L2) and assume that $xz \in \Omega$ and $yx \in \Omega$. By (L1) there exists a decomposition $x = x_1 x_2$ such that $x_1(x_2 z) \in \Omega$, $(yx_1)x_2 \in \Omega$, $x_1 \in \Omega$ and $x_2 \in \Omega$. Hence $x \in \Omega$.

(L2) $\Rightarrow$ (L3) is trivial; the fact that (L3) will imply (L2) is not.

(L3) $\Rightarrow$ (L4): If $xyx \in \alpha(Z)$, then $x(yx) \in \alpha(Z)$ and $(xy)x \in \alpha(Z)$. Hence $x\Sigma \cap \alpha(Z) \neq \emptyset$, $\Sigma x \cap \alpha(Z) \neq \emptyset$, and so, by (L3), $x \in \Omega$.

(L4) $\Rightarrow$ (L5): Let $s = r + k$ and suppose that $yxz \in \alpha(U)$ and $\Sigma x \cap \Omega \neq \emptyset$. Let U_1 be a prefix of U such that $|y| \leqslant |\hat{U}_1| < |y| + k$. Then $U = U_1 U_2$ and we write $x = x_1 x_2$ where $|\hat{U}_1| = |yx_1|$. Hence $|x_1| < k$ and $|x_2| > r$. Clearly $yx_1 \in \alpha(U_1)$, $x_2 z \in \alpha(U_2)$. Since $wx \in \Omega$ for some $w \in \Sigma$, $x_2 zwx = x_2(zwx_1)x_2 \in \Omega$ with $|x_2| > r$. By (L4), $x_2 \in \Omega$. But $yx_1 \in \Omega$ and so $yx = yx_1 x_2 \in \Omega$. Hence the first statement of the conclusion is proved. The proof for the second statement is analogous and starts by taking U_2 to satisfy $|z| \leqslant |\hat{U}_2| < |z| + k$.

(L5) $\Rightarrow$ (L1): Let $t = 2s + k$ and suppose that $yxz \in \alpha(W)$ with $|x| \geqslant t$. Clearly there exists a prefix W_1 of W such that $|y| + s \leqslant |\hat{W}_1| < |y| + s + k$ and a decomposition of $x = x_1 x_2$ such that $yx_1 \in \alpha(W_1)$ and $x_2 z \in \alpha(W_2)$ where $W = W_1 W_2$. Observe that $s \leqslant |x_1| < s + k$ and $s < |x_2|$. Suppose now that $uxv \in \Omega$. Then we have $uxv = ux_1(x_2 v) = (ux_1)x_2 v \in \Omega$ with $yx_1 \in \Omega$ and $x_2 z \in \Omega$. Hence we may apply (L5) to conclude that $ux_1 \in \Omega$ and $x_2 v \in \Omega$. So (L5) $\Rightarrow$ (L1).

Each of the equivalent statements of Lemma 2.1 will now be termed an *L-type statement for* Ω. In this terminology a code (A, α) is synchronizable iff (A, α) is correcting and an L-type statement for Ω holds. From [PML43], (A, α) is correcting iff (A, α) is precorrecting and irredundant. Hence (A, α) is synchronizable iff (A, α) is irredundant, precorrecting, and an L-type statement for Ω holds. Recall however that precorrecting was an Ω-property; explicitly, (A, α) was precorrecting iff $L \cap R = \Omega$ where $L = \{x : x \in \Sigma, x\Omega^+ \cap \Omega^+ \neq \emptyset\}$ and $R = \{x : x \in \Sigma, \Omega^+ x \cap \Omega^+ \neq \emptyset\}$. Therefore, the statement '$L \cap R = \Omega$ and an L-type statement for Ω holds' expresses an Ω-property. It follows that (A, α) is synchronizable iff (A, α)

is irredundant and a certain Ω-property holds. We now give a pleasant formulation of this property in the next lemma. As before (see [PML44]) we let $D = \{x: x \in \Sigma, x\Omega^+ \cap \Omega^+ x \neq \emptyset\}$.

Lemma 2.2. The following propositions are equivalent for Ω.

(PS1) $D = \Omega$.

(PS2)   If $xy \in \Omega$ and $yx \in \Omega$, then $x, y \in \Omega$.

(PS3) $L \cap R = \Omega$ and an L-type statement for Ω holds.

Proof. (PS1) $\Rightarrow$ (PS2): If $x = \emptyset$ or $y = \emptyset$, then $x, y \in \Omega$. If not, then $xy \in \Omega^+$, $yx \in \Omega^+$ and so $xyx \in \Omega^+ \cap \Omega^+ x$ and $yxy \in y\Omega^+ \cap \Omega^+ y$. By (PS1) we have $x, y \in D$ and hence $x, y \in \Omega$.

(PS2) $\Rightarrow$ (PS1): If $x \in D$, then $xy \in \Omega^+$ and $zx \in \Omega^+$ for some $y \in \Omega^+$ and $z \in \Omega^+$. Hence $(yz)x \in \Omega^+$ and $x(yz) \in \Omega^+$. By (PS2) we have $x \in \Omega$.

(PS3) $\Rightarrow$ (PS1): Let us suppose for convenience that (PS3) is $L \cap R = \Omega$ and (L2). If $x \in D$, then $xw = yx$ with $w, y \in \Omega$, $xw, yx \in \Omega$. By [19], there exists a non negative integer h and $u, v \in \Sigma$ such that $w = uv$, $y = vu$, and $x = (vu)^h v$. If $u = \emptyset$, then $w = v = y = x$ and hence $x \in \Omega$. If $v = \emptyset$, then $w = u = y$, $x = u^h$ and so $x \in \Omega$. Hence if $u = \emptyset$ or $v = \emptyset$, then $x \in \Omega$. If $u \neq \emptyset$ and $v \neq \emptyset$, choose h' so that $z = (uv)^{h'} u$ and $|z| \geqslant r$ where r is the integer of (L2). Then $zv = w^{h'+1} \in \Omega$ and $vz = y^{h'+1} \in \Omega$. By (L2), $z \in \Omega$ because $|z| \geqslant r$. But now $xz = (vu)^{h+h'+1} \in \Omega$ and $zx = (uv)^{h'+h+1} \in \Omega$. Hence $x \in L \cap R$ and by (PS3) we have $x \in \Omega$. Therefore (PS3) $\Rightarrow$ (PS1).

(PS1) $\Rightarrow$ (PS3): As above we take (L2) for our L-type statement. To begin the proof recall that $\Omega \subset L \cap R \subset D$. Hence $D = \Omega$ implies $L \cap R = \Omega$. To establish (L2) we let $x\Sigma \cap \Omega \neq \emptyset$ and $\Sigma x \cap \Omega \neq \emptyset$ and claim that if x is 'long enough', then $x \in \Omega$. By hypothesis there exists $y, u \in \Sigma$ and $z, v \in \Omega$ such that $xy = z$ and $ux = v$. Now $z = \hat{Z}'$ for some $Z' \in \Sigma(\alpha(A))$ and $v = \hat{V}'$ for some $V' \in \Sigma(\alpha(A))$. Let us assume that $Z' = (z_1, z_2, \ldots, z_m)$ and that $V' = (v_1, v_2, \ldots, v_n)$ so that $z = z_1 z_2 \ldots z_m$ and $v = v_1 v_2 \ldots v_n$. Hence $xy = z_1 z_2 \ldots z_m$, $ux = v_1 v_2 \ldots v_n$, and we may certainly choose x long enough to contain words of Z' and V'. It follows that for some $1 \leqslant m' \leqslant m$ and $1 \leqslant i \leqslant n$ we have $x = z_1 z_2 \ldots z_{m'} p$ and $x = s v_i v_{i+1} \ldots v_n$ with $p \in P(\alpha(A))$ and $s \in S(\alpha(A))$. We illustrate this situation in Figure 1(a). The vertical marks indicate the beginning or end of a word of $\alpha(A)$. If $p = \emptyset$ or $s = \emptyset$, then $x \in \Omega$ so we may assume that $p \neq \emptyset$ and $s \neq \emptyset$.

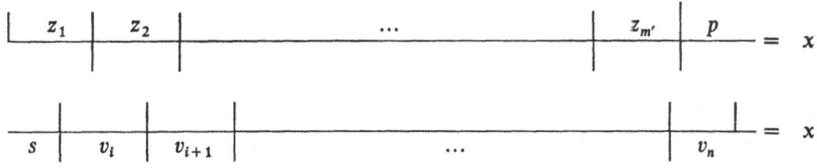

(a) $x = z_1 z_2 \ldots z_{m'} p = s v_i v_{i+1} \ldots v_n$

(b) $x = z_1 z_2 \ldots z_j v_{l+1} \ldots v_n \in \Omega$

(c) $w \hat{Z}_2' = \hat{V}_2' w \Rightarrow w = \hat{W}'$ for $W_\cdot' \in \Sigma(\check{\alpha}(A))$

$\hat{V}_2' = \hat{W}' \hat{V}_4'$ $x = \hat{Z}_1' \hat{V}_4' \hat{V}_3'$

Fig. 1.

Regardless of the length of x, if there exists some $1 \leqslant j \leqslant m'$ and $i \leqslant l < n$ such that the words z_j and v_l end at the same place in x, then we may write $x = z_1 z_2 \ldots z_j v_{l+1} \ldots v_n$ and observe that $x \in \Omega$. This situation is depicted in Figure 1(b). In the earlier terminology of [PML43], if the relation $x = z_1 z_2 \ldots z_{m'} p = s v_i v_{i+1} \ldots v_n$ is reducible, then $x \in \Omega$, so we assume that the relation is irreducible. Our claim now is that, by Lemmas 2.1 and 2.2 of [PML43], if x is sufficiently long, then there exists $Z_1', Z_2', Z_3' \in \Sigma(\alpha(A))$, $V_1', V_2', V_3' \in \Sigma(\alpha(A))$, and $w \in Q(\alpha(A))$ such that the following conditions are satisfied:

$$\widehat{Z_1' Z_2' Z_3'} = z_1 z_2 \ldots z_{m'}, \qquad \widehat{V_1' V_2' V_3'} = v_i v_{i+1} \ldots v_n$$
$$\hat{Z}_1' = s \hat{V}_1' w, \qquad w \hat{Z}_2' = \hat{V}_2' w, \qquad w \hat{Z}_3' p = \hat{V}_2'.$$

These somewhat complicated relationships are pictured in Figure 1(c).

It is clear that $w \in D$ and so $w \in \Omega$ because of (PS1). Hence $w = \hat{W}'$ for $W' \in \Sigma(\alpha(A))$. But then $\hat{V}_2' = \hat{W}' \hat{V}_4'$. It follows that we may write $x = \hat{Z}_1' \hat{V}_4' \hat{V}_3'$ and conclude that $x \in \Omega$ as required. Hence (PS1) does imply (PS3). It should be pointed out that some explicit r for (L2) can be provided, for example, $r = 8qk$ where q is the number of elements in $Q(\alpha(A))$.

It is time to name the Ω-property expressed by (PS1). We say that a code (A, α) is *presynchronizable* iff $D = \Omega$ and observe that presynchronizable codes are predecodable codes because $\Omega \subset L \cap D \subset D$ and that presynchronizable codes are precorrecting codes because of the equivalence of (PS1) and (PS3) in Lemma 2.2. It now follows trivially from our earlier remarks that (A, α) is synchronizable iff (A, α) is irredundant and presynchronizable.

We give the promised equivalence theorem for synchronizability.

THEOREM 2.3. The following statements are equivalent for a code (A, α):

(S1) (A, α) is correcting and an L-type statement for Ω holds.

(S2) $D = \Omega$ and if $\alpha(a) \cap \alpha(X) \neq \emptyset$, then $a = X$.

(S3)   If $x\alpha(Y) \cap \alpha(Z)x \neq \emptyset$, then $XY = ZX$ with $x \in \alpha(X)$.

(S4)   If $x \neq \emptyset$ and $x\alpha(Y) \cap \alpha(Z)x \neq \emptyset$, then $|x| \geqslant |Z(1)|$.

(S5)   If $x \neq \emptyset$ and $x\alpha(Y) \cap \alpha(Z)x \neq \emptyset$, then $|x| \geqslant |Y(*)|$.

(S6) $(\alpha(A), \iota)$ is synchronizable.

Proof. The equivalence of (S1) and (S2) was established above; recall that (A, α) is irredundant iff whenever $\alpha(a) \cap \alpha(X) \neq \emptyset$, then $a = X$.

With $x = \emptyset$, (S3) shows that (A, α) is correcting and hence that (A, α) is irredundant. Clearly (S3) implies that $D = \Omega$ and so (S3) yields (S2). Conversely, (S2) implies (S3) as follows: first (S2) yields that (A, α) is precorrecting and irredundant and so by Theorem 3.4 of [PML44], (A, α) is correcting. Now in (S3) if $x\alpha(Y) \cap \alpha(Z)x \neq \emptyset$, then (S2) implies that $x \in D$ and hence that $x \in \alpha(X)$ for some $X \in \Sigma(A)$. We then have $\alpha(X)\alpha(Y) \cap \alpha(Z)\alpha(X) \neq \emptyset$ and using the fact that α is a homomorphism we obtain $\alpha(XY) \cap \alpha(ZX) \neq \emptyset$. But (S2) shows that (A, α) is correcting and hence that α is separating and so $XY = ZX$ and (S2) implies (S3).

Obviously, (S3) gives (S4) and (S5). So we show that (S4) yields (S3); the proof that (S5) implies (S3) is analogous. First observe that (S4) implies Statement (C12) in Theorem 3.4 of [PML44] and hence (A, α) is correcting. If $x\alpha(Y) \cap \alpha(Z)x \neq \emptyset$ and $x = \emptyset$, then $\alpha(Y) \cap \alpha(Z) \neq \emptyset$ and $Y = Z$ because (A, α) is correcting. So we assume that $x\alpha(Y) \cap \alpha(Z)x \neq \emptyset$ with $x \neq \emptyset$, that is, $x\alpha(Y(1)\,Y(2)\ldots Y(*)) \cap \alpha(Z(1)Z(2)\ldots Z(*))x \neq \emptyset$. Let $|Z(1)\ldots Z(i)| \leqslant |x| < |Z(1)\ldots Z(i+1)|$ and set $X = (Z(1), \ldots, Z(i))$. If the equality sign holds, then $x \in \alpha(X)$ and, because (A, α) is correcting, $XY = ZX$. If the strict inequality holds, then $x = x_1 x_2$ with $|x_2| < |Z(i+1)|$ and $x_2\alpha(Y) \cap \alpha(Z(i+1)X)x_2 \neq \emptyset$ in violation of (S4). Hence (S4) implies (S3).

It remains to prove that (S3) is equivalent to (S6), that is, that synchronizability is an expandable property. The equivalence of (S1) and (S2) shows that (A, α) is synchronizable iff (A, α) is presynchronizable and irredundant. It follows that $(\alpha(A), \iota)$ is synchronizable iff $(\alpha(A), \iota)$ is presynchronizable and irredundant. Now clearly presynchronizability is an expandable property because it is an Ω-property and so we would be finished if we knew that irredundance was an expandable property. However, this fact was established by the equivalence of (IR1) and (IR2) of Theorem 4.1 of [PML43]. Hence synchronizability is an expandable property.

3. COMMA-FREE CODES

In [PML35] a code (A, α) was said to be *comma-free* iff the following statement holds:

(CF2) If $a, b, c \in A$, $u\alpha(a)v \cap \alpha(bc) \neq \emptyset$, then $a = b$ and $u = \emptyset$ or $a = c$ and $v = \emptyset$.

A result of [PML35] was that comma-free codes are both prompt and synchronizable codes and so are decodable and correcting codes. In addition, they are irredundant codes.

We shall say that a code (A, α) is *precomma-free* iff $x\Omega^+ y \cap \Omega^+ \neq \emptyset$ implies $x, y \in \Omega$. Two facts should be mentioned: first, the property expressed is a property of Ω only and not directly of (A, α) and so is an Ω-property; second, the condition can be read as: if $x\alpha(W)y \cap \alpha(Z) \neq \emptyset$, then $\alpha(XWY) \cap \alpha(Z) \neq \emptyset$ with $x \in \alpha(X)$ and $y \in \alpha(Y)$. From this last formulation it is clear that precomma-freedom together with correcting would give $XWY = Z$ if $x\alpha(W)y \cap \alpha(Z) \neq \emptyset$.

It is fairly routine to establish that if (A, α) is precomma-free, then it is preprompt and presynchronizable and hence predecodable and precorrecting. Indeed, all statements are immediate except the assertion that precomma-free codes are presynchronizable so we make good this claim. If $x\alpha(Y) \cap \alpha(Z)x \neq \emptyset$, that is, if $x \in D$, and $x = \emptyset$, then $x \in \Omega$. If $|x| < |\hat{Z}|$, then $xy \in \alpha(Z_1)$ for some $y \in \Sigma$ and for some prefix Z_1 of Z and then $x\alpha(Y)y \cap \alpha(Z)xy = x\alpha(Y)y \cap \alpha(ZZ_1) \neq \emptyset$ and $x \in \Omega$ because (A, α) is precomma-free. If $|x| > |\hat{Z}|$, we use our standard device of choosing some $h > 0$ such that $x\alpha(Y^h) \cap \alpha(Z^h)x \neq \emptyset$ and $|x| < |\hat{Z}^h|$. We then repeat the argument as above to conclude that $x \in \Omega$ and hence that (A, α) is presynchronizable.

We now state and prove our equivalence theorem for comma-freedom. Observe that when we prove below the equivalence of (CF1) and (CF3) for an arbitrary code (A, α), then we also prove the equivalence for the code $(\alpha(A), \imath)$. We use this fact to prove the equivalence of (CF6) and (CF7).

THEOREM 3.1. The following statements are equivalent for a code (A, α):

(CF1) $x\alpha(W)y \cap \alpha(Z) \neq \emptyset$ implies $XWY = Z$ with $x \in \alpha(X)$ and $y \in \alpha(Y)$.

(CF2) If $a, b, c \in A$, $u\alpha(a)v \cap \alpha(bc) \neq \emptyset$, then $a = b$ and $u = \emptyset$ or $a = c$ and $v = \emptyset$.

(CF3) (A, α) is precomma-free and irredundant.

(CF4) If $x \neq \emptyset$, $x\alpha(W)y \cap \alpha(Z) \neq \emptyset$, then $|x| \geqslant |Z(1)|$.

(CF5) If $y \neq \emptyset$, $x\alpha(W)y \cap \alpha(Z) \neq \emptyset$, then $|y| \geqslant |Z(*)|$.

(CF6) $(\alpha(A), \imath)$ is precomma-free and irredundant.

(CF7) $(\alpha(A), \imath)$ is comma-free.

Proof. (CF1) $\Rightarrow$ (CF2): If $u\alpha(a)v \cap \alpha(bc) \neq \emptyset$, then $UaV = bc$ for sentences $U, V \in \Sigma(A)$. Clearly, $U = \emptyset$ and $a = b$ or $V = \emptyset$ and $a = c$.

(CF2) $\Rightarrow$ (CF4): Let $x\alpha(W)y \cap \alpha(A) \neq \emptyset$. If $Z(*) = Z(1)$, then for $a \in A$ we have $x\alpha(W)(ya) \cap \alpha(Za) \neq \emptyset$ contradicting (CF2). Thus we may assume that Z has at least two words. If $|x| < |Z(1)|$, then $x\alpha(W(1))t \cap \alpha(Z(1)Z(2)) \neq \emptyset$ for some $t \in \Sigma$ or else $u\alpha(Z(2))v \cap \alpha(W(1)) \neq \emptyset$ with $u \neq \emptyset$, $v \neq \emptyset$. In the first case we violate (CF2); in the second we can write $u\alpha(Z(2))(va) \cap \alpha(W(1)a) \neq \emptyset$; again we violate (CF2). Hence (CF2) implies (CF4).

The proof that (CF4) implies (CF3) is similar to the proof in Theorem 2.3 above that (S4) implies (S3).

(CF3) $\Rightarrow$ (CF1): Because precomma-free implies precorrecting, (CF3) yields the fact that (A, α) is correcting in virtue of (C11) of Theorem 3.4 of [PML44]. If $x\alpha(W)y \cap \alpha(Z) \neq \emptyset$ in (CF1), then $\alpha(XWY) \cap \alpha(Z) \neq \emptyset$ with $x \in \alpha(X)$ and $y \in \alpha(Y)$ by (CF3). But then $XWY = Z$ because (A, α) is correcting and so (CF3) $\Rightarrow$ (CF1).

The proof that (CF2) $\Rightarrow$ (CF5) is similar to the proof that (CF2) $\Rightarrow$ (CF4) and the proof that (CF5) $\Rightarrow$ (CF3) is similar to the proof that (CF4) $\Rightarrow$ (CF3).

We now show that (CF3) and (CF6) are equivalent. Now (A, α) is pre-comma free iff $(\alpha(A), \iota)$ is precomma-free by definition because pre-comma freedom is an Ω-property. By Theorem 4.1 of [PML43] irredundance is an expandable property and so (CF3) is equivalent to (CF6).

The equivalent of (CF6) and (CF7) follows from the equivalence of (CF1) and (CF3) for $\alpha = \iota$. Hence comma-freedom is an expandable property.

4. DIAGRAMS AND TABLES

In this section we summarize some of our basic results. We first show by diagrams the relationships between the various classes of codes over a fixed alphabet J. We then use tables to indicate the similarities (and differences) between statements characterizing different code properties.

We make the following notational agreements:

$\mathscr{K}$ denotes the class of all codes over J.

$\mathscr{I}$ denotes the class of all irredundant codes over J.

$\mathscr{C}$ denotes the class of all correcting codes over J.

$\mathscr{D}$ denotes the class of all decodable codes over J.

$\mathscr{S}$ denotes the class of all synchronizable codes over J.

$\mathscr{P}$ denotes the class of all prompt codes over J.

$\mathscr{F}$ denotes the class of all (comma)-free codes over J.

Because each comma-free code is both prompt and synchronizable, we have $\mathscr{F} \subset \mathscr{P} \cap \mathscr{S}$ where, as usual, $\mathscr{P} \cap \mathscr{S}$ denotes the class of all codes that are both prompt and synchronizable and $\subset$ denotes inclusion of classes. In a similar fashion we have the following statements:

$$\mathscr{F} \subset \mathscr{P} \cap \mathscr{S} \subset \mathscr{P} \subset \mathscr{D} \subset \mathscr{C} \subset \mathscr{I} \subset \mathscr{K}$$

and

$$\mathscr{F} \subset \mathscr{P} \cap \mathscr{S} \subset \mathscr{S} \subset \mathscr{D} \subset \mathscr{C} \subset \mathscr{I} \subset \mathscr{K}.$$

We now turn to the so-called 'pre' code properties. Recall that these properties are actually concerned with the subset $\Omega(A)$ of $\Sigma(J)$ determined by the code (A, α) and that $\Omega(A) = \Omega(\alpha(A))$. Hence they are expandable properties. We make the following conventions:

$\mathscr{C}_p$ denotes the class of all precorrecting codes over J.

$\mathscr{D}_p$ denotes the class of all predecodable codes over J.

$\mathscr{S}_p$ denotes the class of all presynchronizable codes over J.

$\mathscr{P}_p$ denotes the class of all preprompt codes over J.

$\mathscr{F}_p$ denotes the class of all pre-(comma)-free codes over J.

As we observed before, $\mathscr{F}_p \subset \mathscr{P}_p \cap \mathscr{S}_p$, that is, each pre-(comma)-free code is both preprompt and presynchronizable. More generally we have:

$$\mathscr{F}_p \subset \mathscr{P}_p \cap \mathscr{S}_p \subset \mathscr{P}_p \subset \mathscr{D}_p \subset \mathscr{C}_p$$

and

$$\mathscr{F}_p \subset \mathscr{P}_p \cap \mathscr{S}_p \subset \mathscr{S}_p \subset \mathscr{D}_p \subset \mathscr{C}_p.$$

We can now relate these classes in terms of past theorems which we cite. In this abstract formulation the theorems are particularly simple to express. We have:

(1)	$\mathscr{C} = \mathscr{I} \cap \mathscr{C}_p$	(C11)	of Theorem 3.4 of [PML44]
(2)	$\mathscr{D} = \mathscr{I} \cap \mathscr{D}_p$	(D7)	of Theorem 4.7 of [PML44]
(3)	$\mathscr{P} = \mathscr{I} \cap \mathscr{P}_p$	(P5)	of Theorem 5.1 of [PML44]
(4)	$\mathscr{S} = \mathscr{I} \cap \mathscr{S}_p$	(S2)	of Theorem 2.3 of this chapter
(5)	$\mathscr{F} = \mathscr{I} \cap \mathscr{F}_p$	(CF3)	of Theorem 3.1 of this chapter.

More explicitly, (1) says that each correcting code is both irredundant and precorrecting and that each irredundant and precorrecting code is correcting. Analogous statements for the other theorems. All these relationships are expressed in Figure 2. For example, $\mathscr{C}_p$ is represented by a solid disk and $\mathscr{I}$ by a solid half-disk; the intersection $\mathscr{I} \cap \mathscr{C}_p$ is then represented by the solid half-disk $\mathscr{C}$. Because all codes considered are codes in $\mathscr{K}$, we represent $\mathscr{K}$ by the largest solid disk.

Figure 2 gives the structural relaltionships which exist within the class $\mathscr{K}$ of codes. The explicit characterizations of the codes, of course, are not indicated in Figure 2. We remedy this somewhat by turning now to the presentation of three tables similar to those given in [PML43] for the properties of irredundance, precorrecting, and correcting. For a fixed

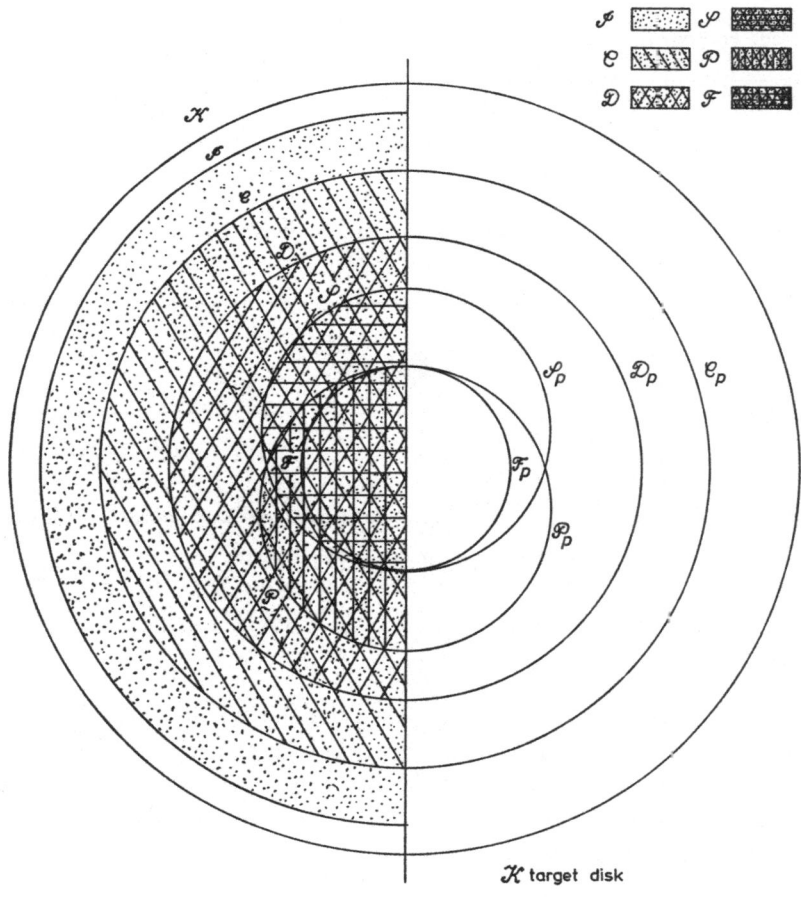

Fig. 2.

code (A, α) we consider the appropriate code properties in the first column and a statement equivalent to the property in the second column; the numbering of the statements refers to the numbering of [PML43] or of this paper as the case may be. For Table I the statements are all of the same 'form'. We have the following with $X, Y, Z, U, V \in \Sigma^+(A)$ and $x, u, v \in \Sigma(J)$:

TABLE I

Code Property of (A, α)			Equivalent Statement	
correcting			(C17) $\alpha(Y)x \cap \alpha(Z) \neq \emptyset$ and $x \in L$ $\Rightarrow YX = Z.$	
decodable			(D10) $\alpha(Y)x \cap \alpha(Z) \neq \emptyset$ and $x \in D$ $\Rightarrow YX = Z.$	
prompt			(P1) $\alpha(Y)x \cap \alpha(Z)$ $\neq \emptyset \Rightarrow YX = Z.$	
	synchronizable			(S3) $x\alpha(Y) \cap \alpha(Z)x$ $\neq \emptyset \Rightarrow XY = ZX$
comma-free			(CF1) $x\alpha(Y)v \cap \alpha(Z) \neq \emptyset \Rightarrow$ $XYV = Z$ with $x \in \alpha(X)$, $v \in \alpha(V)$	

Each property implies the properties listed above it and so each equivalent statement on the right implies those above it. The similarities and the differences in the statements are then easy to observe. Observe that the precise formulations given here are not precisely those given before; however, they are trivially equivalent.

Each assertion says that if a sequence satisfies a certain kind of condition, then the sequence belongs to Ω in a particular way. More explicitly but still vaguely, each statement says that if a sequence x satisfies special statements involving the ranges of certain sentences, then x belongs to the range of a unique sentence and that sentence satisfies an equation involving those same sentences. From this point of view, all of our statements in the right hand column of Table I are 'equational' in character. In still other terms, the hypothesis of each involves Ω and $\Sigma(J)$ and the conclusion is stated in terms of $\Sigma(A)$ alone.

We now present Table II of the same kind. This time we consider 'length' statements, all involving inequalities. For simplicity we restrict ourselves to nonempty sequences. As before we have a set format for our statements. Each says that whenever $x \neq \emptyset$ and x satisfies certain statements about Ω^+ and the range of a particular sentence, then x is at least as long as the length of the last word of that sentence. As before we give trivial modifications of earlier formulations. For each statement, $Z \in \Sigma^+(A)$; $Z(*)$ is the last of word of Z and $|Z(*)|$ is its length.

TABLE II

Code Property of (A, α)		Equivalent Statement	
correcting		(C15) $x \neq \emptyset$, $\Omega^+ x \cap \alpha(Z) \neq \emptyset$ and $x \in L$ $\Rightarrow |x| \geq |Z(*)|$	
decodable		(D6) $x \neq \emptyset$, $\Omega^+ x \cap \alpha(Z) \neq \emptyset$ and $x \in D$ $\Rightarrow |x| \geq |Z(*)|$.	
prompt		(P4) $x \neq \emptyset$, $\Omega^+ x \cap$ $\alpha(Z) \neq \emptyset \Rightarrow$ $|x| \geq |Z(*)|$	
	synchronizable		(S5) $x \neq \emptyset$, $x\alpha(Z)$ $\cap \Omega^+ x \neq \emptyset \Rightarrow$ $|x| \geq |Z(*)|$
comma-free		(CF5) $x \neq \emptyset$, $y\Omega^+ x \cap \alpha(Z) \neq \emptyset$ $\Rightarrow |x| \geq |Z(*)|$.	

Table III presents still another set of statements. As modifications of previous statements, they all have the same 'form': a statement whose hypotheses involve sequences and Ω^+ and whose conclusion is that the sequences are in Ω^+ and the statement that the code is irredundant. The format of the table again indicates the relationships that exist between the code properties. It shows quite explicitly which requirements must be adjoined to irredundance to obtain the desired code property; in the obvious sense, it is the analogue of our diagram above for the case of a particular code.

TABLE III

Code Property of (A, α)			Equivalent Statement	
correcting			(C11) $\quad x\Omega^+\cap\Omega^+\neq\emptyset$ and $\Omega^+x\cap\Omega^+\neq\emptyset$ $\Rightarrow x\in\Omega$ and $\alpha(a)\cap\alpha(X)\neq\emptyset\Rightarrow a=X.$	
decodable			(D7) $\quad \Omega^+x\cap\Omega^+\neq\emptyset$ and $x\Omega^+\cap\Omega^+x\neq\emptyset$ $\Rightarrow x\in\Omega$ and $\alpha(a)\cap\alpha(X)\neq\emptyset\Rightarrow a=X.$	
prompt			(P5) $\quad \Omega^+x\cap\Omega^+\neq\emptyset$ $\Rightarrow x\in\Omega$ and $\alpha(a)\cap\alpha(X)\neq\emptyset$ $\Rightarrow a=X$	
	synchronizable			(S2) $\quad x\Omega^+\cap\Omega^+x\neq\emptyset$ $\Rightarrow x\in\Omega$ and $\alpha(a)\cap\alpha(X)\neq\emptyset$ $\Rightarrow a=X$
comma-free			(CF3) $\quad x\Omega^+y\cap\Omega^+\neq\emptyset\Rightarrow x, y\in\Omega$ and $\alpha(a)\cap\alpha(X)\neq\emptyset\Rightarrow a=X.$	

CHAPTER 6

A STUDY OF ERROR-CORRECTING CODES, IV:
CODE PROPERTIES AND UNAMBIGUOUS SETS

L. CALABI AND W. E. HARTNETT

EDITORIAL NOTE

The search for alternative formulations and presentations goes on unabated in this paper. The basic motivation for the treatment was the desire to utilize the intuitive notion of a comma of a received sequence. In an earlier version [PML 45], elaborate implications involving the unambiguity of members of a large collection of exotic sets were derived. The effort however reduced only to the somewhat meager results of this chapter. At the time (February 1967), the crucial significance of the notion of a comma or separation was masked by the nature of the model being considered. We later realized what was really involved: the idea was there but the import was missed.

1. Introduction

This report is the seventh in a series devoted to the study of codes and their properties. The general program was outlined in [PML44] and will not be repeated here. We recall only that irredundant codes and correcting codes were studied in [PML43], decodable codes and prompt codes were discussed in [PML44], and that synchronizable codes and comma-free codes were characterized in [PML46].

We assume that the reader is familiar with [PML43], [PML44], and [PML46]. Some of the basic definitions and notations will be recalled but prior results will not be listed. The reader may consult the cited references for specific results that are needed here.

In this paper we continue our earlier work on the characterization of code properties. The approach is somewhat different from our previous one and may be summarized as follows. Given a simple code (A, i), we first extend the notion of scansion, originally defined in Ω (see [PML43]), to other sets constructed from A. We then define the notion of unambiguity, which extends that of unique decipherability. Finally

W. E. Hartnett (ed.), Foundations of Coding Theory, 97–105. All Rights Reserved.
Copyright © 1974 by D. Reidel Publishing Company, Dordrecht-Holland.

we shall show that each of the code properties of irredundance, correctability, decodability, and synchronizability can be characterized by the unambiguity of a set. Such a property has been called a code-related property (see [PML45]).

It should be remarked that because our code properties are expandable in the sense of [PML44] it suffices to consider only simple codes here.

2. EXTENSION OF CONCEPTS

We begin by recalling a few notions used in past reports. As usual J will denote a finite nonempty set, called the *alphabet*, $\Sigma = \Sigma(J)$ the set of all finite sequences over J, Σ^+ the nonempty finite sequences in Σ. A *code* is a pair (A, α) in which A is a finite nonempty subset of Σ^+ and α is an admissibility mapping on A as defined in [PML43]. Explicitly, α is a map from A into the subsets of Σ such that: (1) for each $a \in A$, $a \in \alpha(a)$, (2) if $a, b \in A$, $a \neq b$, then $\alpha(a) \cap \alpha(b) = \emptyset$, (3) for each $a \in A$, if $x, y \in \alpha(a)$, then $|x| = |y|$ where $|x|$ denotes the length of x. We also let $\Sigma(A)$ denote the set of finite sequences of members of A, $\Sigma^+(A)$ denotes the set of nonempty sequences in $\Sigma(A)$. Members of A are called *words*; members of $\Sigma(A)$ are called *sentences over A*. Hence sentences are finite sequences of words.

Σ with juxtaposition of sequences over J and $\Sigma(A)$ with juxtaposition of sentences over A are cancellation semigroups. There is a natural map from $\Sigma(A)$ to Σ defined as follows: if $X \in \Sigma(A)$ and X is the void sequence, then $\hat{X}$ is the void sequence in Σ; if X is not void and $X = (a_1, a_2, ..., a_n)$, then $\hat{X} = a_1 a_2 ... a_n \in \Sigma^+$. From the definition it follows that $\widehat{XY} = \hat{X} \, \hat{Y}$, that is, $\wedge$ is a homomorphism from $\Sigma(A)$ into Σ.

The mapping α is defined on $\Sigma^+(A)$ by requiring that when $X = (a_1, a_2, ..., a_n) \in \Sigma^+(A)$, then $\alpha(X) = \alpha(a_1)\alpha(a_2)...\alpha(a_n)$ where the right side is the usual induced juxtaposition product of the sets $\alpha(a_i)$, $i = 1, 2, ..., n$. It follows that $\alpha(XY) = \alpha(X)\alpha(Y)$. It should be noticed that $\hat{X} \in \alpha(X)$ for each $X \in \Sigma^+(A)$.

Each code, (A, α) has an *expanded code* $(\alpha(A), \iota)$ where $\alpha(A) = \bigcup \{\alpha(a): a \in A\}$ and for each $x \in \alpha(A)$, $\iota(x) = \{x\}$. $\Sigma^+(\alpha(A))$ is the set of nonvoid sentences over $\alpha(A)$ and if $X' \in \Sigma^+(\alpha(A))$, $X' = (x'_1, x'_2, ..., x'_k)$, then $\hat{X}' = x'_1 x'_2 ... x'_k$ and $\iota(X') = \{\hat{X}'\}$. A code (B, ι) for which $\iota(b) = \{b\}$ for each $b \in B$ is a *simple code* and hence each expanded code is a simple code.

Each code (A, α) generates the set $\Omega^+ = \alpha(\Sigma^+(A)) = \bigcup \{\alpha(X) : X \in \Sigma^+(A)\}$ and it is routine to observe that $\alpha(\Sigma^+(A)) = \iota(\Sigma^+(\alpha(A)))$. It follows that (A, α) and $(\alpha(A), \iota)$ both generate Ω^+. Hence, if we propose to use Ω^+ to talk about code properties we may use a code or its expanded code. Put another way: if we deal with Ω^+ then we may always assume that we have a simple code.

From this point on, unless noted, we shall assume that we have a fixed simple code (A, ι), shall let X, Y, Z denote members of $\Sigma^+(A)$, and write $\hat{X}$ for $\{\hat{X}\}$. Our three sets A, $\Sigma^+(A)$, and Ω^+ are related as in the diagram of Figure 1.

$$A \longrightarrow \Sigma^+(A) \longrightarrow \Omega^+ \subset \Sigma^+$$

Fig. 1.

The basic scheme of the diagram is this: we start with A, form all nonempty *finite* sequences $\Sigma^+(A)$ over A, and then apply $\wedge$ to the set $\Sigma^+(A)$ to obtain the subset Ω^+ of Σ^+. We now want to do the same kind of thing with what we will call infinite sequences and doubly infinite sequences. To do so we need more notation.

Let $\mathbb{N}$ denote the set $\{1, 2, ..., n, ...\}$ of natural numbers and let $J^{\mathbb{N}}$ denote the set of all functions from $\mathbb{N}$ into J. In usual terminology, $J^{\mathbb{N}}$ is the set of all *infinite sequences over* J. If $x \in J^{\mathbb{N}}$, then we write $x = x_1 x_2...x_n...$ where each $x_i \in J$. In a similar fashion we let $A^{\mathbb{N}}$ denote the set of all sequences over A; each X in $A^{\mathbb{N}}$ will be called an *infinite sentence over* A. We may define a mapping $\wedge$ from $A^{\mathbb{N}}$ into $J^{\mathbb{N}}$ in the obvious way: if $X = (a_1, a_2, ..., a_n, ...) \in A^{\mathbb{N}}$, then $\hat{X} = a_1 a_2 a_3 ... a_n ... \in J^{\mathbb{N}}$.

We let $\mathbb{Z}$ denote the set of all integers and form $J^{\mathbb{Z}}$ and $A^{\mathbb{Z}}$. The elements of $J^{\mathbb{Z}}$ are the *doubly infinite sequences over* J and the elements of $A^{\mathbb{Z}}$ are the *doubly infinite sentences over* A. We may again define a map from $A^{\mathbb{Z}}$ into $J^{\mathbb{Z}}$: if $X = (..., a_{-2}, a_{-1}, a_0, a_1, a_2, ...) \in A^{\mathbb{Z}}$, then $\hat{X} = (...x_{-2} x_{-1} x_0 x_1 x_2...) = (...a_{-2} a_{-1} a_0 a_1 a_2...) \in J^{\mathbb{Z}}$ where x_0 is the first alphabet symbol of the word a_0.

The three constructions are indicated in Figure 2 in which we have repeated the set A.

In the diagram we let Ω_i^+ denote the set of all elements of J^N obtained by applying $\wedge$ to the members of A^N and let Ω_d^+ denote the similar subset of J^Z obtained by applying $\wedge$ to the members of A^Z. We indicate the application of $\wedge$ by putting $\wedge$ above the appropriate arrow.

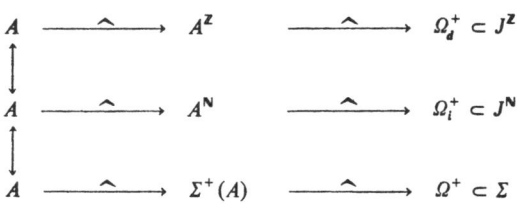

Fig. 2.

In the next section we shall define a notion of unambiguity which can be predicated of each of the sets Ω^+, Ω_i^+, and Ω_d^+. It will turn out that various code properties of A can be described in terms of this notion of unambiguity and so we shall obtain still another alternative characterization of these code properties.

3. SCANSIONS

The notion of scansion will now be defined for each level of our diagram. We then use this concept to define the idea of an unambiguous set.

We say that $X \in \Sigma^+(A)$ is *a scansion of* $x \in \Omega^+$ iff $\hat{X} = x$. Each $x \in \Omega^+$ has at least one scansion by the definition of Ω^+. In a similar fashion we say that $X \in A^N$ is *a scansion of* $x \in \Omega_i^+$ iff $\hat{X} = x$; again, each $x \in \Omega_i^+$ has scansions.

To define scansions of members of Ω_d^+ we need to exercise a little care. Recall that when we defined $\hat{X}$ for $X \in A^Z$ we essentially agreed on an 'origin' in the following sense: given $X = (\ldots, a_{-2}, a_{-1}, a_0, a_1, a_2, \ldots)$, it was clear that $\hat{X}$ should be formed by an 'infinite' juxtaposition $\ldots a_{-2}a_{-1}a_0a_1a_2\ldots$ of the words of X. In order to make this juxtaposition an element $x = (\ldots x_{-2}x_{-1}x_0x_1x_2\ldots)$ of J^Z it was necessary to select some alphabet symbol as x_0. We agreed to take the first symbol of a_0 as x_0. This amounted to the stipulation that a word of X always begins at x_0 in $\hat{X}$.

With this agreement we may say that $X \in A^Z$ is *a scansion of* $x \in \Omega_d^+$ iff $\hat{X} = x$. The doubly infinite sequence x is a function from $\mathbb{Z}$ into J, of course, and it may happen that for a different doubly infinite sequence y there exists a nonzero integer h such that $y(i) = x(i+h)$. In this case we say that y is a *shift of* x. If now, given $x \in \Omega_d^+$ and X a scansion of x, there exists a $Y \in A^Z$ such that $\hat{Y}$ is a shift of z, then we shall regard Y as the same scansion of x as X whenever Y is a shift of X, that is, if $Y(i) = X(i+k)$ for some nonzero integer k. The fact that we have doubly infinite sequences demands this kind of agreement on scansions.

We shall say that a set of sequences with scansions is *unambiguous* iff each sequence has exactly one scansion. In this form the definition applies to subsets of Ω^+, Ω_i^+, and of Ω_d^+. In the following two lemmas we show how the concept may be used.

Lemma 3.1. (A, ι) is an irredundant code iff A is unambiguous.
Proof. By Theorem 4.1 of [PML43] we know that (A, ι) is irredundant iff $a = \hat{X}$ implies $(a) = X$. For each $a \in A$, (a) is a scansion of a and so $a = \hat{X}$ implies $(a) = X$ iff A is unambiguous. Hence the lemma.

Our next lemma indicates how unambiguity is a generalization of unique decipherability.

Lemma 3.2. (A, ι) is a correcting code iff Ω^+ is unambiguous.
Proof. As in the proof of Lemma 3.1 the statement that Ω^+ is unambiguous means that if $t \in \Omega^+$ and $t = \hat{X} = \hat{Y}$, then $X = Y$. But this last statement is equivalent to the fact that (A, ι) is correcting by Theorem 5.1 of [PML43]. Hence the lemma is established.

These lemmas are not overly impressive in that they only restate what we already knew. Other results in this same general vein have been obtained but will not be given here. They are phrased in terms of two weaker notions that can be defined for scansions; both involve the concept of the reducibility of scansions. This latter concept has been used before (see Section 2 of [PML43]; section 4, particularly Lemma 4.5, of [PML44]; and Section 2 of [PML46]); the other notions have been elaborately treated in [PML45] in a more extended setting. At the end of Section 4 we indicate the extended setting. Characterizations for decodability and synchronizability can be given using these concepts but they require considerable detail. We prefer to give equivalent characterizations in terms of the notion of unambiguity at the two other levels of our diagram and we turn to those levels now.

4. CODE-RELATED PROPERTIES

In this section we are primarily concerned with the code-related property of unambiguity and we want to connect it with some of our code properties. The diagram of our next lemma suggests how to do this.

Lemma 4.1. The following implication diagram holds for a simple code (A, ι):

(A, ι) is synchronizable		Ω_d^+ is unambiguous
$\Downarrow$		$\Downarrow$
(A, ι) is decodable		Ω_i^+ is unambiguous
$\Downarrow$		$\Downarrow$
(A, ι) is correcting	$\Longleftrightarrow$	Ω^+ is unambiguous
$\Downarrow$		$\Downarrow$
(A, ι) is irredundant	$\Longleftrightarrow$	A is unambiguous

where $\Rightarrow$ denotes implication and $\Leftrightarrow$ denotes equivalence.

Proof. The left implications are classic results (see [PML35], for example). The lowest equivalence is Lemma 3.1; the next lowest is Lemma 3.2. Because $A \subset \Omega^+$, the lower right implication is obvious and so it remains to prove the two upper right implications. The proofs are similar and so we prove only that the unambiguity of Ω_i^+ implies the unambiguity of Ω^+. If Ω^+ is not unambiguous, then there exists X and Y in $\Sigma^+(A)$ such that $X \neq Y$ but $\hat{X} = \hat{Y}$. Clearly, $X_0 = XXX...$ and $Y_0 = YYY...$ are different infinite sentences over A but $\hat{X}_0 = \hat{Y}_0$. Hence, if Ω^+ is not unambiguous, then neither is Ω_i^+. It follows that the implication we want is established.

The implication diagram suggests two conjectures which are verified in the two theorems which follow.

THEOREM 4.2. (A, ι) is decodable iff Ω_i^+ is unambiguous.

Proof. Our proof can be summarized in the diagram:

(D2) of Theorem 4.7 [PML44] $\Rightarrow \Omega_i^+$ is unambiguous $\Rightarrow$ (D9) of Theorem 4.7 [PML44].

By (D2) there exists some integer $m>0$ such that if $x, y, z \in \Sigma$, $Y, Z \in \Sigma(A)$, $|x| \geqslant m$, $xy = \hat{Y}$, and $xz = \hat{Z}$, then $Y(1) = Z(1)$. Suppose now that $t \in \Omega_i^+$ and that Y_0 and Z_0 are scansions of t in A^N. Then $t = \hat{Y}_0 = \hat{Z}_0$. Clearly, we may choose $x \in \Sigma$ such that $|x| \geqslant m$, $xy = Y_0(1) Y_0(2)...Y_0(l)$ for some l and y, and $xz = Z_0(1) Z_0(2)...Z_0(n)$ for some n and z. By (D2), $Y_0(1) = Z_0(1)$. Cancelling $Y_0(1)$ and $Z_0(1)$ in t we repeat the argument to conclude that $Y_0(2) = Z_0(2)$. Clearly, for each i, $Y_0(i) = Z_0(i)$ and hence Ω_i^+ is unambiguous.

For the other implication, suppose that $Y, Z \in \Sigma^+(A)$ and that $\hat{Y}x = \hat{Z}$ with $x \in D$ where $D = \{u : u \in \Sigma$, there exists some $W, V \in \Sigma(A)$ such that $u\hat{W} = \hat{V}u\}$. Letting $x\hat{W} = \hat{V}x$ we claim that $\hat{Y}\hat{V}\hat{V}... = \hat{Z}\hat{W}\hat{W}\hat{W}... = t \in \Omega_i^+$. Because Ω_i^+ is unambiguous, $YVVV... = ZWWW...$ and because $|\hat{Y}| \leqslant |\hat{Z}|$, Y is a prefix of Z and $Y(1) = Z(1)$. Hence (D9) holds.

We next prove the appropriate theorem characterizing synchronizability of (A, ι). In the proof we use statement (S1) of Theorem 2.3 [PML46] which involves an L-type statement; we shall choose statement (L5) of Lemma 2.1 [PML46] for our L-type statement.

THEOREM 4.3. (A, ι) is synchronizable iff Ω_d^+ is unambiguous.

Proof. Our proof diagram is:

(S1) of Theorem 2.3 [PML46] $\Rightarrow \Omega_d^+$ is unambiguous $\Rightarrow$ (S3) of Theorem 2.3 [PML46].

Suppose $t \in \Omega_d^+$ and choose any 'piece' x in t such that $|x| \geqslant s$ where s is the positive integer of (L5). Then (L5) guarantees that there is a decomposition $x = x_1 x_2$ such that all scansions of t have a word that ends where x_1 ends. If we consider the s alphabet symbols in t following x_1 and denote them by y, then (L5) tells us that all scansions of t have a word that ends at y_1 where $y = y_1 y_2$ is the decomposition furnished by (L5). Hence y_1 is a member of Ω^+ between x_1 and y_2. Because (A, ι) is correcting, y_1 has a unique scansion. Hence all scansions of t induce the same scansion on

y_1. But our original x was arbitrarily picked and hence Ω_d^+ is unambiguous. The diagram below shows what is happening.

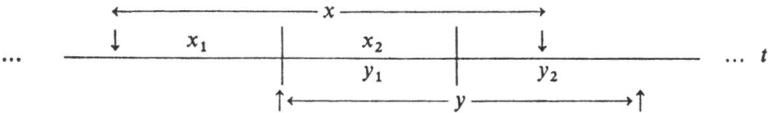

$|y| = s$

To establish (S3) we must show that whenever $x\hat{Y} = \hat{Z}x$ for $Y, Z \in \Sigma(A)$, then $XY = ZX$ with $x = \hat{X}$. If x is the void sequence, then the implication is clear because (A, ι) is correcting by Lemma 4.1. If x is not void, then we observe that

$$\ldots\hat{Z}\hat{Z}x\,\hat{Y}\,\hat{Y}\,\hat{Y}\ldots = \ldots\hat{Z}\hat{Z}\hat{Z}x\,\hat{Y}\,\hat{Y}\ldots$$

and hence that

$$\ldots\hat{Z}\hat{Z}\hat{Z}\ldots = \ldots\hat{Y}\,\hat{Y}\,\hat{Y}\ldots.$$

Because Ω_d^+ is unambiguous we have

$$\ldots ZZZ\ldots = \ldots YYY\ldots.$$

It follows that each word $Y(i)$ of Y is a word of Z and so $Y(1) = Z(j)$ for some $1 \leqslant j \leqslant$ the number of words of Z. Pictorially we have the following situation for $Y = (Y(1), Y(2), \ldots, Y(n))$ and $Z = (Z(1), Z(2), \ldots, Z(m))$:

	x		$Y(1)$	$Y(2)$		$\ldots$		$Y(n)$		$x\hat{Y}$

$Z(1)$		$\ldots$	$Z(j-1)$	$Z(j)$	$Z(j+1)$		$\ldots$	$Z(m)$		x		$\hat{Z}x$

Clearly, $x = Z(1)Z(2)\ldots Z(j-1)$ and so $x \in \Omega^+$. Hence, $x = \hat{X}$ for some $X \in \Sigma(A)$ and we have $\hat{X}\hat{Y} = \hat{Z}\hat{X}$. But (A, ι) is correcting and so $XY = ZX$ with $x = \hat{X}$ and (S3) is established.

We conclude this report by indicating how to generalize the notion of scansion in Ω^+. Let us assume that Σ_1 and Σ_2 are nonempty subsets of Σ each of which contains the void sequence $\emptyset$ and form the juxtaposition product $\Sigma_1\Omega^+\Sigma_2$. If $u \in \Sigma_1$, $v \in \Sigma_2$, and $X \in \Sigma^+(A)$, then we shall say that

(u, X, v) is a (Σ_1, Σ_2)-*scansion* of $t \in \Sigma_1 \Omega^+ \Sigma_2$ iff $t = u\hat{X}v$. If G is a subset of $\Sigma_1 \Omega^+ \Sigma_2$, then we say that G is *unambiguous* (*for* Σ_1 *and* Σ_2) iff each $t \in G$ has exactly one (Σ_1, Σ_2)-scansion.

We let $P(A)$ denote the set of all prefixes of A, $S(A)$ denote all suffices of A, and let $Q(A) = P(A) \cap S(A)$. In [PML45] the following sets were studied in terms of unambiguity and two other code-related properties of weak synchronizability and of synchronizability: Ω^-, $S(A)\Omega^+ P(A)$, $\Omega^+ Q(A)$, $Q(A)\Omega^+$, and $Q(A)\Omega^+ Q(A)$. A sample result of [PML45] is the following: For a certain positive integer t, (A, i) is synchronizable iff Ω^+ is unambiguous and the set of all sequences in $Q(A)\Omega^+ Q(A)$ whose length is greater than or equal to t is synchronizable. The reader is referred to [PML45] for the complete details.

CHAPTER 7

SOME GENERAL RESULTS OF
ABSTRACT CODING THEORY WITH APPLICATIONS
TO THE STUDY OF CODES FOR THE CORRECTION
OF SYNCHRONIZATION ERRORS

L. CALABI AND W. E. HARTNETT

EDITORIAL NOTE

This paper, written during the last months of the study in 1968 and revised in 1969, presents the results of rumination about past endeavors and concentrates on the three important code properties: error-correction, error-decoding, and error-limitation. Attempts to generalize the results of Chapter 11 forced a logical analysis of the relationships involved. As usual, such an analysis was initially cast into a highly symbolic form amenable to manipulation. Somewhat surprisingly, it became apparent exactly what was involved in error-correction irrespective of the model: it was possible to characterize the property of error-correction for arbitrary models. With minor restrictions on the models, decodability was likewise characterized after it became clear precisely what the real definition of decodability should be. Once this was done, it was obvious how synchronizability should be defined for these now essentially arbitrary models. All of the critical implications established for the classical models in Chapters 2–6 held for the general models with modest restrictions and the classical models appeared, as they indeed should, as a special case of the general model. The final result is a simple, conceptual, and adequate frame-work for a consideration of the four basic problems of Coding Theory.
This paper appeared in *Information and Control* **15** (1969) 235–249.

1. INTRODUCTION

The three properties of unique decipherability, decodability with bounded delay, and synchronizability for variable length codes have been described and studied extensively. For the most part, however, they were treated under the assumption of a noiseless channel and the necessary definitions were formulated in that setting. It is only in recent years that attempts have been made to deal with those properties in the presence of noise. Such attempts have faced a number of problems: how to describe the allowable error patterns, how to give suitable generalizations of the

W. E. Hartnett (ed.), Foundations of Coding Theory, 107–121. All Rights Reserved.
Copyright © 1974 by D. Reidel Publishing Company, Dordrecht-Holland.

definitions, how to characterize codes having those properties in a noise context, and finally how to construct such codes.

Our approach to those problems has already proved fruitful in Hartnett [PML42] and in Calabi and Hartnett [PML48]. We use it again here to give very general definitions of, and theorems on, error-correcting codes, decodable codes with bounded delay and error-limiting codes. We will not impose any restriction on the alphabet or the words of the code, nor on the channel noise and its effects. We will then apply our results to the study of codes capable of correcting synchronization errors.

Our tools seem sufficiently different from those generally used to warrant some explanation of the basic ideas (for more background and examples see Hartnett [PML42]). We let J denote the *alphabet*, a set of $q \geqslant 2$ elements, let $\Sigma(J)$ denote the set of all finite sequences over J, let A denote a nonempty finite subset of $\Sigma(J)$ and let $\Sigma(A)$ denote the set of all finite sequences over A. The elements of A are called *words* and the elements of $\Sigma(A)$ are called *sentences*. To each sentence $X = (a_1, a_2, ..., a_k)$ there corresponds an element $\hat{X}$ in $\Sigma(J)$ defined by $\hat{X} = a_1 a_2 ... a_k$ and obtained by the juxtaposition of the words $a_1, a_2, ..., a_k$ of X. If X is a sentence and $\hat{X}$ is transmitted over a channel, we let $\alpha(X)$ denote the set of all members of $\Sigma(J)$ which, when received, should be decoded as X. Notice that we place no restrictions on the lengths of the words or on the kinds of errors the channel may produce; explicitly, this formulation permits substitution errors (replacement of symbols) and/or synchronization errors (insertions and/or deletions of symbols) and/or erasures (replacement of any symbol by one not used in the words of A). Notice also that our formalism describes the error patterns occurring in a sentence, not necessarily in each word. For instance we may talk of 'up to n errors in every t consecutive symbols' instead of 'up to n errors per word'. Our only restriction on $\alpha(X)$ is that it contains $\hat{X}$: if no errors occur in transmission, we certainly want to decode correctly.

If we assume that the channel is noiseless, then $\alpha(X) = \{\hat{X}\}$ for each sentence and then unique decipherability requires that $\hat{X} \neq \hat{Y}$ whenever X and Y are different sentences. Observe that this property can also be described by saying that $\alpha(X) \cap \alpha(Y) = \emptyset$, the empty set, whenever X and Y are different sentences. That is also a precise formulation of the notion of correcting ability: no received sentence which ought to be interpreted as X should be also decodable into Y. So it seems natural to call the pair (A, α) a *code* and to say that it is (*error*) *correcting* (for α) if and only if $\alpha(X) \cap \alpha(Y) \neq \emptyset$ implies $X = Y$ for all sentences X and Y.

In Section 3 the notion of correcting code is analyzed in some detail; a general set-theoretical result of Section 2 yields then a set of necessary and sufficient conditions for a code to be correcting. Section 4 and 5 deal with decodability and error-limiting ability (or synchronizability), respectively. Throughout we need to introduce auxiliary properties, to help isolate the most important features of the concepts involved.

In the second part we apply some of our results to the study of block codes capable of correcting synchronization and/or substitution errors. After a general study of the Levenshtein distance (Section 6), we characterize in Section 7 the correcting ability of those block codes whose words have pairwise Levenshtein distance $2e + 1$ or larger. The last section, Section 8, gives sufficient conditions for such codes to be decodable with bounded delay, generalizing a result of Calabi and Hartnett [PML48].

2. Separation for a binary relation

We now prove a general theorem which will be used in Section 3 to characterize correcting codes. We let A be an arbitrary nonempty set, $\Sigma(A)$ the set of finite sequences over A, $|X|$ the length of a sequence $X \in \Sigma(A)$ and α an arbitrary mapping from $\Sigma(A)$ into a set H. We identify $a \in A$ with the one-term sequence $(a) \in \Sigma(A)$ and set $\alpha(A) = H_0 \subset H$. If S is a binary relation between elements of H, that is if $S \subset H^2$, we say that the pair (A, α) is *S-separating* if and only if from $(\alpha(X), \alpha(Y)) \in S$ follows $X = Y$ for all sequences X, Y over A. If $S \subset H^2$ contains the diagonal (i.e. all the pairs (c, c) for $c \in H$), we shall say for short that S is a *reflexive relation* in H. We than have the following characterization:

THEOREM 2.1. Let $S \subset H^2$. Then, of the following two statements, the second implies the first; and if $S \cap H_0^2$ is a reflexive relation in H_0, then also the first implies the second:

(a) $(\alpha(X), \alpha(Y)) \in S$ implies $X = Y$ for all X, Y in $\Sigma(A)$;

(b) $(\alpha(X), \alpha(Y)) \in S$ implies $|X| = |Y|$. Moreover there exists $R \subset H_0^2$ such that:

(1) $(\alpha(a), \alpha(b)) \in R$ implies $a = b$ for all a, b in A;

(2) $(\alpha(X), \alpha(Y)) \in S$ and $X = (a_1, a_2, \ldots, a_k)$,
         $Y = (b_1, b_2, \ldots, b_k)$ implies $(\alpha(a_i), \alpha(b_i)) \in R$ for $i = 1, 2, \ldots, k$.

Proof. Assume (b) and $(\alpha(X), \alpha(Y)) \in S$. Then $|X| = |Y|$ and hence, say, $X = (a_1, a_2, \ldots, a_k)$, $Y = (b_1, b_2, \ldots, b_k)$. Consequently $(\alpha(a_i), \alpha(b_i)) \in R$ by (2), and $a_i = b_i$ for each i, by (1), which implies $X = Y$. Conversely assume now (a) and $S \cap H_0^2$ reflexive, and set $R = S \cap H_0^2$. If $(\alpha(X),$ $\alpha(Y)) \in S$ we know $X = Y$; hence certainly $|X| = |Y|$. If $(\alpha(a), \alpha(b)) \in R$ then also $(\alpha(a), \alpha(b)) \in S$ and thus $a = b$. Finally if $(\alpha(a_1, a_2, \ldots, a_k),$ $\alpha(b_1, b_2, \ldots, b_k)) \in S$ then $a_i = b_i$, $\alpha(a_i) = \alpha(b_i)$ and by reflexivity, $(\alpha(a_i),$ $\alpha(b_i)) \in R$.

As an immediate consequence we obtain:

Corollary 2.2. Let $S \subset H^2$ and assume $S \cap H_0^2$ to be reflexive. Then (A, α) is *S*-separating if and only if

(a) $(\alpha(X), \alpha(Y)) \in S$ implies $|X| = |Y|$ for all $X, Y \in \Sigma(A)$;

(b) $(\alpha(a), \alpha(b)) \in S$ implies $a = b$ for all $a, b \in A$;

(c) $(\alpha(a_1, a_2, \ldots, a_k), \alpha(b_1, b_2, \ldots, b_k)) \in S$ implies $(\alpha(a_i), \alpha(b_i)) \in S$ for $i = 1, 2, \ldots, k$ for all equally long sequences $(a_1, a_2, \ldots, a_k), (b_1, b_2, \ldots, b_k)$ over A.

3. ERROR-CORRECTING CAPABILITY

We apply now the results of Section 2 to Coding Theory. For convenience we write $\alpha(X) \equiv \alpha(Y)$ if and only if $\alpha(X) \cap \alpha(Y) \neq \emptyset$. Observe that $\equiv$ is then a binary, reflexive relation between subsets of $\Sigma(J)$. Reformulating the definition given in the Introduction, we say that the code (A, α) is *correcting* if and only if the following statement holds:

(A) $\alpha(X) \equiv \alpha(Y)$ implies $X = Y$ for all X, Y in $\Sigma(A)$.

In the Terminology of Section 2, then, (A, α) is correcting if and only if it is $\equiv$-separating. Corollary 2.2 suggests the consideration of the following three properties that a code (A, α) might have:

(B)   Given   sentences $X = (a_1, a_2, \ldots, a_k)$, $Y = (b_1, b_2, \ldots, b_k)$,
         $\alpha(X) \equiv \alpha(Y)$ implies $\alpha(a_i) \equiv \alpha(b_i)$ for $i = 1, 2, \ldots, k$;

(C) $\alpha(a) \equiv \alpha(b)$ implies $a = b$ for all words a, b in A;

(D) $\alpha(X) \equiv \alpha(Y)$ implies $|X| = |Y|$ for all sentences
         X, Y in $\Sigma(A)$.

Those statements may be interpreted as follows. Assume that, because of channel noise, two sentences X and Y be received as the same sequence. Then (D) requires them to have the same number of words, say k. If $k = 1$, (C) will assure $X = Y$. If $k > 1$, we may use (B) to conclude that, after transmission, each word a_i of X, may be decoded into the corresponding word b_i of Y. Notice that (D) is always satisfied when all the words of A have equal length ('block codes') and when the channel noise cannot change the length of the transmitted sequences.

It is evident that, together, (B), (C) and (D) imply (A); Corollary 2.2 yields also the converse. We state:

THEOREM 3.1. A code (A, α) is correcting if and only if statements (B), (C) and (D) hold.

4. ERROR-DECODING CAPABILITY

In the noiseless case it is usual to say that we have decodability with bounded delay k if and only if, for sentences $X = (a_1, a_2, ..., a_h)$ and $Y = (b_1, b_2, ..., b_n)$ and a sequence w, whenever $\hat{X}w = \hat{Y}$ and $|\hat{X}| \geqslant k$, then X and Y have the same first word which can be left-cancelled to obtain $a_2a_3...a_hw = b_2b_3...b_n$. It is tempting to try a straightforward generalization and say that (A, α) is decodable with delay k, if and only if $\alpha(X)w \equiv \alpha(Y)$ and $|\hat{X}| \geqslant k$ imply that the first words of X and Y are the same. Now, however, we cannot, in general, conclude $\alpha(a_1)\alpha(a_2, ..., a_n)w \equiv \alpha(a_1)\alpha(b_2, ..., b_m)$, nor can we left-cancel to obtain $\alpha(a_2, ..., \alpha_n)w = \alpha(b_2, ..., b_m)$. Hence we lose the basic notion that decodability suggests, namely, that of successive determination of the words of the sentence X when $\hat{X}$ is received.

An adequate definition, which reduces to the classical one when $\alpha(X) = \{\hat{X}\}$ for all X, is obtained as follows: we say that (A, α) is *decodable with delay* k if and only if the following statement holds:

(E_k)   Given sentences X, Y in $\Sigma(A)$ and a sequence w, $\alpha(X)w \equiv \alpha(Y)$ and $|\hat{X}| \geqslant k$ imply $X = ZX_2$, $Y = ZY_2$ for some sentences Z, X_2, Y_2 with Z nonempty and $\alpha(X_2)w \equiv \alpha(Y_2)$.

The next theorem is rich in consequences and has proven very useful (see Section 8 below and Calabi and Hartnett [PML48]).

THEOREM 4.1. The code $(A\ \alpha)$ is decodable with delay k if the following two statements hold:

(F_k) Given sentences X, Y in $\Sigma(A)$ and a sequence w, $\alpha(X)w \equiv \alpha(Y)$ and $|\hat{X}| \geqslant k$ imply $X = X_1 X_2$, $Y = Y_1 Y_2$ with nonempty sequences X_1, Y_1 such that $\alpha(X_1) \equiv \alpha(Y_1)$ and $\alpha(X_2)w \equiv \alpha(Y_2)$;

(A_k) $\alpha(X) \equiv \alpha(Y)$ and $|\hat{X}| \leqslant k$ imply $X = Y$ for all sentences X, Y in $\Sigma(A)$.

Notice that (A) could be denoted (A_∞) and that (A_1) and (C) are identical. A code satisfying (A_k) or (F_k) has been called k-separating or, respectively, k-exact in Calabi and Hartnett [PML48].

Proof. If $\alpha(X)w \equiv \alpha(Y)$ repeated applications of (F_k) yield decompositions $X = X_1 X_2$, $Y = Y_1 Y_2$ with $0 < |\hat{X}_1| \leqslant k$; then (A_k) implies $X_1 = Y_1$: that is, (E_k) holds.

As an immediate consequence we have:

Corollary 4.2. The code (A, α) is decodable with delay k if it is correcting and has property (F_k).

Though (E_k) implies (F_k), the converse of the last result does not seem to hold: (E_k) does not imply (A) in our very general context. A partial converse may be formulated as follows:

THEOREM 4.3. Let (A, α) be decodable with delay k; assume that statement (D) holds as well as (G): $\alpha(X)\hat{Y} \subset \alpha(XY)$ for all sentences X, Y in $\Sigma(A)$. Then (A, α) is correcting.

Proof. Suppose $\alpha(X) \equiv \alpha(Y)$. Then we have $\alpha(X)\widehat{X^k} \equiv \alpha(Y)\widehat{X^k}$ and hence $\alpha(XX^k) \equiv \alpha(YX^k)$. With $U = XX^k$ and $V = YX^k$, decodability yields $U = U_1 U_2$, $V = U_1 V_2$ with $\alpha(U_2) \equiv \alpha(V_2)$. Hence X, Y and U_1 have a prefix in common. By assumption, $|X| = |Y|$, hence if $|X| < |U_1|$, then $X = Y$. If not, repeat the construction to conclude that $X = Y$ and so that (A, α) is correcting.

Using also Theorem 3.1, we now obtain a characterization of decodability:

Corollary 4.4. Let (A, α) have properties (C), (D) and (G). Then (A, α) is decodable with delay k if and only if (B) and (F_k) hold.

5. ERROR-LIMITING CAPABILITY

It seems very important to distinguish clearly between two synchronizability properties that a code may have. One is the ability of correcting synchronization errors, i.e., of reconstructing the original sentence in its entirety even in the presence of certain deletions or insertions (see below Sections 6 to 8). The other is the ability to re-synchronize, i.e., to use an unintelligible portion of a message to determine the beginning of some word and, there, to resume the decoding process. A code with this second property has been called *error-limiting*. We adopt that terminology because it avoids misunderstandings and well describes the most important aspect of the code capability. (In previous work we have used the term 'synchronizable' for what we now call error-limiting.)

Here too we have to generalize the classical definition. Let us first agree to say that a sequence x is a *message infix* of (A, α) if and only if there are sequences y, z (possibly empty) and a sentence W such that $yxz \in (\alpha(W)$. We then say that a code (A, α) is *error-limiting with delay k* if and only if it is correcting and satisfies:

(I_k) every message infix x with $|x| \geqslant k$ has a decomposition $x = x_1 x_2$ such that from $yxz \in \alpha(W)$ follows the existence of a decomposition $W = W_1 W_2$ with $yx_1 \in \alpha(W_1)$ and $x_2 z \in \alpha(W_2)$.

The interpretation is easy: whenever we receive at least k consecutive symbols with allowable errors (or none at all), we can find a 'comma', or word separation; from there normal decoding can resume. The independence of that comma from the particular sentence being transmitted is also assured since the decomposition $x = x_1 x_2$ is the same for all W. It is apparent that our definition reduces to the usual one when the channel is noiseless (see e.g., Scholtz [28] or Hartnett [PML42]).

Decodability and error-limiting capability are related by our next result:

THEOREM 5.1. Let (A, α) be error-limiting with delay k, and assume that there is an integer h such that from $x \in \alpha(X)$ and $|\hat{X}| \geqslant h$ follow $|x| \geqslant k$. Then (A, α) is decodable with delay h.

Proof. In view of Corollary 4.2 it is enough to show that (A, α) has property (F_h). Assume $\alpha(X)w = \alpha(Y)$ and $|\hat{X}| \geqslant h$; there is then $x \in \alpha(X)$ with $|x| \geqslant k$ (by assumption) and $xw \in \alpha(Y)$. Since the code satisfies (I_k), there are decompositions $x = x_1x_2$, $X = X_1X_2$ and $Y = Y_1Y_2$ such that $x_1 \in \alpha(X_1)$, $x_2 \in \alpha(X_2)$ (taking y, z empty in statement (I_k)) and $x_1 \in \alpha(Y_1)$, $x_2w \in \alpha(Y_2)$ (with y empty and $z = w$). Consequently $x_1 \in \alpha(X_1) \cap \alpha(X_2) \neq \emptyset$ and $x_2w \in \alpha(X_2)w \cap \alpha(Y_2) \neq \emptyset$, showing indeed that (A, α) has property (F_h).

6. On the Levenshtein Distance

We start here the second part of our paper, devoted to the study of block codes capable of correcting substitution and synchronization errors (irrespective of their error-limiting capability). In this context the Levenshtein distance plays the central role that the Hamming distance has when only substitution errors occur. Because of the numerical difficulties encountered in the usage of the Levenshtein distance, we present in this section some helpful results of general interest, even if they are not logically needed in the sections to follow.

The Hamming distance $H(x, y)$ between two equally long sequences x, y may be defined as the smallest number of substitutions necessary to transform x into y. In order to study synchronization errors (deletions and insertions), alone or in conjunction with substitution errors, Levenshtein [15] has introduced two new distance functions. For arbitrary sequences x, y (not necessarily equally long), $L(x, y)$ denotes the smallest number of deletions and insertions necessary to transform x into y; and similarly $D(x, y)$, called the *Levenshtein distance* of x and y, denotes the smallest number of deletions, insertions and substitutions necessary to transform x into y.

It is not difficult to show that L and D are indeed distance functions, that is

$$L(x, y) = 0 \text{ if and only if } x = y; \qquad D(x, y) = 0 \text{ if and only if } x = y$$
$$L(x, y) = L(y, x); \qquad D(x, y) = D(y, x)$$
$$L(x, y) \leqslant L(x, z) + L(z, y); \qquad D(x, y) \leqslant D(x, z) + D(z, y).$$

Given a sequence x, a sequence z will be called a *subsequence* of x if and only if it can be obtained from x by deletions. Denote by $S(x, -r)$ the set of those subsequences of x obtained by r deletions; and by $S(x, +r)$ the set of those sequences obtained from x by r insertions. The following easy results will help in computing L and D.

Lemma 6.1. Given x and y, let z be a longest sequence which is a subsequence of both x and y. Then $L(x, y) = |x| + |y| - 2|z|$.

As customary, we use the Hamming distance $H(A, B)$ between two sets A, B to denote min $H(a, b)$ for $a \in A$ and $b \in B$. We then have:

Lemma 6.2. Let $|x| = m + k$, $|y| = m$ and set $D(x, y; r) = k + 2r + H(S(x, -(k+r)), S(y, -r))$. Then

$$D(x, y) = \min\{D(x, y; r), \quad r = 0, 1, ..., h\}$$

where $2h = L(x, y) - k$.

If x is a sequence of length n, the Levenshtein ball $B(x, e)$ of radius e around x is the set of all the sequences y with $D(x, y) \leqslant e$ (and then $n - e \leqslant |y| \leqslant n + e$). We shall denote by $B(x, e, m)$ the subset of $B(x, e)$ of those sequences whose length is m. If $m \leqslant n$ and $e \geqslant 2(n - m)$, $B(x, e, m)$ contains, among others, all sequences having Hamming distance at most $e - 2(n - m)$ from some element of $S(x, m - n)$; and similarly if $m > n$.

If A is a set of sequences of length n with mutual Levenshtein distances at least $2e + 1$, we say here for short that A is an (n, e)-*set*. How many elements can an (n, e)-set have? Very little is known and the difficulties involved in answering that question are many. It may be enough to remember that the corresponding question for the Hamming distance is still open, in spite of great efforts by many scientists; and in spite of the fact that the Hamming balls are very easy to describe and the number of their elements depend only upon n and e, not upon the center x. On the contrary, the number of elements in $B(x, e)$ and $S(x, -r)$ depends also upon x itself.

If $M(n, e)$ is the maximal number of elements in an (n, e)-set, Levenshtein has shown that, for binary sequences,

$$2^{n-1}/n \leqslant M(n, 1) \leqslant 2^n/(n+1).$$

For $n = 7$ this yields $10 \leqslant M(7, 1) \leqslant 16$. In Table I we give a $(7, 1)$-set A with 12 elements to which no further sequence may be added; indeed for every sequence x of length 7 there is $a \in A$ with $S(x, -1) \cap S(a, -1) \neq \emptyset$.

Only asymptotic bounds are known for $e > 1$. Table II gives a $(13, 2)$-set of 12 elements.

TABLE I	TABLE II
A set of 12 sequences of length 7, with mutual Levenshtein distance of at least 3	A set of 12 sequences of length 13, with mutual Levenshtein distance of at least 5
1100000	0000000000000
1000101	0001001100111
1110011	1010001010010
1101111	1001010011110
0000011	0110001111110
0101001	0001101111000
1010110	1110010000111
1111100	1001110000001
0010000	0110101100001
0001100	0101110101101
0111010	1110110011000
0011111	1111111111111

Denoting with vertical bars the number of elements in a set, Levenshtein has also shown, for the binary case,

$$0 \leqslant \binom{r(x) - s + 1}{s} \leqslant |S(x, -s)| \leqslant \binom{r(x) + s - 1}{s} \leqslant \binom{n + s - 1}{s}$$

$$\sum_{i=0}^{s} \binom{|x|}{i} 2^{s-i} \leqslant |S(x, +s)| \leqslant \sum_{i=0}^{s} \binom{|x|}{i}\binom{s}{i} 2^{s-i}$$

if $r(x)$ denotes the number of runs in x. (Remember that a *run* in a sequence x is a maximal subsequence of equal, consecutive terms.) For $s = 1$, those inequalities become

$$|S(x, -1)| = r(x)$$
$$|S(x, +1)| = |x| + 2.$$

If we consider a sequence over a more general alphabet we obtain very easily:

Lemma 6.3. If x is a sequence over an alphabet with q symbols, then

$$|S(x, -1)| = r(x)$$
$$|S(x, +1)| = |x|(q-1)+q.$$

Notice that, in the last relation, only the length of x appears.

Lemma 6.4. On the average (over all sequences of length $|x|$, over an alphabet with q symbols) $S(x, -1)$ has $\{|x|(q-1)+1\}/q$ elements.
Proof. If $y \in S(x, -1)$, then and only then, $x \in S(y, +1)$. Thus Lemma 6.3 tells us that each one of the q^{n-1} elements y of length $n-1$ belongs to exactly $|y|(q-1)+q = (n-1)(q-1)+q$ sets $S(x, -1)$ with $|x| = n$. Thus $\sum |S(x, -1)|$, extended over the q^n elements of length n, counts each element y exactly $(n-1)(q-1)+q$ times. Consequently

$$\text{average size} = \frac{\sum |S(x,-1)|}{q^n} = \frac{q^{n-1}[(n-1)(q-1)+q]}{q^n} =$$

$$= \frac{q^{n-1}[(|z|-1)(q-1)+q]}{q^n}$$

yielding the desired result.

Notice that, again by Lemma 6.3, $\{|x|(q-1)+1\}/q$ is then also the average number of runs in a sequence. Since $B(x, 1)$ consists of $S(x, -1) \cup S(x, +1)$ and of the Hamming ball around x of radius 1, we also obtain:

Lemma 6.5. For each x,

$$|B(x, 1)| = r(x) + 2|x|(q-1)+q+1.$$

On the average (over all sequences of length $|x|$), $B(x, 1)$ has a number of elements given by

$$\frac{|x|(2q^2 - q - 1) + q^2 + q + 1}{q}$$

It may be interesting to remark that, for $q = 2$, the average size is the arithmetic mean of the maximal size $(r(x) = |x|)$ and the minimal size $(r(x) = 1)$. The following two results may also prove useful in the present context.

Lemma 6.6. The number of sequences of length n, over an alphabet with q symbols, having exactly r runs is given by $\binom{n-1}{r-1} q \, (q-1)^{r-1}$.

Proof. If $N(n, r, q)$ denoted the number of the lemma, consideration of the subsequences obtained by deletion of the last term yields

$$N(n, r, q) = (q-1) N(n-1, r-1, q) + N(n-1, r, q).$$

Since also $N(n, 1, q) = q$, $N(n, n, q) = q(q-1)^{n-1}$ and $N(n, n+r, q) = 0$, our result follows.

If $\xi_1, \xi_2, \ldots, \xi_q$ are the alphabet symbols, denote by x_n that sequence whose i-th term is ξ_q if $i = rq+j$, $r = 0, 1, \ldots$:

$$x_n = \xi_1 \xi_2 \ldots \xi_q \xi_1 \xi_2 \ldots$$

Let also $f(n, r, q) = \max\{|S(x, -r)|, \text{ for } |x| = n\}$. Then we have

Lemma 6.7. For all n, r and q, $f(n, r, q) = |S(x_n, -r)|$. Moreover $f(n, r, q)$ is the coefficient of z^n in the generating function

$$\phi(z) = (\sum_{j=1}^{q} z^j)^{n-r} \, (\sum_{i \geq 0} z^i).$$

The proof is rather involved and may be found in Calabi [PML53]. For $q = 2$ we obtain

$$f(n, r, 2) = \sum_{i=0}^{r} \binom{n-r}{i},$$

a much better bound than Levenshtein's $\binom{n+r-1}{r}$.

7. ERROR-CORRECTING FOR THE LEVENSHTEIN METRIC

Hamming has shown that a block code can correct up to e substitution errors per word if and only if the Hamming distance between any two distinct words is at least $2e+1$. It is our aim to present here the corresponding result for the Levenshtein distance. The complexity apparent throughout Section 6 suggests that a straightforward generalization of Hamming's theorem is not to be hoped for. That is indeed the case and our result may be stated informally as follows: a block code of length n can correct up to $e (2e < n)$ substitution errors *per word* or (but not both) up to e substitution and synchronization errors *per sentence* if and only if the Levenshtein distance between any two distinct words is at least $2e+1$.

For a formal statement, and to prove it, let A be a set of sequences. Denoting Hamming balls by B_H, we define a mapping α_e on $\Sigma(A)$ by setting $\alpha_e(X) = B(\hat{X}, e) \cup B_H(a_1, e) B_H(a_2, e) \ldots B_H(a_r, e)$ if $X = (a_1, a_2, \ldots, a_r)$. Notice that, then, $\alpha(a) = B(a, e)$ for $a \in A$.

THEOREM 7.1. Let A be a set of sequences of length n, e an integer with $2e < n$. Then (A, α_e) is correcting if and only if $D(a, b) \geqslant 2e+1$ for every pair of distinct words a, b.

Proof. If (A, α_e) is correcting, then in particular $\alpha_e(a) \equiv \alpha_e(b)$ implies $a = b$. Thus $D(a, b) < 2e+1$ implies $a = b$ and the easy half of the theorem is established. To prove the other half we use Theorem 3.1. Let $\alpha_e(X) \equiv \alpha_e(Y)$. If $z \in \alpha_e(X) \cap \alpha_e(Y)$, then $n|X| - e \leqslant |z| \leqslant n|X| + e$ and similarly for Y. Consequently $n|Y| - e \leqslant n|X| + e$ or $|Y| \leqslant |X| + 2e/n$. Since $2e < n$, $|Y| \leqslant |X|$. By symmetry, $|X| \leqslant |Y|$ and $|X| = |Y|$ establishing Property (D). Property (C) holds because $D(a, b) \geqslant 2e+1$.

Let us establish Property (B). Assuming $\alpha_e(a_1, a_2, \ldots, a_k) \equiv \alpha_e(b_1, b_2, \ldots, b_k)$, let z be in both sets. Then there are (not necessarily unique) decompositions $z = x_1 x_2 \ldots x_k = y_1 y_2 \ldots y_k$ with $x_i \in \alpha_e(a_i)$ and $y_i \in \alpha_e(b_i)$. If, for some decomposition, $x_i = y_i$ for all i, then $D(a_i, b_i) \leqslant D(a_i, x_i) + D(y_i, b_i) \leqslant 2e$ and $\alpha_e(a_i) \equiv \alpha_e(b_i)$, terminating the proof. Thus assume that for any decomposition, $x_i \neq y_i$ for some i; then certainly synchronization errors have occurred and, for appropriate sequences u_i, v_i, one of the three cases obtains: $y_i u_i = v_i x_i$, $x_i u_i = v_i y_i$, or $u_i y_i v_i = x_i$. It will be enough to consider in detail the first case, the others being similar. Let $l(Y, i)$ and $r(Y, i)$ be the number of synchronization errors which have occurred in the first $i-1$ and, respectively, in the last $k-i$ words of Y; define similarly $l(X, i)$ and $r(X, i)$. Since $D(z, \hat{X}) \leqslant e$, *a fortiori* $D(b_i, y_i) \leqslant e - l(Y, i) - r(Y, i)$ and similarly $D(a_i, x_i) \leqslant e - l(X, i) - r(X, i)$. Clearly $|v_i| \leqslant l(X, i) + l(Y, i)$ and $|u_i| \leqslant r(X, i) + r(Y, i)$. Then

$$D(a_i, b_i) \leqslant D(a_i, x_i) + D(x_i, y_i) + D(y_i, b_i)$$
$$\leqslant [e - l(X, i) - r(X, i)] + [|v_i| + |u_i|] + [e - l(Y, i) - r(Y, i)]$$
$$\leqslant 2e$$

and again $\alpha_e(a_i) \equiv \alpha_e(b_i)$.

It is interesting to speculate whether the mapping α_e is, in some sense, the 'best' for which Theorem 7.1 holds. The question is open even when 'best' means 'largest': is there another mapping α, with $\alpha(X) \supset \alpha_e(X)$ for all X, for which our theorem holds?

8. A SUFFICIENT CONDITION FOR DECODABILITY

We begin by recalling that a block code capable of correcting substitution errors is automatically decodable. This is manifestly not so if one allows synchronization errors as we do here. Hence it is of considerable interest to have conditions for decodability even for block codes. In Calabi and Hartnett [PML48] we have presented an infinite family of block codes capable of correcting substitution or synchronization errors and decodable (with some delay). We generalize here the results of that paper, disregarding for the time being the corresponding generalization of the code construction.

Let A be a set of sequences, e and t two integers with $2e < t$; define a new mapping α_{et} on $\Sigma(A)$ as follows:

> if $|X| \leqslant t$, $\alpha_{et}(X)$ consists of all those sequences which may be obtained from $\hat{X}$ by either up to e substitution errors in each one of $t - 2e$ words, or up to e deletions in $\hat{X}$, or up to e insertions in $\hat{X}$;
> if $|X| > t$, $\alpha_{et}(X) = \bigcap \alpha_{et}(X_1)\alpha_{et}(X_2)\alpha_{et}(X_3)$ where the intersection is extended over all the decompositions $X = X_1 X_2 X_3$ with $|X_2| = t$.

In intuitive words, $\alpha_{et}(X)$ consists of all those sequences which may be obtained from $\hat{X}$ by making, in each block of t consecutive words, up to e substitution errors in each of $t - 2e$ words, or up to e deletions, or up to e insertions.

THEOREM 8.1. Let A be a set of sequences of length n and let e and t be integers with $2e < n$, $2e < t$. Suppose that $D(a, b) \geqslant 2e + 1$ for every pair of distinct words a, b in A and suppose that A satisfies:

(P_e): $au = vb$ for a, $b \in A$ implies $|u| > 2e$.

Then (A, α_{et}) is decodable with delay nt.

Proof. In view of Theorem 4.1, it is enough to show that (A, α_{et}) has properties (F_k) and (A_k) for $k = nt$. Let then $\alpha_{et}(X) \equiv \alpha_{et}(Y)$ with $|\hat{X}| \leqslant nt$ and thus $|X| \leqslant t$. By a reasoning parallel to that used in the proof of Theorem 7.1, we obtain $|Y| = |X|$ and thus also $|Y| \leqslant t$. But then $\alpha_{et}(X) \subset \alpha_e(X)$ and $\alpha_{et}(Y) \subset \alpha_e(Y)$ and by Theorem 7.1, $X = Y$. Thus indeed (A, α_{et}) has property (A_{nt}). To establish (F_{nt}), let $X = (a_1, a_2, ..., a_k)$, $Y = (b_1, b_2, ..., b_h)$ and $z \in \alpha_{et}(X)w \cap \alpha_{et}(Y)$ with $k > t$. It follows as above that then also $h \geqslant t$. Let $z = x_1 x_2...x_k w = y_1 y_2...y_h$, $x_i \in \alpha_{et}(a_i)$, $y_i \in \alpha_{et}(b_i)$. If there is an $i \leqslant t$ such that $x_1 x_2...x_i = y_1 y_2...y_i$, then the sentences $X_1 = (a_1, ..., a_i)$, $X_2 = (a_{i+1}, ..., a_k)$, $Y_1 = (b_1, ..., b_i)$, $Y_2 = (b_{i+1}, ..., b_h)$ satisfy the reducibility requirements. If such a subscript i does not exist, we have in particular $|x_1| \neq |y_1|$; and since we limit ourselves to consideration of only the first t words of X and Y, we may assume $|y_1| < |x_1|$ without any loss of generality. Then x_1 is obtained by up to e insertions in a_1, or y_1 is the result of up to e deletions in b_1, or both. If both, then $x_1 a_2 a_3...a_t x_{t+1}...x_k w = y_1 b_2 b_3...b_t y_{t+1}...y_h$ and $ua_2 = b_2 v$ with $|u| \leqslant 2e$ contradicting (P_e). If $|y_1| = |b_1| < |x_1|$, the inequality $t > 2e$ insures that there is at least one subscript $j \leqslant t$ such that $y_j = b_j$, $x_j = a_j$ and $ua_j = b_j v$ with, again, $|u| \leqslant 2e$. If $|y_1| < |x_1| = |a_1|$ the conclusion is the same. In any case we obtain a contradiction. Thus necessarily $x_1 x_2...x_i = y_1 y_2...y_i$ for some $i \leqslant t$. The theorem is established.

We remark that, in view of Theorem 7.1, for (A, α_{et}) to be decodable (with some delay) it is necessary that A be an (n, e)-set. Condition (P_e) however does not seem to be necessary. Notice though that A cannot contain with $a = xu$ also $b = ux$ if $|u| \leqslant 2e$. Indeed, if it does, write $u = u_1 u_2$ with $|u_1| \leqslant e$, $|u_2| \leqslant e$; and consider $z = u_2 a^h$. Then $z \in \alpha_{et}(a^t)$ (obtained by $|u_2|$ insertions), and $z \in \alpha_{et}(b^t)u$ preventing reducibility. As a consequence, A cannot contain the sequence $00...0$ or $11...1$. Similarly one can show that if A contains a, b, c, d with $ua = bv$ and $vc = du$, (A, α_{et}) cannot satisfy statement (F_{nt}) if $|u| \leqslant 2e$.

PART III

TESTS AND CONSTRUCTIONS

OVERVIEW

The model in Chapter 8 is for the noiseless channel; no errors are allowed. The basic notion needed for the three theorems of the chapter is that of the residual quotient set of a pair of sets of sequences over some alphabet. The notion is defined and then certain residual quotient sets are characterized in Propositions 2 and 4, the latter being the more useful formulation. Unique decipherability is characterized in Theorem I, unique decipherability with bounded delay (= decodability with bounded delay) in Theorem II, and synchronizability (= error-limitation) in Theorem III. All proofs involve residual quotient sets. The chapter closes with the establishment of numerical bounds concerning the algorithms described in the three theorems.

Chapter 9 furnishes a fairly complete treatment of the standard model because it was the first published account of our work in Abstract Coding Theory. It anticipates the more general model treated in Chapter 11. Essentially an extension of Riley's paper to the standard model, it relies heavily on his results. In addition, it uses the fact that the three code properties of correcting, decodability, and error-limitation are all expandable code properties in the sense of Chapter 4. This fact implies that the theorems of Chapter 8 are tests for the code properties even for the standard model. However the tests must be applied to the set of code words of the expanded code which, in general, is much larger than the original set of code words. The aim of the paper is to show that matters can be improved especially in special cases of interest.

The residual quotient sets of Riley are generalized by using the notion of a gauged set, a pair consisting of a set and a set-valued mapping. Standard model codes are special gauged sets and many examples of codes are given for motivation and for later illustration of the tests.

Following the examples, a rather elaborate construction involving gauged sets is given and then applied to gauged sets obtained from quasi-metrics on the alphabet. Theorems 1, 2, 3 and Corollary 4 provide the technical details of the computation involved in the construction for the quasi-metric case.

Using the prior results, Theorem 7 characterizes correctability for standard model codes, Theorem 8 does the same for decodability, and Theorem 9 provides necessary and sufficient conditions for error-limitation. Technical modifications of the scheme being employed yield Theorem 12, another and more pleasant characterization of error-limitation. A final theorem deals with the specialization of the last theorem to the case of an indexed set, a special and important case of a code. The chapter ends with illustrative applications of the tests to specific codes.

Chapter 10 generalizes a construction due to Neumann to provide a family of error-correcting and error-limiting binary codes which are standard model codes. First, certain uniquely specified sets of binary sequences, called N-sets, are introduced and the codes are then defined to be special but not uniquely determined subsets of N-sets. It is shown that the codes have the properties in question for all values of the parameters involved. Actually the codes were constructed to have the properties and hence the proof mainly consists of showing how codes satisfying the specified conditions achieve the desired behavior. The important N-sets are studied in considerable detail. They are characterized in Theorem 1 and valuable additional information about them is presented in other lemmas and theorems. Computer generated examples of N-sets and codes are given and tabular results are furnished.

The model studied in Chapter 11 was the result of our first attempt to treat substitution and synchronization errors. The Levenshtein metric was the obvious tool for such a study and it entered into the construction in an essential way. The chapter begins with the explicit construction of the family of block codes, deals with average code size, computes the redundancy of the average sized code, and tabulates descriptions of some of the codes. The next section introduces a model which depends on three integral parameters and defines correcting and decodability for such models. Levenshtein distance is defined and studied and a necessary distance condition on a code for the correction of substitution and synchronization errors is given. In a sequence of lemmas which culminate in a single theorem it is shown that a block code, which satisfies the necessary condition for correcting and an additional length type condition, is decodable. It is then observed that the deductive pattern involved in the proofs is applicable to still more general models; it was used in our later paper, Chapter 7. Finally, it is demonstrated that the codes constructed in the early part of the paper satisfy the sufficient conditions of the theorem and hence are decodable even in the presence of certain substitution and synchronization errors.

CHAPTER 8

THE SARDINAS/PATTERSON
AND LEVENSHTEIN THEOREMS

J. A. RILEY

EDITORIAL NOTE

It was said of the mathematician, Jacques Hadamard, that he never read the proofs for other peoples theorems; if he was unable to furnish a proof himself, then he went through life never knowing one. In the case of the present paper, some but not all of the proofs of the theorems were available when the paper was written (November,1965). As a consequence, the author had to construct proofs of his own. In the best of mathematical tradition, he isolated the essential algebraic properties of binary sequences needed and so proceeded to give elegant and elementary proofs for these valuable theorems.

This paper appeared in *Information and Control* **10** (1967) 120–136.

1. INTRODUCTION

The purpose of this paper is to supply complete proofs of the following three theorems, each of which is a basic result in the theory of variable length codes (cf. the text for the meaning of the terminology employed):

(I) (Sardinas and Patterson, 1953): a finite code C is uniquely decipherable if and only if $\mathcal{R}_n(C)$ does not contain an element of C for any $n \geq 1$, where the $\mathcal{R}_n(C)$ are certain sets of sequences derived from C;

(II) (Even, 1963 and Levenshtein, 1962): a finite code C is uniquely decipherable with bounded delay if and only if it is uniquely decipherable and if $\mathcal{R}_{n_0}(C)$ is empty, for some $n_0 \geq 1$;

(III) (Levenshtein, 1962): a finite code C is synchronizable if and only if it is uniquely decipherable and if $\mathcal{R}_{n_0}(C, \text{Suff } C)$ is empty, for some $n_0 \geq 1$ (again with the $\mathcal{R}_n(C, \text{Suff } C)$ denoting certain sets constructed from C).

There are a number of proofs of (I) in the literature: by Sardinas and Patterson, in an unpublished report of theirs [25]; in Bandyopadhyay (1963 [3]), Levenshtein (1964 [15]), and Ash (1965 [2]). These proofs are

W. E. Hartnett (ed.), Foundations of Coding Theory, 129–145. All Rights Reserved.
Copyright © 1974 by D. Reidel Publishing Company, Dordrecht-Holland.

somewhat complicated, and not as 'clean' as one might wish. The treatment given here is, I believe, a good deal simpler, being based explicitly on certain fundamental properties of sequences. In particular, the notion of *residual quotient* of sequences seems to be quite a useful one in the general theory of variable length codes.

(II) has been discussed at length in Even (1963 [9]) and proved in Levenshtein (1964 [15]). The latter paper, indeed, gives a detailed exposition with proofs, of each of (I)–(III), along with other interesting results concerning codes. It is an expanded version of Levenshtein's preliminary announcement (1962 [14]), which stimulated our present study.

Our proof of (II) is more or less straightforward, using a general finiteness criterion for the residual sets $\mathcal{R}_n$ (cf. the text: Proposition 6).

The latter criterion is also applied to (III); the proof depends, in addition, on certain equivalent forms of the notion of synchronizability due to Even (1964 [10]) and to Calabi and Arquette (1965 [PML39] and [PML40]).

Other references to work having a bearing on our discussion are: Golomb and Gordon (1965 [12]), Markov (1960 [20], 1962 [21]), and Blum (1965 [5]) (the latter giving an ingenious alternative approach to these matters).

2. THE RESIDUAL QUOTIENT

Denote by Σ the collection of finite sequences of 0's and 1's. Juxtaposition of sequences is a binary operation on Σ, and, as is well known, Σ, together with this operation, is the free semigroup generated by the set $\{0, 1\}$. We will use the symbol $\emptyset$ to denote the empty sequence; $\emptyset$ is the unit element of Σ: $\emptyset x = x\emptyset$ for all sequences x in Σ. We will also use the same symbol $\emptyset$ for the empty *set*; this will not lead to any confusion since it will be clear from the context which meaning of $\emptyset$ is to be understood.

If x is a sequence in Σ, the length, $|x|$, of x, is the number of 0's and 1's of which it is composed. The length of the empty sequence is of course defined to be 0.

If x, y are two elements of Σ, we define the *residual* (quotient), $x|y$, of x and y as follows:

(i) if x is a proper prefix of y, i.e. if $y = xy'$ for some nonempty sequence y' in Σ, then $x|y = y'$;

(ii) similarly, if y is a proper prefix of x, $x = yx'$, then $x|y = x'$;

(iii) otherwise, i.e. if neither x nor y is a proper prefix of the other, $x|y$ is left undefined.

In particular, if x and y are of the same length, $x|y$ is not defined.

In algebraic terminology, $(x, y) \rightarrow x|y$ is a *partial* operation on Σ, which is defined if and only if either x is a *left divisor* of y, or if y is a left divisor of x. It is to be observed that the residual operation is commutative, in the sense that when defined, $x|y = y|x$, but not associative.

If C, C' are two subsets of Σ, the residual operation may be extended to define the residual quotient $C|C'$: $C|C'$ is the collection of all elements r of Σ such that either $x = x'r$ or $x' = xr$, for some x, x' in C, C' respectively. Symbolically, $C|C' = \{x|x'; x \in C, x' \in C'\}$. If it happens that $x|x'$ is not defined for *any* pair $x \in C$, $x' \in C'$, then, of course, we consider that $C|C'$ is also not defined.

Let C be any subset of Σ. The set, $\mathscr{R}(C)$, of residuals of C is defined as the smallest subset of Σ which

(a) contains C;
and (b) contains $r|c$, for all $r \in \mathscr{R}(C)$, $c \in C$.

Of course, such subsets of Σ exist: Σ itself is one. $\mathscr{R}(C)$ is in fact the intersection of all subsets of C which satisfy both properties (a) and (b),

In a similar fashion, we define the set, $\mathscr{R}(C, D)$, of residuals of C *with respect to D* (D another subset of Σ) to be the intersection of all subsets N of Σ which:

(a) contain D;
and (b) contain $r|c$, for all $r \in N$, $c \in C$.

Evidently $\mathscr{R}(C) = \mathscr{R}(C, C)$.

The set $\mathscr{R}(C, D)$ may be 'graded' by defining the sets $\mathscr{R}_n(C, D)$ of residuals of n-th *order*, for $n = 0, 1, \ldots$:

$$\mathscr{R}_0(C, D) \quad = D;$$
$$\mathscr{R}_1(C, D) \quad = \{x \in \Sigma; x = d|c \quad \text{for some } d \in D, c \in C\};$$
$$\mathscr{R}_{n+1}(C, D) = \{x \in \Sigma; x = r_n|c \quad \text{for some } r_n \in \mathscr{R}_n, c \in C\}.$$

It is clear that the sets $\mathscr{R}_n(C, D)$, $n = 0, 1, \ldots$, are well-defined by induction. It is also obvious that the $\mathscr{R}_n(C, D)$ are just the repeated 'products' of C and D:

$$\mathcal{R}_0 = D;$$
$$\mathcal{R}_1 = D|C;$$
$$\mathcal{R}_2 = (D|C)|C;$$

and so on.

Proposition 1. $\mathcal{R}(C, D) = \mathcal{R}_0(C, D) \cup \mathcal{R}_1(C, D) \cup \mathcal{R}_2(C, D) \cup \dots$.

Proof. Denote the union on the right by U; then U has the properties (a) and (b) of the definition of $\mathcal{R}(C, D)$. Thus $\mathcal{R}(C, D) \subseteq U$. To prove the opposite inclusion, let $x \in \mathcal{R}_n(C, D)$. We will show by induction on n that x is in $\mathcal{R}(C, D)$. If $n = 0$, $x \in \mathcal{R}_0 = D$, and since $D \subseteq \mathcal{R}(C, D)$, $x \in \mathcal{R}(C, D)$. Assume that $\mathcal{R}_n(C, D) \subseteq \mathcal{R}(C, D)$, and let x be in $\mathcal{R}_{n+1}(C, D)$. Then, by definition of the latter, $x = r_n|c$, for some $r_n \in \mathcal{R}_n$, and $c \in C$. By induction, $r_n \in \mathcal{R}(C, D)$, and so, by (b) of the definition of $\mathcal{R}$, $x \in \mathcal{R}(C, D)$. Thus $\mathcal{R}_{n+1} \subseteq \mathcal{R}(C, D)$ and the proposition is proved.

The sets $\mathcal{R}_n$ are just the *right classes* of the Levenshtein paper; when $D = C$, $\mathcal{R}_n(C, C) = \mathcal{R}_n(C)$ is the 'Seg$_n$' of Sardinas and Patterson.

Now we wish to show that a sequence x is in $\mathcal{R}(C, D)$ if and only if there exists $d \in D$, and $c_1, \dots, c_n \in C$ such that x has the following form:

$$(*) \qquad x = (\dots(((d|c_1)|c_2)|c_3)|\dots)|c_n.$$

It will be convenient for us to use the Lukasiewicz parenthesis-free notation for products; in this notation $(*)$ is written as: $x = |\dots|||dc_1c_2c_3\dots c_n$. Such a product, in which the operation symbols '$|$' are grouped at the left, followed by the sequence symbols $d, c_1, \dots, c_n$, will be said to be *simple*. Using this notion, together with Proposition 1, a more detailed restatement of what we wish to prove is:

Proposition 2. x is an element of $\mathcal{R}_n(C, D)$, $n \geqslant 1$, if and only if it is a simple product of the form:

$$x = |\dots||dc_1c_2\dots c_n, \text{ where } d \in D \text{ and } c_1, \dots, c_n \in C.$$

Proof. The proof is by induction on n. If $n = 1$, $x \in \mathcal{R}_1(C, D)$ if and only if $x \in D|C$, i.e. if and only if $x = d|c$, for some $d \in D$, $c \in C$. Assume the result true for n. Then $x \in \mathcal{R}_{n+1}(C, D)$ if and only if $x = r_n|c$ for some $r_n \in \mathcal{R}_n(C, D)$, $c \in C$. By our induction hypothesis, $r_n \in \mathcal{R}_n$ if and only if r_n is a simple product, $r_n = |...||d'c_1c_2...c_n$; thus $x \in \mathcal{R}_{n+1}$ if and only if $x = (|...||d'c_1c_2...c_n)|c$, i.e. if and only if $x = ||...||d'c_1c_2...c_nc$. The proof is finished.

3. Characterization of $\mathcal{R}_n(C, D)$

Let $a_1, ..., a_r$ and $b_1, ..., b_s$ be two sets of elements of Σ such that the products $a_1...a_r$ and $b_1...b_s$ are equal, $a_1...a_r = b_1...b_s$. We will say that this equality is *irreducible* if no shorter 'terminal' sub-products are equal, i.e. if $a_i...a_r = b_j...b_s$ for any $i, j \Rightarrow i = 1, j = 1$ (e.g. (10) (00) (11) (0110) = (100) (011) (01) (10) contains the shorter equality $0110 = (01)$ (10)...).

If the equality $a_1...a_r = b_1...b_s$ is irreducible, then, in particular $a_r \neq b_s$, so that, also, a_r and b_s have different lengths.

Proposition 3. Let $a_1, ..., a_r$ and $b_1, ..., b_s$ be two ordered sets of sequences such that $a_1...a_r = b_1...b_s$ and suppose the equality to be irreducible. Then the shorter of a_r and b_s is a residual of the set $\{a_1, ..., a_r, b_1, ..., b_s\}$, and is, in fact, a simple product of the form $|...||xyz...w$, in which the 'innermost' factors x, y are either a_1, b_1 or b_1, a_1 respectively.

Proof. By induction on $r+s$. If $r+s = 3$ then, $a_1 = b_1b_2$, say, and $b_2 = |a_1b_1$. Assume the proposition true for $r+s = n \geqslant 3$. Let $a_1...a_r = b_1...b_s$ with $r+s = n+1$, and suppose that no shorter subproducts are equal. If $r = 1$, then $a_1 = b_1...b_s$, and $b_s = |...||a_1b_1b_2...b_{s-1}$, so that the proposition holds in this case. Similarly for $s = 1$. We may assume then that $r, s \geqslant 2$.

Now $a_1 \neq b_1$ (since otherwise the shorter product equality $a_2...a_r = b_2...b_s$ would hold), so that a_1, say is shorter than b_1. Then, since a_1 is a prefix of the sequence $a_1...a_r$, and hence a prefix of $b_1...b_s$, we have $b_1 = a_1b_1'$. Cancelling a_1, we obtain the equality:

$$a_2 ... a_r = b_1'b_2 ... b_s.$$

Now, again this last equality is irreducible, so that our induction hypothesis applies, and we conclude that the shorter of a_r and b_s is a simple product of the form $|...|b_1'a_2....$ Since $b_1' = |a_1b_1$, this product is equal to $|...||a_1b_1a_2...$; this is what we wished to prove.

Now let C, D be, as before, two subsets of Σ. The following proposition is Levenshtein's Lemma 2, and affords a characterization of the sets $\mathcal{R}_n$ in a form suitable for our subsequent applications.

Proposition 4. A nonempty sequence x is in $\mathcal{R}_n(C, D)$, $n \geqslant 1$, if and only if there exists a_0 in D, n elements $a_1, \ldots, a_n$ of C, and an integer r, $1 \leqslant r \leqslant n$, such that:

(A)   either (i) $a_0 a_1 \ldots a_{r-1} x = a_r \ldots a_n$,

        or   (ii) $a_0 a_1 \ldots a_{r-1} = a_r \ldots a_n x$,

                    with, in either case, an irreducible equality, and

(B)   with x strictly shorter than a_n, if case (i) holds, and strictly shorter than the last factor of $a_0 a_1 \ldots a_{r-1}$ if case (ii) holds (this last factor is a_0, if $r = 1$, and a_{r-1}, if $r > 1$).

Proof. If $a_0, a_1, \ldots, a_n$ exist such that (A) and (B) hold, then Proposition 3 applies to show that x is a simple product of the form $x = |\ldots|a_0 a_r \ldots a_n$, and hence, by Proposition 2, belongs to $\mathcal{R}_n(C, D)$. The converse, that if $x \in \mathcal{R}_n$ then (A), (B) hold, is proved by induction on n. If $n = 1$, then $x \in \mathcal{R}_1(C, D)$, and so either $dx = c$, or $d = cx$, for some $d \in D$, $c \in C$. Clearly (A), (B) hold in this case. Assume the desired result true for $n \geqslant 1$, and let $x \in \mathcal{R}_{n+1}(C, D)$. Then there exists $x_n \in \mathcal{R}_n(C, D)$, and $c \in C$, such that either (a) $x_n = cx$ or (b) $x_n x = c$. By our induction hypothesis, there exist $a_0 \in D$, $a_1, \ldots, a_n \in C$, and r, such that either (i) $a_0 \ldots a_{r-1} x_n = a_r \ldots a_n$, or (ii) $a_0 \ldots a_{r-1} = a_r \ldots a_n x_n$. Combining cases (a), (b) with (i), (ii), there are four possible situations:

(1) $x_n = cx$,   and $a_0 \ldots a_{r-1} x_n = a_r \ldots a_n$;

(2) $x_n = cx$,   and $a_0 \ldots a_{r-1} = a_r \ldots a_n x_n$;

(3) $x_n x = c$,   and $a_0 \ldots a_{r-1} x_n = a_r \ldots a_n$; and

(4) $x_n x = c$,   and $a_0 \ldots a_{r-1} = a_r \ldots a_n x_n$.

Multiply the second equality in (3), (4) by x on the right, and substitute c for $x_n x$ to obtain: (3') $a_0 \ldots a_{r-1} c = a_r \ldots a_n x$, and (4') $a_0 \ldots a_{r-1} x = a_r \ldots a_n c$. In (1) and (2) replace x_n by cx to obtain: (1') $a_0 \ldots a_{r-1} cx = a_r \ldots a_n$; and (2') $a_0 \ldots a_{r-1} = a_r \ldots a_n cx$. So far, then, we have shown, writing $a_{n+1} = c$, that if $x \in \mathcal{R}_{n+1}$, there exists $a_0 \in D$, and $a_1, \ldots, a_{n+1} \in C$ such that either

[(1') or (3')], or [(2') or (4')] holds. It is clear that condition (A) of the statement of the proposition is satisfied. It is not difficult to check that x is strictly shorter than the appropriate last factor in each of the cases (1')–(4'). Thus (B) holds and the Proposition is proved.

In what follows Proposition 4 will be used quite heavily, and it will be convenient to use an abbreviated statement of the conditions (A) and (B). A subset C of Σ will generally (but not always) be called a *code* and its elements, *words*, or *code words*. Products of words, such as $a_1 \ldots a_{r-1}$ and $a_r \ldots a_n$ will be called *messages*; the collection $\mathcal{M}(C)$ of all messages formed from the elements of C is the subsemigroup of Σ generated by C. The empty message, $\emptyset$, is to be identified with the empty sequence. If m is a message, $m = c_1 \ldots c_r$, say, the number of *words* in m is just the number of factors, viz. r.

One should really be a bit more precise in speaking of 'the' factors of a message; *a priori*, it is of course quite possible that a given sequence may be factored into code words in more than one way. Another way of saying this is that a given sequence m may be the 'multiplied-out' version of two *different* ordered sets, $(a_1, \ldots, a_r)$ and $(b_1, \ldots, b_s)$, of code words: $m = a_1 \ldots a_r = b_1 \ldots b_s$. What we mean, therefore, by a message, is an *ordered set*, $(a_1, \ldots, a_r)$ of code words, together with their product $m = a_1 \ldots a_r$.

The equalities (i) and (ii) of (A) above may then be written as $dmx = m'$ or $dm = m'x$, $d \in D$, $m, m' \in \mathcal{M}(C)$. In this form, we allow the possibility that $m = \emptyset$. In an equality of the form $b_1 \ldots b_r x = c_1 \ldots c_s$, we will say that x is *short* if its length is strictly smaller than the length of the last factors c_s of $c_1 \ldots c_s$.

Using this terminology and notation, Proposition 4 may be rendered in a more compact form as:

Proposition 5. A sequence x is an element of $\mathcal{R}_n(C, D)$, $n \geqslant 1$, if and only if there exists an irreducible equality $dmx = m'$, or $dm = m'x$ in which x is short, $d \in D$, and m, m' are messages from C having together a total of exactly n words.

4. UNIQUE DECIPHERABILITY

A code C is said to be *uniquely decipherable*, abbreviated '*UD*', if, intuitively, two equal messages must have the same factors, in the same order. Precisely, C is UD if whenever $a_1 \ldots a_r = b_1 \ldots b_s$, for $a_1, \ldots, b_1, \ldots$ in C, then $r = s$ and $a_i = b_i$, $i = 1, \ldots, r$.

THEOREM I. C is UD if and only if no one of the sets $\mathscr{R}_n(C)$, for $n \geqslant 1$, contains an element of C.

Proof. If $x \in C$ is also an element of $\mathscr{R}_n(C)$ for some $n \geqslant 1$, then by applying Proposition 5 with $D = C$ there exists an irreducible equality $mx = m'$, with m, m' and x in $\mathscr{M}(C)$ and with short x. Because of this latter property, x is not equal to the last factor of m', and we have two equal messages with different factors. Thus C is not UD. Conversely, if C is not UD, there exists an equality $m = m'$ with different factors. Let m, m' together have n factors; then $n \geqslant 3$. We may assume that the equality is irreducible (otherwise, cancel ...). In particular the last factor of m is not equal to the last factor of m', and so one of them must be short. By Proposition 5, then, this short factor is an element of $\mathscr{R}_{n-2}$, and $n - 2 \geqslant 1$. The theorem is proved.

It should be observed, and this is the express purpose of the Sardinas/ Patterson paper, that the theorem provides an algorithm for deciding whether a given finite code is UD. The idea is this: since, as is easily verified, the elements of $\mathscr{R}_n(C)$, $n \geqslant 1$, are *suffixes of* code words, and since C is finite, with each word of C a sequence of finite length, the sets $\mathscr{R}_n(C)$, if not empty, must sooner or later start repeating themselves. That is, there exists $n_0 \geqslant 1$ such that $\mathscr{R}_{n_0}$ is either empty, or equal to $\mathscr{R}_{n'_0}$ for some $n'_0 < n_0$. In practice one need carry the construction of the $\mathscr{R}_n$ only as far as $\mathscr{R}_{n_0}$. Then C is UD if and only if no one of the $\mathscr{R}_n$, $1 \leqslant n \leqslant n_0$, contains a code word from C.

Another remark, which, from the standpoint of cultural completeness, needs to be made, concerns the relation of unique decipherability to the theory of free semigroups. The connection is this: a subsemigroup of Σ, with minimal generating set C, is (isomorphic to) the free semigroup generated by C, if and only if the code C is UD. In view of the fact that the classification problem for free subsemigroups of Σ is as yet, except for small generating sets consisting of one and two elements, completely unresolved, the characterization just mentioned, together with the algorithmic aspects of the theorem, may well be of considerable interest.

5. A FINITENESS CONDITION. CODES WITH BOUNDED DELAY

As mentioned in the Introduction, the properties of synchronizability and of unique decipherability with bounded delay are bound up with the vanishing of some one of the sets $\mathscr{R}_n$. There is a general 'finiteness' condition which is both necessary and sufficient for this. We first point out the (quite easily proved) fact that if $\mathscr{R}_{n_0}(C, D)$ is empty, for a particular n_0, then $\mathscr{R}_n(C, D)$ is empty for all $n \geqslant n_0$ as well.

Proposition 6. Let C be a finite code, and let D be any subset of Σ. Then the two following statements are equivalent:

(A) $\mathscr{R}_{n_0}(C, D)$ is empty, for some $n_0 \geqslant 1$.

(B)   there exists an integer $N \geqslant 1$ such that if an irreducible equality holds in either of the forms $dmx = m'$ or $dm = m'x$, with $|m| + |m'| \geqslant N$, then x is not short.

Proof. (A) $\Rightarrow$ (B). Suppose that $\mathscr{R}_{n_0}$ is empty, for a particular $n_0 \geqslant 1$. Choose $N = n_0 \cdot l_{\max}$, where $l_{\max}$ denotes the longest length of an element of C, and suppose that there exists an irreducible equality $dmx = m'$ (or $dm = m'x$) with $|m| + |m'| \geqslant N$. Suppose that m and m' together contain s words. Then $|m| + |m'| \leqslant s \cdot l_{\max}$, so that $N \leqslant s \cdot l_{\max}$, and hence $n_0 \leqslant s$. If x were short, then Proposition 5 would apply to show that $x \in \mathscr{R}_s(C, D)$. This, however, is impossible since $\mathscr{R}_{n_0} = \emptyset$, and so $\mathscr{R}_s = \emptyset$, also, by virtue of the inequality $s \geqslant n_0$. Thus x is not short, and (B) holds.

Conversely, suppose that (B) holds, for a certain $N \geqslant 1$. Let n_0 be any integer larger than $N/l_{\min}$, $l_{\min}$ denoting the length of the shortest elements of C, and suppose that $\mathscr{R}_{n_0}(C, D)$ is not empty: let $x \in \mathscr{R}_{n_0}(C, D)$. By Proposition 5, there exist $d \in D$, and messages m, m' with a total of n_0 words, such that one or the other of the two following irreducible equalities holds with short x: $dmx = m'$, or $dm = m'x$. Now $|m| + |m'| \geqslant n_0 \cdot l_{\min} \geqslant N$, and hence (B) applies to show that x is not short. This is a contradiction. Thus $\mathscr{R}_{n_0}$ is empty, and (B) $\Rightarrow$ (A).

A code C is said to be uniquely decipherable with *bounded delay*, '*UBD*', if there exists an integer $N \geqslant 1$ (called the 'delay') such that, loosely, products from C of length N or more uniquely determine their first factors. More precisely, 'C is *UBD*' is defined to mean that there exists an N such that if $b_1 b_2 \ldots$ and $c_1 c_2 \ldots$ are two messages whose first N terms are equal, then $b_1 = c_1$.

Proposition 7. A code C is *UBD* if and only if the following condition is satisfied: (∗) there exists N' such that if $my = m'$ with y a prefix of an element of C, and if $|m'| \geqslant N'$, then either m and m' have the same first word, or else y is strictly longer than the last word of m'.

Proof. If C is *UBD*, with delay N, choose $N' = N$, and suppose that $my = m'$, y a prefix, and $|m'| \geqslant N'$. Then $yy' = C$, for some c in C, and mc is a message having the same first N terms as m'. Since C is *UBD*, with delay N, this entails that mc and m' have the same first word, and thus m and m' also have the same first word. Thus (∗) holds.

Conversely, suppose that C satisfies (∗); choose $N = N' + l_{max}$. If $m = b_1 b_2 \dots$, $m' = c_1 c_2 \dots$ are two messages having the same first N terms, suppose that the N-th term occurs in the words b_{t+1}, c_{u+1} respectively. Then $b_{t+1} = yy'$, $c_{u+1} = zz'$, and $b_1 \dots b_t y = c_1 \dots c_u z$, each of the two sides of this equality being of length N. One or the other of y and z is the longer, say $|y| \leqslant |z|$. Since $b_1 \dots b_t y = c_1 \dots c_u z$, we have $z = z'y$ with z' a prefix of c_{u+1}. Cancelling y, then, we have the equality $b_1 \dots b_t = c_1 \dots c_u z'$. Now if z' is longer than b_t, cancel b_t, obtaining $b_1 \dots b_{t-1} = c_1 \dots c_u z''$, where $z' = z'' b_t$. If z'' is longer than b_{t-1}, cancel b_{t-1}, and so on…. Ultimately we arrive at an equality of the form $b_1 \dots b_r = c_1 \dots c_u z^{(0)}$, with $|z^0| \leqslant |b_r|$, and with, of course, z^0 a prefix of c_{u+1}. Also, $|c_1 \dots c_u z^{(0)}| \geqslant |c_1 \dots c_u z| - l_{max} = N - l_{max} = N'$. Thus the hypothesis of the condition (∗) is fulfilled, and $z^{(0)}$ is not strictly longer than b_r, the last word of the product $b_1 \dots b_r$. The conclusion of (∗) then yields: $b_1 = c_1$, i.e. m and m' have the same first word. Thus C is *UBD* and the proposition is proved.

It will have been observed that it was not really necessary to include the phrase 'or else y is strictly longer than the last word of m'' in the conclusion of (∗): our proof also shows, essentially, that C is *UBD* if and only if there exists N' such that if $my = m'$, with y a prefix of an element of C, and with $|m'| \geqslant N'$, then m and m' have the same first word. We will however need the seemingly stronger version (∗) for the next result.

A useful characterization of *UBD* codes can be derived by combining Propositions 6 and 7: C is *UBD* if and only if $\mathscr{R}_{n_0}(C)$ is empty, for some $n_0 \geqslant 1$. This equivalence was, apparently, first conceived by Sardinas and Patterson, and asserted to be true in (Even, 1963 [9]) and by Levenshtein. As far as we know the following proof is the only published version.

THEOREM II. Let C be a finite, uniquely decipherable code. The following conditions are equivalent.

(A) $\mathcal{R}_{n_0}(C)$ is empty, for some $n_0 \geq 1$,

(B)   There exists N such that if an irreducible equality $mx = m'$ holds, with $|m| + |m'| \geq N$, then x is not short;

(C)   There exists N' such that if $my = m'$, with y a prefix of a word in C, and if $|m'| \geq N'$, then either m and m' have the same first word, or else y is strictly longer than the last word of m'.

(D) C is *UBD*.

Proof. The equivalence of (A) and (B) is just Proposition 6, with $D = C$; likewise, the equivalence of (C) and (D) is just Proposition 7. We have to show that (B) is equivalent to (C).

(B) $\Rightarrow$ (C). Choose $N' = N$. Suppose that $my = m'$, with y a prefix of an element of C, and with $|m'| \geq N'$. Then $|m| + |m'| \geq |m'| \geq N' = N$, and $|m| + |m'| \geq N$. If the equality $my = m'$ is irreducible, then (B) applies to give: y is not short. In this case, also, because of irreducibility, y is not equal to the last word of m' so that y must be strictly longer than the last word of m'. If the equality is not irreducible, then $m = m_1 m_2 y$ and $m' = m'_1 m'_2$, with $m_1 = m'_1$, $m_2 y = m'_2$, for certain m_1, m_2, m'_1, m'_2. Since C *is UD* the equality $m_1 = m'_1$ implies that m_1 and m'_1, and hence m, m' have the same first word. Since the equality is either irreducible or not, we have proved that either m, m' have the same first word, or else y is strictly longer than the last word of m'. This proves (C).

Conversely, assume that (C) holds. Choose $N = 2(N' + l_{max})$, and suppose that the equality $mx = m'$ is irreducible, with $|m| + |m'| \geq N$. Assume that (B) is false; i.e. assume that x is short. Then x is strictly shorter than the last word of m': writing $m = a_1 \ldots a_r$, $m' = a_{r+1} \ldots a_s$, this means that $a_1 \ldots a_r x = a_{r+1} \ldots a_s$, with $|x| < |a_s|$. Then $a_s = yx$, y a prefix of a_s, and, cancelling x, we obtain the equality $a_1 \ldots a_r = a_{r+1} \ldots a_{s-1} y$. If y is strictly longer than a_r we may write $y = y' a_r$, and hence, cancelling a_r, $a_1 \ldots a_{r-1} = a_{r+1} \ldots a_{s-1} y'$. If, again, y' is longer than a_{r-1}, cancel a_{r-1}, and so on .... Eventually we obtain an equality $a_1 \ldots a_t = a_{r+1} \ldots a_{s-1} y''$, in which $|y''| \leq |a_t|$, y'' a prefix of a_s. Now $|m| = |m'| - |x|$, so that $|m| + |m'| = 2|m'| - |x| \geq N$. Thus $|m'| \geq N/2 = N' + l_{max}$. Also, since y'' is a prefix of a_s, $|a_{r+1}...a_{s-1}y''| \geqslant |a_{r+1}...a_s| - l_{max} = m' - l_{max}$, and thus $|a_{r+1}...a_{s-1}y''| \geqslant m' - l_{max} \geqslant N'$. Condition (C) now applies to the equality $a_1...a_t = a_{r+1}...a_{s-1}y''$, and since y'' is not strictly longer than a_t we conclude that the first words of $a_1...a_t$ and $a_{r+1}...a_{s-1}$ are the same, i.e. $a_1 = a_{r+1}$. This however contradicts the irreducibility of the equality $mx = m'$. Hence our assumption that x is short has led to a contradiction, and therefore x is *not* short. (B) is proved, and with it, the theorem.

We have already remarked above that the construction of the sets $\mathcal{R}_n(C)$ for a finite code will eventually lead either to an empty set, $\mathcal{R}_{n_0} \neq \emptyset$, for some $n_0 \geqslant 1$, or to a repetition of a previously constructed class. It is clear therefore that an effective algorithm can be given for deciding whether a given code is *UBD*.

It should be remarked, finally, that the concept '*UBD*' is related to the question of unique factorization of *infinite* messages. Reference may be made to Levenshtein's paper, in which he defines the concept of 'strongly free' codes, and to (Gilbert and Moore, 1959 [11]).

6. SYNCHRONIZABLE CODES

A second application of our finiteness condition (Proposition 6) is to synchronizability. This notion is a basic one in the theory of variable length codes; Levenshtein's definition is (essentially): a code C, finite and uniquely decipherable, is *synchronizable* if there exists an integer N such that whenever ax and xb are messages, for given sequences a, b and x, then x is also a message, provided that it is longer than N. A more intuitive formulation is given by Even (1964 [10]); his definition has been refined, and presented in a more precise form by Calabi and Arquette (1965 [PML39] and [PML40]). The latter reference also contains a study of certain other equivalent definitions of synchronizability. In the following theorem we present our proof of the equivalence of several of these conditions, together with the proof of Levenshtein's result: C is synchronizable if and only if $\mathcal{R}_{n_0}(C, \text{Suff } C)$ is empty, for some $n_0 \geqslant 1$. Here Suff C denotes a certain set of sequences derived from C, viz. Suff C is the collection of proper suffixes of elements of C, i.e. those sequences x which are not themselves words in C, but for which $x'x \in C$ for some sequences x'.

THEOREM III. Let C be a finite uniquely decipherable code. The following statements are equivalent.

(A) $\mathcal{R}_{n_0}(C, \text{Suff } C)$ is empty, for some $n_0 \geq 1$.

(B)   There exists N such that in any irreducible equality of either the form $dmx = m'$ or the form $dm = m'x$, with $d \in \text{Suff } C$, and with $|m| + |m'| \geq N$, x is not short.

(C)   There exists N' such that if $|x| \geq N'$, and if, for certain sequences a, b both ax and xb are messages from C then x is itself a message.

(D)   There exists N'' such that:
        (1) if $|x| \geq N''$, and ax is a message, for some sequence a, then whenever $a'xb'$ is a message, so is $a'x$;
        (2) if $|x| \geq N''$, and xb is a message, for some sequence b, then whenever $a'xb'$ is a message, so is xb'.

(E)   There exists N''' such that if $|x| \geq N'''$, and if x is part of a message, i.e. if axb is a message, for certain sequences a, b, then x can be factored, $x = x_1 \cdot x_2$, the two factors having the property that whenever $a'xb'$ is a message, then so are $a'x_1$ and x_2b'.

Proof. The equivalence of (A) and (B) is just Proposition 6, with $D = \text{Suff } C$. We will show that (B) $\Rightarrow$ (C) $\Rightarrow$ (D) $\Rightarrow$ (E) $\Rightarrow$ (B). (B) $\Rightarrow$ (C): choose $N' = N$, and let $ax = m$, $xb = m'$ for certain sequences a, b, and messages m, m'. Suppose that $|x| \geq N'$. We wish to show that x is a message. Since $ax = m$, and m is a product of words from C, we may 'cancel' words from the left sides of the equality to show that $x = x'm''$, in which x' is a suffix of a code word. Further, we may assume that x' is in D, i.e. is a *proper* suffix, since if x' is itself a code word, then $x = x'm''$ is already a message. Again, by 'chopping' words from the right side of the equality $xb = m'$, we may write $b = b'm'''$, and $m' = m^{iv}m'''$, where now b' is shorter than the last word of m^{iv}. (If b' *is* the last word of m^{iv}, then b, and hence x, is a message, and again we are done.) We have now $xb' = m^{iv}$, and so $x'm''b' = m^{iv}$. In this last equality $x' \in \text{Suff } C$, and b' is short. Also, $|m''| + |m^{iv}| \geq |x|$ (since $m^{iv} = xb'$) and so $|m''| + |m^{iv}| \geq N' = N$. If the equality $x'm''b' = m^{iv}$ is irreducible, then (B) applies to yield: b' is not short. This however would contradict the fact that, by construction, b' *is* short. Thus the equality is not irreducible, and so $x'm^{v} = m^{vi}$, for certain 'sub-messages' m^v, m^{vi} of m'', m^{iv} respectively. But then $x'm''$ is also a message; i.e. x is a message. Hence (C) is proved.

(C) $\Rightarrow$ (D): Choose $N'' = N' + l_{max}$. Suppose that $|x| \geqslant N''$, and that ax is a message, for some sequence a. Let $a'xb'$ be a message, for given a', b'. We want to show that part (1) of (D) holds, viz., that $a'x$ is a message. Consider the sequence consisting of the first l_{max} terms of x; since $a'xb'$ is a message, i.e. a product of words from C, and since each word is of length at most l_{max}, there must be a 'comma' somewhere in this sequence, i.e. one of the terms in this sequence must be the first term of a factor of the message $a'xb'$. We have therefore a factorization of x, $x = x_1x_2$, such that $a'x_1$ and x_2b' are 'sub-messages' of $a'xb'$. In particular x_2 is a prefix of a message (viz. x_2b'). Also, by assumption, x, and hence x_2, is a suffix of a message (viz. ax). Further, $|x_2| \geqslant |x| - l_{max} \geqslant N'' - l_{max} = N'$. Thus (C) applies, and we may conclude that x_2 is itself a message. But then $a'x = a'x_1 \cdot x_2$ is also a message, and (D), (1) is proved. The proof of (2) is quite similar, the construction starting off this time with the right-most l_{max} terms of x....

(D) $\Rightarrow$ (E): Choose $N''' = 2N'' + l_{max}$. Let axb be a message, and suppose that $|x| \geqslant N'''$. Consider the sequence consisting of the 'middle' l_{max} terms of x. Again, the first term of some word of the message axb must lie in this sequence so that we have a factorization $x = x_1 \cdot x_2$, with ax_1 and x_2b being 'sub-messages' of axb. Now the lengths of both x_1 and x_2 are not smaller than $\frac{1}{2}(|x| - l_{max}) \geqslant \frac{1}{2}(N''' - l_{max}) = N''$. Thus (D) applies, and we conclude that if $a'xb'$ is a message, then $a'x_1$ and x_2b' are both messages. This proves (E).

(E) $\Rightarrow$ (B): Choose $N \geqslant 2(N''' + 2l_{max})$ and suppose that the irreducible equality $dmx = m'$ holds, with $d \in$ Suff C, and $|m| + |m'| \geqslant N$. If x is short (of length less than that of the last word of m'), then, since $|m| = |m'| - |d| - |x|$, $|m| + |m'| = 2|m'| - |d| - |x|$, and so $2|m'| - |d| - |x| \geqslant N$. Hence $|m'| \geqslant N/2$, and $|m| \geqslant N/2 - |d| - |x| \geqslant N/2 - 2l_{max} \geqslant N'''$. (E) now applies, since $|m| \geqslant N'''$, and since m is part of the message $dmx = m'$. We conclude that $m = y_1y_2$, with dm_1 and m_2x being messages. Since C is UD, the equality $dm_1 \cdot m_2x = m'$ means that dm_1 and m_2x are 'sub-messages' of m', and hence the equality $dmx = m'$ is not irredudible. This is a contradiction. Hence the assumption that x is short is untenable; x is *not* short. The conclusion of (B) holds in this case. Again, suppose that the irreducible equality $dm = m'x$ holds, with d in Suff C, and with

$|m| + |m'| \geqslant N$. Since d is a suffix, pd is an element of C for some sequence p, and $pdm = pm'x$ is a message. Now $|m'| = |m| + |d| - |x|$, and $|m| + |m'| = 2|m| + |d| - |x|$, so that $2|m| + |d| - |x| \geqslant N$, and $|m| \geqslant \{N + |x| - |d|\}/2$. Thus $|m'| = |m| + |d| - |x| \geqslant \{N + |x| - |d|\}/2 + |d| - |x|$ or $|m'| \geqslant N/2 - |x|/2 + |d|/2 \geqslant N/2 - |x|/2$. If x is short, this last inequality becomes $|m'| \geqslant N/2 = l_{max}/2 \geqslant N/2 - l_{max} \geqslant N'''$. Hence (E) applies to m' as a part of the message $pm'x$, and we conclude that m' may be written as $m' = m'_1 \cdot m'_2$, with pm'_1 and $m'_2 x$ messages. Thus $pdm = pm'_1 \cdot m'_2 x$. Now again since C is uniquely decipherable, pm'_1 and $m'_2 x$ must be 'sub-messages' of pdm, so that, since pd is (by unique decipherability) the first factor of pdm and hence of pm'_1, we must obtain a further factorization of m, $m = m_1 m_2$, such that $pdm_1 = pm'_1$, and $m_2 = m'_2 x$. But this contra-dicts the irreducibility of the equality $dm = m'x$. The assumption that x is short has again led to a contradiction, and so x is not short. The con-clusion of (B) holds in both cases, and the proof of the theorem is complete.

It should be remarked that D,(1) and D,(2) are *equivalent* statements; it was convenient for us to retain the separate statements.

It is not really necessary to point out that, again, we have a finite algorithm for testing synchronizability.

Finally, as in the case of *UD* and *UBD* codes, there is a certain connec-tion with 'freedom'; for this, reference must be made to Levenshtein's paper.

7. SOME NUMERICAL BOUNDS

In connection with the algorithmic aspects of Theorems I–III, there are certain numerical bounds which are of considerable practical interest.

Let C be a finite code, and D another subset of Σ. As before we will write $\mathscr{R}_n$ instead of $\mathscr{R}_n(C, D)$, and $\mathscr{R}$ instead of $\mathscr{R}_1 \cup \mathscr{R}_2 \cup \ldots$.

Lemma. If for some $i \geqslant 1$, $\mathscr{R}_i(C, D)$ is contained in $D \cup \mathscr{R}_1(C, D) \cup \ldots \cup \mathscr{R}_{i-1}(C, D)$, then $\mathscr{R} = \mathscr{R}_1 \cup \ldots \cup \mathscr{R}_i$.

Proof. Suppose that $\mathscr{R}_i$ is contained in $D \cup \mathscr{R}_1 \cup \ldots \cup \mathscr{R}_{i-1}$, for some $i \geqslant 1$. Let $x \in \mathscr{R}_{i+1}$. Then $x = x'|c$, $x' \in \mathscr{R}_i$, $c \in C$. Since $\mathscr{R}_i \subseteq D \cup \mathscr{R}_1 \cup \ldots \cup \mathscr{R}_{i-1}$, either $x' \in D$, or $x' \in \mathscr{R}_j$, for some j such that $1 \leqslant j \leqslant i-1$. If $x' \in D$, $x = x'|c$ is in $\mathscr{R}_1$. If $x' \in \mathscr{R}_j$, $1 \leqslant j \leqslant i-1$, then x is in $\mathscr{R}_{j+1}$; in either case x is in $\mathscr{R}_1 \cup \ldots \cup \mathscr{R}_i$. This shows that $\mathscr{R}_{i+1} \subseteq \mathscr{R}_1 \cup \ldots \cup \mathscr{R}_i$. But now $\mathscr{R}_{i+1}$ is also contained in $D \cup \mathscr{R}_1 \cup \ldots \cup \mathscr{R}_i$, so that a repetition of the argument just concluded shows that $\mathscr{R}_{i+2} \subseteq \mathscr{R}_1 \cup \ldots \cup \mathscr{R}_{i+1} \subseteq \mathscr{R}_1 \cup \ldots \cup \mathscr{R}_i$. And so on...; each $\mathscr{R}_n$ is contained in $\mathscr{R}_1 \cup \ldots \cup \mathscr{R}_i$, and so $\mathscr{R} \subseteq \mathscr{R}_1 \cup \ldots \cup \mathscr{R}_i$. Thus $\mathscr{R} = \mathscr{R}_1 \cup \ldots \cup \mathscr{R}_i$.

Proposition 8. Take $D = C$, and denote by t the number of suffixes of elements of C which are not themselves elements of C. Then $\mathscr{R} = \mathscr{R}_1 \cup \ldots \cup \mathscr{R}_{t+1}$.

Proof. Suppose that $\mathscr{R} \neq \mathscr{R}_1 \cup \ldots \cup \mathscr{R}_{t+1}$. Then by the Lemma, no one of $\mathscr{R}_1, \ldots, \mathscr{R}_{t+1}$ is contained in the union of C and the preceding $\mathscr{R}_i$'s. In particular, $\mathscr{R}_1 \nsubseteq C$, so that there is an element $x_1 \in \mathscr{R}_1$, $x_1 \notin C$. Likewise, there is an $x_2 \in \mathscr{R}_2$, $x_2 \notin C \cup \mathscr{R}_1$. And so on; we construct in this way a set of $t+1$ distinct residuals $x_1, \ldots, x_{t+1}$. Now the x_i are suffixes of code words, by definition of the $\mathscr{R}_i$. Since they are not in C, we have a contradiction to our assumption that there are exactly t suffixes of this type. Hence $\mathscr{R} = \mathscr{R}_1 \cup \ldots \cup \mathscr{R}_{t+1}$.

As an immediate corollary we have a useful bound on the test for *UD*: the idea being that in view of the proposition, if *any* $\mathscr{R}_{n_0}$ contains an element of C, then so does $\mathscr{R}_1 \cup \ldots \cup \mathscr{R}_{t+1}$.

Corollary. A code C is *UD* if and only if no one of the residual sets $\mathscr{R}_1, \ldots, \mathscr{R}_{t+1}$ contains an element of C.

Turning to the tests for *UBD* and synchronizability, we see that in these cases also it is not necessary to construct more than the first $t+1$ residual sets in order to see whether any of the $\mathscr{R}_i$ are empty.

Proposition 9. Let C be a uniquely decipherable code, D any other subset of Σ, and let t denote the number of suffixes of elements of $C \cup D$ which are not themselves in C (i.e., if z is one of these suffixes, then $z \notin C$). Then if for any value n_0 of n, $\mathscr{R}_{n_0}(C, D)$ is empty, so is $\mathscr{R}_{t+2}(C, D)$. Further, if the elements of D are suffixes of elements of C, $\mathscr{R}_{t+1}$ is also empty.

Proof. Suppose that $\mathscr{R}_{t+2}$ is *not* empty. Let x_{t+2} be in $\mathscr{R}_{t+2}$, and let $x_0, x_1, \ldots, x_{t+1}, x_{t+2}$ be a residual 'chain' giving rise to x_{t+2} (meaning, of course, that x_1 is a residual, $x_0 | c$, of x_0, x_2 is a residual, $x_1 | c'$, of x_1, and so on). Then, first of all, no two of the x_i are equal, since if $x_i = x_j$, say, with $i \neq j$, then by construction, x_i is also an element of $\mathscr{R}_{j+(j-i)}$,

$\mathscr{R}_{j+2(j-i)}, \ldots$, and in general, x_i belongs to $\mathscr{R}_{j+n(j-i)}$ for all n. This implies that no $\mathscr{R}_n$ is empty, and hence contradicts our assumption. Furthermore, the chain $x_0, \ldots, x_{t+2}$ can contain at most one element of C: if x_i and x_j are in C, $i \neq j$, then x_j actually belongs to $\mathscr{R}_{j-i}(C, C)$; this, however, contradicts our assumption that C is UD. We have therefore a set of $t+2$ residuals, which are distinct, and of which at most one belongs to C. Again, the x_i, with the possible exception of x_0 which belongs to D, are all suffixes of elements of $C \cup D$. This yields a contradiction to the assumption that there are exactly t such suffixes. The proposition is proved.

Corollary. Let C be a uniquely decipherable code, and let t denote the number of suffixes of elements of C which do not belong to C. Then C is *UBD* and/or synchronizable if and only if $\mathscr{R}_{t+1}(C, C)$ and/or $\mathscr{R}_{t+1}(C, \text{Suff } C)$, respectively, is empty.

A last remark: the methods used above enable us to prove the following rather general result:

Proposition 10. Let C be a code, and D another subset of Σ. If u denotes the number of proper suffixes of elements of $C \cup D$ (including those which may be equal to other elements of C), then $\mathscr{R} = \mathscr{R}_1 \cup \ldots \cup \mathscr{R}_{u+1}$. If any one of the $\mathscr{R}_n$ is empty, then, in particular, so is $\mathscr{R}_{u+1}$.

CHAPTER 9

GENERALIZATION OF TESTS
FOR CERTAIN PROPERTIES
OF VARIABLE-LENGTH CODES

W. E. HARTNETT

EDITORIAL NOTE

In a 1964 report, Riley had already indicated how to generalize the Sardinas/Patterson and Levenshtein theorems for per word errorless models to special per word substitution error models and it seemed obvious to Calabi that the same kind of theorems should hold for general per word substitution error models. This paper established such theorems; as usual, more ideas were introduced and more technical tools were created. The paper relies very heavily on the fact that our models insure the expandability of our code properties. Such expandability is essential for the tests.

The paper was originally submitted for publication in August 1966; after substantial editorial and refereeing delay, it was accepted in 1968. Taking advantage of the ensuing two years, the author provided a new introduction which updated the conceptual framework of the earlier version. The paper appeared in *Information and Control* **13** (1968) 20–45.

1. INTRODUCTION

The three properties of unique decipherability, decodability with bounded delay, and synchronizability for variable length codes have been described and studied in the literature of Coding Theory. For the most part, the properties were treated under the assumption of a noiseless channel and the necessary definitions were formulated in that setting. It is only in recent years that attempts have been made to deal with these properties in the presence of certain error patterns. Such attempts have faced a number of problems: how to describe the error patterns, how to give suitable generalizations of the definitions, how to characterize codes having these properties in an error context, and finally how to construct codes or families of codes to combat allowable noise.

Since 1964 the Coding Group at Parke Mathematical Laboratories has been attacking these problems and the present paper reports on one

W. E. Hartnett (ed.), Foundations of Coding Theory, 147–172. *All Rights Reserved.*
Copyright © 1974 by D. Reidel Publishing Company, Dordrecht-Holland.

aspect of that work. It provides constructive characterizing tests for the three properties of variable length codes over noisy channels which reduce to the well-known Sardinas-Patterson and Levenshtein tests in the absence of noise. The approach is fairly general in scope and a discussion of basic ideas will be helpful for background and motivation.

The central notion for us is the concept of the *range* $\alpha(X)$ *of a sentence* $X = (a_1, a_2, ..., a_k)$ of variable length code words over some alphabet. For a given channel, $\alpha(X)$ denotes the set of all sequences, which when received, should be decoded as X: for a noiseless channel, $\alpha(X)$ is just $\hat{X}$, the juxtaposition product $a_1 a_2 ... a_k$. The notion of the range of sentence can be used to describe many error patterns and we indicate some of them now. First, we recall that noise may cause two kinds of errors: the change of one alphabet symbol to another, the *substitution* error, and the insertion or deletion of a symbol, the *synchronization* error.

If we choose positive integers e, s, and t, then we could require that $\alpha(X)$ consist of all sequences obtainable from $\hat{X}$ by making up to r substitution errors and/or up to s synchronization errors for each t consecutive symbols transmitted. For an example, we could allow up to 2 substitution errors and up to 1 synchronization error for each 100 consecutive symbols sent. Clearly, there is a wide variety of error patterns describable in this way: in particular, we may deal with only one kind of error if this is desirable.

A second scheme is as follows: for each code word a, specify $\alpha(a)$ in an appropriate fashion, and then for $X = (a_1, a_2, ..., a_k)$ let $\alpha(X) = \alpha(a_1)\alpha(a_2)...\alpha(a_k)$, the set of all sequences obtained from juxtaposing sequences picked from the $\alpha(a_i)$'s. In this case, we say that α is defined *as a homomorphism*: clearly, complete freedom still exists in the specification of α on the code words; both kinds of errors could be considered.

Our generalizations will be established for the case of α a homomorphism and with only substitution errors allowed. The first is an extremely useful technical restriction; the second is a necessary restriction because the corresponding theorems fail for synchronization errors. However within these restrictions we present the most general results achievable.

The sets $\alpha(X)$ may be thought of as 'generalized balls' around the sequences $\hat{X}$; our assumption that α is a homomorphism means that the balls around sequences are generated by the balls around the code words and our assumption that only substitution errors are considered means that all sequences in a given ball around a code word have the same length as the code word. In particular cases, the balls would be described in terms of special distances between sequences.

Later we shall use the notion of the range of a sentence to define three properties of codes for noisy channels: error correctability, decodability, and synchronizability (or error limitability). The first of these generalizes the notion of unique decipherability, the second includes the notion of bounded delay, and the third the notion of re-establishing correct decoding after a finite delay. The definitions given will be general and suitable for any error patterns not just for the patterns we consider in this paper. It should be mentioned in passing that many different equivalent definitions of these properties exist (cf. the papers cited below). For example, our definition of synchronizability reduces to that of Levenshtein (1962 [14]) in the noiseless case.

The description of general error patterns, the formulation of adequate definitions, and characterizations of codes with the properties have been studied extensively by Calabi and Riley (1964 [PML25]), Calabi and Arquette (1965 [PML35]), Calabi and Arquette (1966 [PML43]), Arquette and Hartnett (1966 [PML44]), Arquette, Calabi, and Hartnett (1966 [PML46]), Calabi and Hartnett (1967 [PML47]), and Hartnett (1967 [PML49]). Families of decodable codes for a third type of error pattern involving both kinds of errors have been constructed by Calabi and Hartnett (1967 [PML48]) and families of error correcting and error limiting codes for substitution errors have been constructed by Hatcher (1968 [PML55]).

2. Definitions and examples

For a given alphabet J, we let $\Lambda = \Lambda(J)$ denote the set of all nonempty finite sequences ($=$ words) over J. If X and Y are subsets of Λ, we let $XY = \{xy : x \in X, y \in X\}$ where xy denotes the usual juxtaposition product of words. For $x \in \Lambda$ we let $|x|$ denote the length of x and set $[x] = \{x' : x' \in \Lambda, |x'| = |x|\}$; for a subset X of Λ we let $X^* = \bigcup \{[x] : x \in X\}$ and let Suff X denote the set of all suffixes of members of X which are not members of X. If $x, y \in \Lambda$ and $|x| \neq |y|$, then $x \in [y]u$ or $y \in [x]u$ for a unique $u \in \Lambda$ and we set $r(x, y) = u$.

Now suppose that X and Y are subsets of Λ and define $Q(X, Y) = \{w : w \in \Lambda, \; xw = y \text{ or } yw = x \text{ for } x \in X \text{ and } y \in Y\}$. Notice that each $w \in Q(X, Y)$ is a suffix of a member of X or Y. Notice also that if all members of X and Y have a common length, then $Q(X, Y) = \emptyset$; it follows that if $Q(\{x\}, \{y\}) \neq \emptyset$, then $|x| \neq |y|$ and $x = yu$ or $y = xu$ for a unique $u \in \Lambda$, that is, x is a prefix of y or conversely. Finally observe that if $X \subset [x]$ and $Y \subset [y]$ for some $x \in X$ and $y \in Y$ and if $u \in Q(X, Y)$, then $Q(X, Y) \subset [u]$, that is, all elements of $Q(X, Y)$ have the same length.

We now use these preliminary notions to define objects that will be needed for the rest of the paper. Suppose that A is a finite subset of Λ. A mapping α from A into the set of subsets of A^* will be called *a gauge on A* iff $\alpha(a) \subset [a]$ for each $a \in A$. If α is a gauge on A, then (A, α) is called a *gauged set* and A will be referred to as *the base set* of the pair. The natural interpretation of a gauge is that for each $a \in A$, $\alpha(a)$ is a set of words of the same length as a which are related to a in some fashion; such mapping have been used for a variety of purposes by various authors. For example, we may think of $\alpha(a)$ as the set of sequences that can occur as output when a is transmitted over a channel. Logically, of course, we need not restrict $\alpha(a)$ to consist of words of the same length as a; for our applications, however, this will be necessary so we shall assume it at the outset.

A given set A may have many gauges; normally these are chosen with a particular purpose in mind and we give a number of examples later. For applications, the gauge chosen would reflect some of the properties of the channel. One gauge occurs with considerable frequency and should be noted: for $a \in A$ we let $\iota(a) = \{a\}$, each element a is related only with itself. In this case we say that (A, ι) is *simple*; clearly, we may always identify A and (A, ι). We shall use this identification whenever it is convenient.

Later we construct a sequence of gauged sets and prove a fundamental relationship concerning this sequence. In applications, however, we shall deal only with special gauged sets which reasonably may be termed codes. These are obtained by restrictions on the gauge as follows: a *code* (A, α) is a gauged set such that (1) $a \in \alpha(a)$ for each $a \in A$ and (2) $\alpha(a) \cap a(b) = \emptyset$ for all distinct pairs of words of A.

Gauged sets were introduced in Wolfowitz (1961 [33]) and called codes but only for the case when all elements of A had a common length. Our notion of gauged set is general enough to include many of the definitions of codes in the literature. It covers both block and variable length codes, distance codes, and indexed codes (see Calabi and Riley (1964 [PML25]). It also encompasses the codes with admissibility mappings of Calabi and Arquette (1965 [PML35]); an admissibility mapping α on A has the property that (A, α) is a code in our sense. It should be mentioned that a simple gauged set (A, ι) is a code.

If (A, α) is a gauged set, we let $\alpha(A) = \bigcup \{\alpha(a) : a \in A\}$ and call $(\alpha(A), \iota)$ the *expanded gauged set* of (A, α); if (A, α) is a code, then $(\alpha(A), \iota)$ is the *expanded code* of (A, α). In the cases of a code (A, α), $A \subset \alpha(A)$ but this is not true in general for gauged sets and points up some of the motivation for our definition of a code. We normally think of $\alpha(a)$ as the set of all sequences whose length is the same as a such that, when received, they are to be decoded as a. This view of $\alpha(a)$ requires first that $\alpha(a) \subset [a]$, that is, that α is a gauge on A, second, that $a \in \alpha(a)$, and third, that $\alpha(a) \cap \alpha(b) = \emptyset$ for distinct pairs of words in A. In brief, we would want (A, α) to have those properties that our codes do have.

Examples that will be of continued interest for us can be developed now. We need some background material involving J and Λ. We first indicate how a function g defined on pairs of members of J will yield a useful function defined on pairs of words.

Suppose that g is a function defined on $J \times J$, the set of ordered pairs of members of J, which takes on integral values and has the following properties: (1) $0 \leqslant g(p, q)$ and $g(p, q) = 0$ if $p = q$, (2) $g(p, q) = g(q, p)$, and (3) $g(p, q) \leqslant g(p, r) + g(r, q)$ for p, q, and r in J.

Now suppose that $a, b \in \Lambda$, $a = (a_1, \ldots, a_n)$, $b = (b_1, \ldots, b_m)$ with a_i in J for each i and b_j in J for each j. Let $k = \min\{n, m\}$ and define a function ρ_g by requiring that

$$\rho_g(a, b) = \sum_{i=1}^{k} g(a_i, b_i).$$

It is clear that ρ_g is defined on $\Lambda \times \Lambda$ and that $\rho_g(a, b) \geqslant 0$ for each pair of words (a, b) in $\Lambda \times \Lambda$. Using the fact that q has properties (1), (2), and (3) above, we could prove directly that ρ_g has the following properties: (1) $\rho_g(a, b) = 0$ if a is a prefix of b or b is a prefix of a, (2) $\rho_g(a, b) = \rho_g(b, a)$, and (3) $\rho_g(a, b) \leqslant \rho_g(a, c) + \rho_g(c, b)$ if $|c| \geqslant \min\{|a|, |b|\}$.

Suppose now that A is a nonempty finite subset of Λ. It is clear that ρ_g

is defined on $A \times A$. We say that a function f is an *index on A* if for each $a \in A$, $f(a)$ is a non-negative integer and say that (A, f) is an *indexed set* if f is an index on A. We let

$$S_{f(a)}(a; \rho_g) = \{a' : a' \in [a], \rho_g(a, a') \leqslant f(a)\}.$$

Then $S_{f(a)}(a; \rho_g)$ is the ρ_g-*sphere around a of radius $f(a)$* and if we define α_f^g on A by requiring that $\alpha_f^g(a) = S_{f(a)}(a; \rho_g)$, then α_f^g is a gauge and $a \in \alpha_f^g(a)$ for each f and g. In general, the gauged set (A, α_f^g) is not a code because $\alpha_f^g(a) \cap \alpha_f^g(b) \neq 0$ could hold for certain choices of a, b and f. However, if no two words in A have the same length, then (A, α_f^g) is a code. It is obvious that if we hope to achieve decoding, then we must demand that (A, α_f^g) is a code. If the index f is such that (A, α_f^g) is a code, then we shall call (A, α_f^g) an *indexed code*.

The indexed codes will be of substantial interest in this paper; many of their properties can be described in terms of the integral-valued functions, g, ρ_g and f, and other integral-valued functions obtained from them, if we impose certain restrictions on the function g. For a general function g, it can happen that a ρ_g-sphere around a word a can be just $\{a\}$ despite the fact that $0 < f(a)$, indeed, this can happen for large $f(a)$. In other words, a ρ_g-sphere with positive radius can be nearly empty and such ρ_g-spheres present a number of difficulties which we have to avoid in order to obtain useful results.

We now present a condition which will yield 'good' ρ_g-spheres and then give examples of functions g which have satisfied this condition. We shall say that an integral-valued function g defined on $J \times J$ which satisfied the earlier conditions (1), (2), and (3) is a *quasi-metric* iff the corresponding function ρ_g satisfies the following condition: (*) if $b \in [a]$ and $\rho_g(a, b) = h + k > 1$ for positive integers h and k, then there exists $c \in [a]$ such that $\rho_g(a, c) = h$, $\rho_g(c, b) = k$. An easy argument shows that condition (*) is equivalent to the corresponding condition for g on $J \times J$. For our purposes (*) will be more convenient.

Although (*) is a fairly strong condition, there are a number of quasi-metrics of interest. Throughout the rest of the paper g will denote an arbitrary quasi-metric unless otherwise specified. We now list certain quasi-metrics on an arbitrary alphabet J which can be taken to be $\{0, 1, \ldots, n\}$ for some natural number n; we let i and j denote members of the alphabet J.

(1) Let $g(i, i) = 0$ for each i, $g(i, j) = 1$ iff $i \neq j$. Then ρ_g is the extended Hamming distance (see Calabi and Riley (1964 [PML25])). Clearly, ρ_g satisfies (*).

(2) Let $g(i, j) = |i-j|$, the absolute value of the difference of i and j. We may assume that whenever $|i-j| > 1$, then $i-j > 1$. Now suppose $g(i, j) = i-j = h+k > 1$ for positive integers h and k. Then $i > h > 0$, $i - (i-h) > 0, (i-h) - j = k > 0$ and so $i - h \in J$ and $g(i, j) = i-j = [i-(i-h)]$ $+ [(i-h)-j] = g(i, i-h) + g(i-h, j)$ and $g(i, i-h) = h$ and $g(i-h, j) = k$. Hence g satisfies its (*) condition and therefore is a quasi-metric because it clearly satisfies the condition (1), (2), and (3).

(3) For this example we regard one member of the alphabet as a 'blank' or 'erasure' symbol; denote it by a. Then define $g(i, i) = 0$ for each i, $g(i, a) = 1$ if $i \neq a$, and $g(i, j) = 2$ if $i \neq a, j \neq a, i \neq j$. Informally, one error counts as two erasures. It is routine to show that g has properties (1), (2), and (3). The (*) condition for g need only be checked for $g(i, j) = 2$ and clearly we have $g(i, j) = g(i, a) + g(a, j) = 1 + 1 = 2$ with $g(i, a) = g(a, j) = 1$. Hence g is a quasi-metric.

(4) The (*) condition is trivially satisfied if $g(i, j) \leqslant 1$ for each i and j; this was the situation in example (1). As above in example (3) we may take $g(i, j) > 1$ as long as we satisfy (*) for g. For $J = \{0, 1, 2, 3, 4\}$ we could have the following: $g(i, i) = 0$ each i, $g(0,1) = g(2, 3) = 0$, $g(0, 2) = g(0, 3) = g(1, 2) = g(1, 3) = 1$, and $g(0, 4) = g(1, 4) = g(2, 4) = g(3, 4) = 2$. It then turns out that g is a quasi-metric.

For simplicity we will write ρ instead of ρ_g for the rest of the paper unless otherwise noted assuming that there is a quasi-metric on J. We now give examples of different codes with the same base set A which will be used later to illustrate certain concepts.

Examples of Codes

Throughout the examples we choose $A = \{001, 1010, 01010\} = \{a, b, c\}$ with $a = 001$, $b = 1010$, and $c = 01010$ and fix the quasi-metric g on $J \times J$ by requiring that $g(0, 0) = g(1, 1) = 0$, $g(1, 0) = 1$ where we have chosen $J = \{0, 1\}$; as noted above, $\rho_g = \rho$ is then the extended Hamming distance.

1. The first example is (A, ι) where $\iota(a) = \{a\}$, $\iota(b) = \{b\}$ and $\iota(c) = \{c\}$.

2. The gauge α on A is defined by the following table:

$\alpha(a)$	$\alpha(b)$	$\alpha(c)$
001	1010	01010
010	1100	11000
100	1001	10100
	0110	10010
	0101	10001
	0011	01100
		01001
		00110
		00101
		00011

In this case, each member of $\alpha(x)$ for $x \in A$ has the same number of 1's as x.

3. We define an index f on A as follows: $f(a) = 2$, $f(b) = 1$, and $f(c) = 0$. Assuming that g has been fixed as above we set $\alpha_f(x) = S_{f(x)}(x; \rho)$ for each $x \in A$. We then have the table below:

$\alpha_f(a)$	$\alpha_f(b)$	$\alpha_f(c)$
001	1010	01010
101	0010	
011	1110	
000	1000	
111	1011	
010		
100		

4. Suppose that f is the index on A of the preceding example and that g is fixed as at the beginning of this section. We now wish to define a gauge α^f on A so that, for each $a \in A$, $\alpha^f(x)$ will be a set of sequences such that $y \in \alpha^f(x)$ iff the length of the error-burst of y relative to x is less

than or equal to $f(x)$. More precisely, for each pair z, w of sequences such that $z = (z_1, \ldots, z_k)$, $w = (w_1, \ldots, w_k)$, and $|z| = |w|$, we let

$$D(z, w) = \{i : g(z_i, w_i) \neq 0\}.$$

Because $D(z, w) \subset \{1, \ldots, k\}$, there is a first and a last subscript in $D(z, w)$, say i and j respectively. We then define the length $L(w, z)$ of $D(z, w)$ to be $1 + (j - i)$. Finally we set $\alpha^f(x) = \{y : y \in [x], L(x, y) \leqslant f(x)\}$ for each $x \in A$ and so obtain the table:

$\alpha^f(a)$	$\alpha^f(b)$	$\alpha^f(c)$
001	1010	01010
000	0010	
011	1110	
101	1000	
111	1011	
010		

Several things should be noticed about this example. The strong dependence on g must be kept in mind; for example, if we chose g so that $g(0, 0) = g(1, 1) = g(0, 1) = 0$, then $\alpha^f(c)$ and indeed $\alpha_f(c)$ would consist of all binary sequences of length equal to $|c|$. The influence of the index f can be quite pronounced; for example, if we re-defined $f(c)$ to be 4, then $\alpha^f(c)$ would become a large set instead of just $\{c\}$. Finally, both features would be more striking for codes with long words. These more striking examples are left to the reader.

3. A CONSTRUCTION INVOLVING GAUGED SETS

Suppose that (A, α) and (A_0, α_0) are arbitrary gauged sets, that $a \in A$ and $a_0 \in A_0$. We say that a is *compatible* with a_0 iff $Q(\alpha(a), \alpha_0(a_0)) \neq \emptyset$. If a is compatible with a_0, then $|a| \neq |a_0|$, $r(a, a_0) = u$ for a unique $u \in A$, and $Q(\alpha(a), \alpha_0(a_0)) \subset [u]$.

We now construct a sequence $\{(A_n, \alpha_n) : n = 1, 2, \ldots\}$ of gauged sets as follows. Form the set

$$\{r(a, a_0) : a \in A, a_0 \in A_0, Q(\alpha(a), \alpha_0(a_0)) \neq \emptyset\};$$

because it clearly depends on the gauged sets (A, α) and (A_0, α_0) we denote it by $R_1(A, \alpha; A_0, \alpha_0)$. Notice that while $r(a, a_0)$ exists whenever $a \in A$, $a_0 \in A_0$ and $|a| \neq |a_0|$, $r(a, a_0) \in R_1(A, \alpha; A_0, \alpha_0)$ iff a is compatible with a_0. Notice also that $R_1(A, \alpha; A_0, \alpha_0) \subset \operatorname{Suff} A \cup \operatorname{Suff} A_0$ and that $R_1(A, \alpha; A_0, \alpha_0) = \emptyset$ if no element of A is compatible with any element of A_0.

We denote $R_1(A, \alpha; A_0, \alpha_0)$ in two other ways: as $R_1(A, A_0)$ and as A_1. Whenever any possible confusion can result we shall use the original notation.

A gauge α_1 on A_1 is now defined by the requirement that for each $u \in A_1$

$$\alpha_1(u) = \bigcup \{Q(\alpha(a), \alpha_0(a_0)) : a \in A, a_0 \in A_0, \text{ and } r(a, a_0) = u\};$$

from a previous remark, $\alpha_1(u) \subset [u]$ and hence α_1 is indeed a gauge. If $A_1 = \emptyset$, then α_1 is the void function. In any case we obtain the gauged set (A_1, α_1) and we may repeat the construction with (A, α) and (A_1, α_1).

Assuming that (A_n, α_n) has been defined, we let

$$R_{n+1}(A, \alpha; A_0, \alpha_0) = R_1(A, \alpha; A_n, \alpha_n)$$

and denote this set by A_{n+1} or $R_{n+1}(A, A_0)$. Explicitly, we have

$$A_{n+1} = \{r(a, u) : a \in A, u \in A_n, Q(\alpha(a), \alpha_n(u)) \neq \emptyset\}$$

and we define the gauge α_{n+1} on A_{n+1} by requiring that

$$\alpha_{n+1}(v) = \bigcup \{Q(\alpha(a), \alpha_n(u)) : a \in A, u \in A_n, r(a, u) = v\}$$

for each $v \in A_{n+1}$.

Our construction has now produced the sequence $\{(A_n, \alpha_n) : n = 1, 2, \ldots\}$ of gauged sets. Observe that if $R_n(A, A_0) = \emptyset$ for some n, then α_n is the void function and $R_m(A, A_0) = \emptyset$ whenever $m > n$.

For completeness, we set $R_0(A, \alpha; A_0, \alpha_0) = A_0$, let α_0 be taken as the gauge on A_0, and obtain the sequence $\{(A_n, \alpha_n) : n = 0, 1, \ldots\}$ of gauged sets.

It is worthwhile to observe what happens in the case that both gauged sets are simple. If we start with the simple gauged sets (A, ι) and (A_0, ι), then $a \in A$ is compatible with $a_0 \in A_0$ iff $Q(\{a\}, \{a_0\}) \neq \emptyset$, that is, iff $a = a_0 u$ or $a_0 = au$ for a unique $u \in \Lambda$. If the pair (a, a_0) is compatible, then $Q(\{a\}, \{a_0\}) = \{u\} = \{r(a, a_0)\}$. Hence $R_1(A, A_0) = \{r(a, a_0) : Q(\{a\}, \{a_0\})$

$\neq \emptyset\} = \{Q(\{a\}, \{a_0\}): a \in A, a_0 \in A_0\} = Q(A, A_0)$. It is now easy to check that $\alpha_1(u) = \{u\}$ for each $u \in A_1$ and hence that $\alpha_1 = \iota$; the construction shows that $\alpha_n = \iota$ for all $n \geq 0$. Hence the construction applied to simple gauged sets is the same construction used in Riley (1967 [PML34]).

We now return to Example 2 and indicate the first steps of the construction with $(A, \alpha) = (A_0, \alpha_0)$. Notice that A has 3 elements, $\alpha(A)$ has 19, A_1 has 2, $\alpha_1(A_1)$ has 4, A_2 has 5, and $\alpha_2(A_2)$ has 20. Notice also that while (A, α) and (A_1, α_1) are codes, (A_2, α_2) is not a code because $\alpha_2(01) \cap \alpha_2(10) \neq \emptyset$.

We check compatible pairs in order to obtain the set A_1:

$$Q(\alpha(a), \alpha(b)) = \{1\}, \qquad r(a, b) = 0$$
$$Q(\alpha(a), \alpha(c)) = \{10, 01\}, \qquad r(a, c) = 10$$
$$Q(\alpha(b), \alpha(c)) = \{0\}, \qquad r(b, c) = 0$$

and hence $A_1 = R_1(A, A) = \{0, 10\}$. We then use our definition of α_1 to compute that: $\alpha_1(0) = \{0, 1\}$ and $\alpha_1(10) = \{10, 01\}$. Hence we have the gauged set (A_1, α_1).

We then check compatible pairs for (A, α) and (A_1, α_1) to get A_2:

$$Q(\alpha(a), \alpha_1(0)) = \{01, 10, 00\}, \quad r(a, 0) = 01$$
$$Q(\alpha(b), \alpha_1(0)) = \{010, 100, 001, 110, 101, 011\}, \quad r(b, 0) = 010$$
$$Q(\alpha(c), \alpha_1(0)) = \{1010, 1000, 0100, 0010, 0001, 1100, 1001,$$
$$0110, 0101, 0011\}, \quad r(c, 0) = 1010$$
$$Q(\alpha(a), \alpha_1(10)) = \{0\}, \quad r(a, 10) = 1$$
$$Q(\alpha(b), \alpha_1(10)) = \{10, 01\}, \quad r(b, 10) = 10$$
$$Q(\alpha(c), \alpha_1(10)) = \{100, 010, 001\}, \quad r(c, 10) = 010$$

and so $A_2 = R_1(A, A_1) = \{01, 010, 1010, 1, 10\}$. We then compute that:

$$\alpha_2(1) = \{0\},$$
$$\alpha_2(01) = \{01, 10, 00\},$$
$$\alpha_2(10) = \{10, 01\},$$
$$\alpha_2(010) = \{010, 100, 001, 110, 101, 011\},$$
$$\alpha_2(1010) = \{1010, 1000, 0100, 0010, 0001, 1100, 1001, 0110,$$
$$0101, 0011\}.$$

The gauged set (A_2, α_2) has now been constructed. Continuation should be clear.

The example just given indicates that the problem of constructing the gauged sets (A_n, α_n) could become very tedious for general gauged sets (A, α) and (A_0, α_0). The example also suggests that perhaps for special gauges life might be a good bit simpler. This is actually the case for Example 3 and, indeed, for all gauged sets obtained by means of the ρ-spheres determined by an index. A good deal of simplicity is obtained from the fact that compatibility of words can be characterized in terms of the function ρ_g and the index functions. This, in turn, gives a straightforward way to compute $\alpha_n(u)$ for $u \in A_n$. We show now how this happens.

For $a \in A$ and $a_0 \in A_0$ we define the functions S, F and M as follows:

$$S(a, a_0) = \begin{cases} f(a) & \text{if} \quad |a_0| < |a| \\ f_0(a) & \text{if} \quad |a| < |a_0| \\ \text{undefined otherwise} \end{cases}$$

$$F(a, a_0) = f(a) + f_0(a_0) - \rho(a, a_0)$$
$$M(a, a_0) = \min\{S(a, a_0), F(a, a_0)\}.$$

It should be noted that $S(a, a_0)$ and $M(a, a_0)$ are defined iff $|a| \neq |a_0|$ and that $M(a, a_0) \geqslant 0$ iff $F(a, a_0) \geqslant 0$ and $S(a, a_0)$ exists. We can now state our first theorem.

THEOREM 1. $Q(\alpha_f(a), \alpha_{f_0}(a_0)) \neq \emptyset$ iff $M(a, a_0) \geqslant 0$.
Proof. Suppose $u \in Q(\alpha_f(a), \alpha_{f_0}(a_0))$, then $S(a, a_0)$ exists because $|a| \neq |a_0|$; assume $|a| < |a_0|$. Then there exists $a' \in \alpha_f(a)$ and $a_0' \in \alpha_{f_0}(a_0)$ such that $a_0' = a'u$, $|a'| \geqslant |a|$, $\rho(a, a') \leqslant f(a)$ and $\rho(a_0, a_0') \leqslant f_0(a_0)$. Using property (3) of ρ twice we have $\rho(a, a_0) \leqslant \rho(a, a') + \rho(a', a_0') + \rho(a_0', a_0) \leqslant f(a) + 0 + f_0(a_0)$ because $\rho(a', a_0') = 0$ in view of the fact that a' is a prefix of a_0'. It follows that $F(a, a_0) \geqslant 0$ and hence that $M(a, a_0) \geqslant 0$.

Now assume that $M(a, a_0) \geqslant 0$ and that $|a| < |a_0|$. It is enough to exhibit an $a' \in \alpha_f(a)$ which is a prefix of some $a_0' \in \alpha_{f_0}(a_0)$ in order to show that $Q(\alpha_f(a), \alpha_{f_0}(a_0)) \neq \emptyset$. Because $M(a, a_0) \geqslant 0$ we know that $F(a, a_0) \geqslant 0$ and so $\rho(a, a_0) \leqslant f(a) + f_0(a_0)$. Because $a_0 = a'u$ for $|a'| = |a|$, we see that $\rho(a, a_0) = \rho(a, a') = \rho(au, a') = \rho(au, a'u) \leqslant f(a) + f_0(a_0)$. Clearly, if $0 \leqslant \rho(a, a_0) \leqslant f(a)$, then $a' \in \alpha_f(a)$; if $0 \leqslant \rho(a, a_0) \leqslant f_0(a_0)$, then $au \in \alpha_{f_0}(a_0)$. In either case, $Q(\alpha_f(a), \alpha_{f_0}(a_0)) \neq \emptyset$. We can then assume that $1 < \rho(a, a_0) = h + k \leqslant f(a) + f_0(a_0)$ with h and k positive integers such that $h \leqslant f(a)$ and $k \leqslant f_0(a_0)$. By the (*) condition for ρ, there exists some $b \in [a]$ such that $\rho(a, b) = h$ and $\rho(b, a') = k$. Hence $b \in \alpha_f(a)$, $bu \in \alpha_{f_0}(a_0)$, b is a prefix of bu, and so the proof is complete.

The importance of this theorem is that to check compatibility of elements in our situation we need not construct $\alpha_f(a)$, $\alpha_{f_0}(a_0)$, and $Q(\alpha_f(a)$, $\alpha_{f_0}(a_0))$; we need only compute $M(a, a_0)$ and this really involves only the computation of $F(a, a_0)$. An example later will illustrate this fact.

THEOREM 2. If $M(a, a_0) \geqslant 0$, then

$$Q(\alpha_f(a), \alpha_{f_0}(a_0)) = \{u' : u' \in [r(a, a_0)],$$
$$\rho(u', r(a, a_0)) \leqslant M(a, a_0)\}.$$

Proof. Throughout we assume that $M(a, a_0) \geqslant 0$ and that $|a| < |a_0|$ with $a_0 = a'u$ with $a' \in [a]$ and $r(a, a_0) = u$. Hence $\rho(a, a_0) \leqslant f(a) + f_0(a_0)$.

Now suppose that $u' \in [u]$, $\rho(u', u) \leqslant M(a, a_0)$. If $a' \in \alpha_f(a)$, then $\rho(a, a') \leqslant f(a)$, and because $\rho(a'u', a_0) = \rho(a'u', a'u) = \rho(u', u) \leqslant M(a, a_0) \leqslant S(a, a_0) = f_0(a_0)$, $a'u' \in \alpha_{f_0}(a_0)$. Therefore $u' \in Q(\alpha_f(a), \alpha_{f_0}(a_0))$. If $a' \in \alpha_f(a)$, then $\rho(a, a') > f(a)$, $f(a) - \rho(a, a') = f(a) - \rho(a, a_0) < 0$, and $M(a, a_0) = f_0(a_0) + \{f(a) - \rho(a, a')\} < f_0(a_0)$. By property (*) there exists an $a'' \in [a]$ such that $\rho(a', a'') = \rho(a, a') - f(a)$ and $\rho(a, a'') = f(a)$; hence $a'' \in \alpha_f(a)$ and we form $a_0' = a''u'$ and claim that $a_0' \in \alpha_{f_0}(a_0)$. We have

$$\rho(a_0, a_0') = \rho(a'u, a''u') = \rho(a', a'') + \rho(u, u')$$
$$= \rho(a, a') - f(a) + \rho(u, u') \leqslant \rho(a, a') - f(a) + M(a, a_0)$$
$$= \{\rho(a, a') - f(a)\} + f_0(a_0) + \{f(a) - \rho(a, a')\} = f_0(a_0).$$

It follows that $a'' \in \alpha_f(a)$, $a''u' \in \alpha_{f_0}(a_0)$, and hence that $u' \in Q(\alpha_f(a), \alpha_{f_0}(a_0))$. Therefore

$$\{u' : u' \in [r(a, a_0)], \rho(u', r(a, a_0)) \leqslant M(a, a_0)\}$$
$$\subset Q(\alpha_f(a), \alpha_{f_0}(a_0)).$$

For the opposite inclusion we presume that $u' \in Q(\alpha_f(a), \alpha_{f_0}(a_0))$. Then there exist $a_0' \in \alpha_{f_0}(a_0)$ and $a'' \in \alpha_f(a)$ such that $a_0' = a''u'$. Because $a_0' \in \alpha_{f_0}(a_0)$ we have

$$0 \leqslant \rho(a_0, a_0') = \rho(a'u, a''u') = \rho(a', a'') + \rho(u, u') \leqslant f_0(a_0)$$

and so $\rho(u, u') \leqslant f_0(a_0) - \rho(a', a'')$.

On the other hand, $\rho(a, a_0) = \rho(a', a) \leqslant \rho(a', a'') + \rho(a'', a) \leqslant \rho(a', a'')$

$+f(a)$ because $a'' \in \alpha_f(a)$. Hence $\rho(a, a_0) - f(a) \leqslant \rho(a', a'')$ and we then have

$$\rho(u, u') \leqslant f_0(a_0) - \rho(a', a'') \leqslant f_0(a_0) - \{\rho(a, a_0) - f(a)\}$$
$$= f_0(a) + f(a) - \rho(a, a_0) = F(a, a_0).$$

Clearly, $\rho(u, u') \leqslant S(a, a_0) = f_0(a_0)$ and so $\rho(u, u') \leqslant M(a, a_0)$. Therefore if $u' \in Q(\alpha_f(a), \alpha_{f_0}(a_0))$, then $u' \in [u]$ and $\rho(u, u') \leqslant M(a, a_0)$. Hence the opposite inclusion holds and the proof is complete.

The proof of Theorem 2 is essentially due to Riley [PML34].

Our last theorem of this section shows how to define an index f_n for each of the sets A_n that arise in our construction of the sequence of gauged sets.

THEOREM 3. If (A, f) and (A_0, f_0) are indexed sets, (A, α_f) and (A_0, α_{f_0}) are the corresponding gauged sets, $R_1(A, \alpha_f; A_0, \alpha_{f_0}) = A_1 \neq \emptyset$, then there exists an index f_1 on A_1 such that for each $u \in A_1$, $\alpha_1(u) = \alpha_{f_1}(u)$.
Proof. Our last theorem, phrased in terms of ρ-spheres, says that if $Q(\alpha_f(a), \alpha_{f_0}(a_0)) \neq \emptyset$ and $r(a, a_0) = u$, then

$$Q(\alpha_f(a), \alpha_{f_0}(a_0)) = S_{M(a, a_0)}(u; \rho)$$

where $S_{M(a, a_0)}(u; \rho)$ is the ρ-sphere around u of radius $M(a, a_0)$. If we now recall that, for $u \in A_1$, $\alpha_1(u) = \bigcup \{Q(\alpha_f(a), \alpha_{f_0}(a_0)) : r(a, a_0) = u\}$ then we have $\alpha_1(u) = \bigcup \{S_{M(a, a_0)}(u; \rho) : r(a, a_0) = u\}$.

It is clear that a union of ρ-spheres around u is a ρ-sphere around u, and hence if we define f_1 by requiring that

$$f_1(u) = \max\{M(a, a_0) : r(a, a_0) = u\},$$

then $\alpha_1(u) = S_{f_1(u)}(u; \rho) = \alpha_{f_1}(u)$ and f_1 is obviously an index on A_1. This completes the proof.

Corollary 4. If $\{(A_n, \alpha_n) : n = 0, 1, 2, \ldots\}$ is the sequence of gauged sets that were constructed from the gauged sets (A, α_f) and (A_0, α_{f_0}), then if $A_n \neq \emptyset$, then there exists an index f_n on A_n such that $\alpha_n(u) = \alpha_{f_n}(u)$ for each $u \in A_n$.

It is now clear that in the case of gauged sets obtained from indexed sets, we need deal only with the indexes involved and not with the gauges.

We indicate how this technique would apply to Example 3. We let

$(A,f)=(A_0,f_0)$ and recall that if $x, y \in A$ then x is compatible with y iff $|x| \neq |y|$ and $F(x, y) \geqslant 0$. Using this we see that 001 is compatible with 1010 and with 01010, hence $A_1 = \{r(001, 1010), r(001, 01010)\} = \{0, 10\}$. Because of the simplicity of our example, each $u \in A_1$ is $r(x, y)$ for only one pair (x, y) of words in A, hence $f_1(0) = M(001, 1010) = 1$ and $f_1(10) = M(001, 01010) = 0$. Therefore $\alpha_{f_1}(0) = \{0, 1\}$ and $\alpha_{f_1}(10) = \{10\}$.

If we now apply the procedure to (A, f) and (A_1, f_1) we find 5 compatible pairs (x, y) with $x \in A$ and $y \in A_1$ and compute the $r(x, y)$ to obtain A_2 as

$$A_2 = \{r(001, 0), r(1010, 0), r(01010, 0), r(001, 10) \ r(1010, 10)\}$$
$$= \{01, 010, 1010, 1, 10\}.$$

Again each $u \in A_2$ is $r(x, y)$ for only one pair (x, y) so we easily compute that $f_2(01) = 2, f_2(010) = 1, f_2(1010) = 0, f_2(1) = 0, f_2(10) = 1$ and hence that

$$\alpha_{f_2}(01) = \{01, 11, 00, 10\}, \qquad \alpha_{f_2}(010) = \{010, 110, 000, 011\}$$
$$\alpha_{f_2}(1010) = \{1010\}, \qquad \alpha_{f_2}(1) = \{1\},$$
$$\alpha_{f_2}(10) = \{10, 00, 11\}.$$

The continuation is now obvious. Again notice that (A_2, α_{f_2}) is not a code because $\alpha_{f_2}(01) \cap \alpha_{f_2}(10) \neq \emptyset$.

If we apply our construction to the code of Example 4 with $(A, \alpha^f) = (A, \alpha) = (A_0, \alpha^{f_0}) = (A_0, \alpha_0)$, we obtain the set $A_1 = R_1(A, \alpha^f; A, \alpha^f)$ and the usual gauge α_1. It is not clear that it is possible to define an index f_1 on A_1 so that the gauged set (A_1, α_1) is the same as the gauged set (A_1, α^{f_1}). Of course, all of the gauges α_n may be obtained by the ordinary brute-force method.

4. TESTS FOR CERTAIN PROPERTIES OF CODES

A given code (A, α) may have many properties of interest. Given that it has a particular property, one may ask if the expanded code $(\alpha(A), \iota)$ has the same property; the question, of course, can always be asked in the other direction. Let us say that a property P of a code is *expandable* iff whenever a code has property P, then the expanded code has property P and conversely. It turns out that many of the interesting properties of codes are expandable. Our concern will be with three expandable properties and we define those properties now; the proof that they are expandable follows from the results in the previously cited papers of Arquette, Calabi, and Hartnett (1966 [PML44]).

Given a code (A, α) we say that a finite sequence $X = (x_1, \ldots, x_n)$ of words of A is a *sentence*; we extend α to sentences by the requirement that

$$\alpha(X) = \alpha(x_1)\alpha(x_2)\ldots\alpha(x_n).$$

where the right hand side, as usual, denotes the juxtaposition product of the $\alpha(x_i)$'s. We say that $y \in A$ is *admissible* if $y \in \alpha(X)$ for some sentence X and say that y' is an *infix of* y if $y = uy'v$ for some possibly empty sequences u and v.

Then (A, α) is *correcting* iff whenever X and Y are distinct sentences, $\alpha(X) \cap \alpha(Y) = \emptyset$. We say that (A, α) is *decodable* iff (A, α) is correcting and there exists a positive integer s such that if $x \in A$, $|x| \geqslant s$, Y and Z are sentences, $xy \in \alpha(Y)$ and $xz \in \alpha(Z)$ for some sequences y, z in A, then Y and Z have the same first word. Finally, we say that (A, α) is *synchronizable* iff (A, α) is correcting and there exists a positive integer t such that if $x \in A$, $|x| \geqslant t$, and x is an infix of an admissible sequence in A, then x has a decomposition $x = x_1 x_2$ such that whenever yxz is admissible for sequences y and z, each of yx_1 and x_2z is either admissible or empty.

For each of these three properties there is a theorem which provides a constructive test for the property in question when the code is simple. The theorem for correctability is due to Sardinas and Patterson (1953 [25]) and the theorems for decodability and synchronizability were given by Levenshtein (1962 [14], 1964 [15]); a complete treatment of the theorems can be found in Levenshtein (1962 [14], 1964 [15]) and in Riley (1967 [PML34]). We state them here for reference.

I (A, ι) is correcting iff $A \cap R_n(A, A) = \emptyset$ for all $n \geqslant 1$.

II (A, ι) is decodable iff (A, ι) is correcting and $R_{n_0}(A, A) = \emptyset$ for some $n_0 \geqslant 1$.

III (A, ι) is synchronizable iff (A, ι) is correcting and $R_{n_0}(A, \mathrm{Suff}\, A) = \emptyset$ for some $n_0 \geqslant 1$.

For each of the theorems the test involves the construction of the sets $R_n(A, A_0)$ that we defined before; for I and II we let $A_0 = A$ and for III let $A_0 = \mathrm{Suff}\, A$. In Riley (1964 [PML34]) it is shown that if t denotes the number of elements of $\mathrm{Suff}\, A$, then it is enough to compute the sets

$R_1(A, A_0), \ldots, R_{t+1}(A, A_0)$ and hence the tests are finite. However, the actual utility of the tests is largely determined by the amount of work needed to calculate those sets.

If we now use the fact that our properties of interest are expandable we may write the obvious variants of the above theorems.

I′ (A, α) is correcting iff $\alpha(A) \cap R_n(\alpha(A), \alpha(A)) = \emptyset$ for all $n \geqslant 1$.

II′ (A, α) is decodable iff (A, α) is correcting and $R_{n_0}(\alpha(A), \alpha(A))$
        $= \emptyset$ for some $n_0 \geqslant 1$.

III′ (A, α) is synchronizable iff (A, α) is correcting and $R_{n_0}(\alpha(A),$
        $\mathrm{Suff}\, \alpha(A)) = \emptyset$ for some $n_0 \geqslant 1$.

While the above variants are theorems and do provide tests for the properties in question, they are much more bothersome to deal with than I, II, and III because the sets to be computed now involve the expanded codes and we have already seen examples to indicate that $\alpha(A)$ can be much larger than A. It is clear that the amount of necessary calculation may greatly increase when we switch, say, from I to I′.

The aim of the next few results is to show that we can simplify matters somewhat. We return to our gauged sets.

The basic question that concerns us can be phrased as follows: given gauged sets (A, α) and (A_0, α_0) we may carry out the n-th step of our construction, obtain the gauged set $(R_n(A, A_0), \alpha_n)$, and then form the expanded gauged set $(\alpha_n(R_n(A, A_0)), \iota)$. On the other hand, we may first obtain the expanded gauged sets $(\alpha(A), \iota)$ and $(\alpha_0(A_0), \iota)$ and then carry out the n-th step of our construction and get the simple gauged set $(R_n(\alpha(A), \alpha_0(A_0)), \iota)$. The question: what relationship exists between the gauged sets $(\alpha_n(R_n(A, A_0)), \iota)$ and $(R_n(\alpha(A), \alpha_0(A_0)), \iota)$. The answer: they are the same. We now provide the necessary proofs.

Observe first that if $\{X_i\}$ and $\{Y_j\}$ are families of subsets of Λ, $X = \bigcup X_i$ and $Y = \bigcup Y_j$, then

$$Q(X, Y) = \bigcup \{Q(X_i, Y_j) : X_i \in \{X_i\}, Y_j \in \{Y_j\}\}.$$

Our basic theorem about gauged sets can now be given.

THEOREM 5. Suppose (A, α) and (A_0, α_0) are gauged sets. Then $R_1(\alpha(A), \alpha_0(A_0)) = \alpha_1(R_1(A, A_0))$.
Proof. By an early remark $R_1(\alpha(A), \alpha_0(A_0)) = Q(\alpha(A), \alpha_0(A_0))$ and in

view of our observation just above $Q(\alpha(A), \alpha_0(A_0)) = \bigcup \{Q(\alpha(a), \alpha_0(a_0)): a \in A, a_0 \in A_0\}$. So we must prove that

$$\bigcup \{Q(\alpha(a), \alpha_0(a_0)): a \in A, a_0 \in A_0\}$$
$$= \bigcup \{\alpha_1(u): u \in R_1(A, A_0)\}.$$

By definition $\alpha_1(u) = \bigcup \{Q(\alpha(a), \alpha_0(a_0)): r(a, a_0) = u\}$ and hence the right hand side is contained in the left hand side. To go the other way, suppose $u' \in Q(\alpha(a), \alpha_0(a_0))$. Because $Q(\alpha(a), \alpha_0(a_0)) \neq \emptyset$, $|a| \neq |a_0|$ and hence $r(a, a_0) = u$ for some $u \in R_1(A, A_0)$. It follows that $Q(\alpha(a), \alpha_0(a_0)) \subset \alpha_1(u)$. Therefore the left hand side is contained in the right hand side and we are finished.

We are now in a position to prove that the answer to our question is correct.

Corollary 6. For each $n \geq 1$, $R_n(\alpha(A), \alpha_0(A_0)) = \alpha_n(R_n(A, A_0)) = \alpha_n(A_n)$.
Proof. By induction. For $n = 1$ we apply Theorem 5 to conclude that $R_1(\alpha(A), \alpha_0(A_0)) = \alpha_1(R_1(A, A_0))$ as required. Now assume that the equality holds for $n = k$. Then for $n = k+1$ we have

$$R_{k+1}(\alpha(A), \alpha_0(A_0)) = R_1(\alpha(A), R_k(\alpha(A), \alpha_0(A_0))).$$

By the inductive step,

$$R_k(\alpha(A), \alpha_0(A_0)) = \alpha_k(R_k(A, A_0))$$

and hence

$$R_{k+1}(\alpha(A), \alpha_0(A_0)) = R_1(\alpha(A), \alpha_k(R_k(A, A_0)))$$
$$= R_1(\alpha(A), \alpha_k(A_k)).$$

We then apply Theorem 5 with (A_0, α_0) replaced by (A_k, α_k) to conclude, because of the definitions of α_{k+1} and $R_1(A, A_k)$, that

$$R_{k+1}(\alpha(A), \alpha_0(A_0)) = \alpha_{k+1}(R_1(A, A_k)) = \alpha_{k+1}(R_{k+1}(A, A_0)).$$

Hence the equality holds for $n = k+1$ and, by induction, the theorem is established.

Our last results, applied to the variants I', II', and III', immediately yield the theorems which provide tests for the three properties of codes we have been studying.

THEOREM 7. Let (A, α) be a code. Then the following statements are equivalent.

(1) (A, α) is correcting.

(2) $\alpha(A) \cap \alpha_n(R_n(A, \alpha; A, \alpha)) = \emptyset$ for all $n \geq 1$.

(3)   For each $n \geq 1$, if $u \in R_n(A, \alpha; A, \alpha)$ and $a \in A$, then $\alpha(a) \cap \alpha_n(u) = \emptyset$.

Proof. Corollary 6 and I' immediately show that (1) is equivalent to (2). The equivalence of (2) and (3) is trivial in view of the fact that

$$\alpha(A) \cap \alpha_n(R_n(A, A)) = [\bigcup \alpha(a)] \cap [\bigcup \{\alpha_n(u) : u \in R_n(A, A)]$$
$$= \bigcup [\alpha(a) \cap \alpha_n(u)].$$

If $\alpha = \alpha_f$ for some index f on A, then condition (3) of Theorem 7 may be written as: for each $n \geq 1$, if $u \in R_n(A, A)$ and $a \in A$, then $\rho(a, u) > f(a) + f_n(u)$ where f_n is the index on A_n.

THEOREM 8. Let (A, α) be a code. Then (A, α) is decodable iff (A, α) is correcting and $R_{n_0}(A, \alpha; A, \alpha) = \emptyset$ for some $n_0 \geq 1$.
Proof. Corollary 6 and II' show that (A, α) is decodable iff (A, α) is correcting and $\alpha_{n_0}(R_{n_0}(A, \alpha; A, \alpha)) = \emptyset$ for some $n_0 \geq 1$. But $\alpha_{n_0}(R_{n_0}(A, \alpha; A, \alpha)) = \emptyset$ iff $R_{n_0}(A, \alpha; A, \alpha) = \emptyset$ by our construction and so the theorem is proved.

THEOREM 9. Let (A, α) be a code. Then (A, α) is synchronizable iff (A, α) is correcting and $R_{n_0}(A, \alpha; \mathrm{Suff}\,\alpha(A), \imath) = \emptyset$ for some $n_0 \geq 1$.
Proof. In III' we may write $R_{n_0}(\alpha(A), \mathrm{Suff}\,\alpha(A))$ as $R_{n_0}(\alpha(A), \imath(\mathrm{Suff}\,\alpha(A)))$ and apply Corollary 6 to the gauged sets (A, α) and $(\mathrm{Suff}\,\alpha(A), \imath)$ to conclude that $R_{n_0}(\alpha(A), \imath(\mathrm{Suff}\,\alpha(A))) = \alpha_{n_0}(R_{n_0}(A, \alpha; \mathrm{Suff}\,\alpha(A), \imath)$. But again $\alpha_{n_0}(R_{n_0}(A, \alpha; \mathrm{Suff}\,\alpha(A), \imath)) = \emptyset$ iff $R_{n_0}(A, \alpha; \mathrm{Suff}\,\alpha(A), \imath) = \emptyset$ and so the theorem follows.

An examination of the three theorems reveals that while we need compute only the sets $R_n(A, \alpha; A, \alpha)$ involving A for Theorems 7 and 8, we have to compute the sets $R_n(A, \alpha; \mathrm{Suff}\,\alpha(A), \imath)$ involving $\alpha(A)$ for Theorem 9. From a computational point of view this is still undesirable; a modification due to Calabi allows us to deal with sets that involve only A. The modification depends upon a reformulation of III' in which we replace $\mathrm{Suff}\,\alpha(A)$ by a new set $S(\alpha(A)) = \alpha(A) \cup \mathrm{Suff}\,\alpha(A)$. First we need an easy result.

Lemma 10. Suppose that (B, ι), (C, ι) and (D, ι) are simple gauged sets. Then $(C \cup D, \iota)$ is a simple gauged set and for each $n \geqslant 1$

$$R_n(B, C \cup D) = R_n(B, C) \cup R_n(B, D).$$

Proof. The fact that $(C \cup D, \iota)$ is a simple gauged set is trivial so we turn to the equality. Recall that for the case of simple gauged sets $R_1(B, C \cup D)$ $= Q(B, C \cup D)$ and, by an earlier observation, $Q(B, C \cup D) = Q(B, C) \cup$ $Q(B, D)$. But $Q(B, C) = R_1(B, C)$ and $Q(B, D) = R_1(B, D)$. Therefore $R_1(B, C \cup D) = R_1(B, C) \cup R_1(B, D)$ and so the equality holds for $n = 1$. Assume that it holds for $n = k$. Then $R_{k+1}(B, C \cup D) = R_1(B, R_k(B, C \cup D)) = R_1(B, R_k(B, C) \cup R_k(B, D)) = R_1(B, R_k(B, C)) \cup R_1(B, R_k(B, D)) = R_{k+1}(B, C) \cup R_{k+1}(B, D)$ because of the inductive hypothesis and the case for $n = 1$. Hence, the lemma holds by induction.

We now state and prove what amounts to a variant of III'.

III"   Let (A, α) be a code. Then (A, α) is synchronizable iff (A, α) is correcting and $R_{n_0}(\alpha(A), \iota; S(\alpha(A)), \iota) = \emptyset$ for some $n_0 \geqslant 1$.

Proof. By Lemma 10 we have that for each $n \geqslant 1$

$$R_n(\alpha(A), S(\alpha(A))) = R_n(\alpha(A), \alpha(A) \cup \mathrm{Suff}\,\alpha(A))$$
$$= R_n(\alpha(A), \alpha(A)) \cup R_n(\alpha(A), \mathrm{Suff}\,\alpha(A)).$$

Hence if $R_{n_0}(\alpha(A), S(\alpha(A))) = \emptyset$ for some n_0 and (A, α) is correcting, then $R_{n_0}(\alpha(A), \mathrm{Suff}\,\alpha(A)) = \emptyset$ and hence (A, α) is synchronizable by III'. Conversely, if (A, α) is synchronizable, then (A, α) is correcting and $R_{n_1}(\alpha(A), \mathrm{Suff}\,\alpha(A)) = \emptyset$ for some n_1 by III'. But (A, α) is decodable by Calabi and Arquette (1965 [PML35]) and hence $R_{n_0}(\alpha(A), \alpha(A)) = \emptyset$ for some n_2 by II'. Now let $n_0 = \max\{n_1, n_2\}$. Then, by Lemma 10,

$$R_{n_0}(\alpha(A), \alpha(A)) \cup R_{n_0}(\alpha(A), \mathrm{Suff}\,\alpha(A)) = \emptyset$$
$$= R_{n_0}(\alpha(A), S(\alpha(A)))$$

and so the theorem follows.

In order to apply Corollary 6 in the usual way to III' we must define a gauge α_S on $S(A) = A \cup \mathrm{Suff}\,A$ so that $S(\alpha(A)) = \alpha_S(S(A))$. For $x \in S(A)$ we define $\alpha_S(x) = \bigcup \{[x] \cap S(\alpha(a)) : x \in S(\{a\})\}$ and have the lemma that we need. We say that α_S is the gauge on $S(A)$ *induced by* α and that $(S(A), \alpha_S)$ is *induced by* (A, α).

Lemma 11. With the previous notation we have

(1) $S(\alpha(A)) = \bigcup \{S(\alpha(a)) : a \in A\}$

(2) $S(\alpha(A)) = \alpha_S(S(A)).$

Proof. Because $\alpha(a) \subset \alpha(A)$ for each $a \in A$, $S(\alpha(a)) \subset S(\alpha(A))$ and hence $\bigcup \{S(\alpha(a)) : a \in A\} \subset S(\alpha(A))$. On the other hand, if $y \in S(\alpha(A))$, then there exists some $a' \in \alpha(A)$ such that $a' = uy$. But $\alpha(A) = \bigcup \{\alpha(a) : a \in A\}$ is a disjoint union of the $\alpha(a)$'s and hence $a' \in \alpha(a)$ for some $a \in A$. But then $y \in S(\alpha(a))$ and hence $S(\alpha(A)) \subset \bigcup \{S(\alpha(a)) : a \in A\}$ and (1) is established.

For (2) suppose $y \in \alpha_S(x)$. Then $y \in S(\alpha(a))$ for some $a \in A$ and hence $y \in S(\alpha(A))$. So $\alpha_S(x) \subset S(\alpha(A))$ and then $\alpha_S(S(A)) = \bigcup \{\alpha_S(x) : x \in S(A)\} \subset S(\alpha(A))$. Conversely, if $y \in S(\alpha(A))$, then $y \in S(\alpha(a))$ for some $a \in A$ and $a = ux$ with $|x| = |y|$. But then $y \in \alpha_S(x)$ and so $S(\alpha(A)) \subset \alpha_S(S(A))$. Hence (2) holds.

We now give the expected theorem which furnishes a test for synchronizability of a code.

THEOREM 12. A code (A, α) is synchronizable iff (A, α) is correcting and $R_{n_0}(A, \alpha; S(A), \alpha_S) = \emptyset$ for some $n_0 \geqslant 1$.

Proof. Lemma 11, part (2) and III' together show that the code (A, α) is synchronizable iff (A, α) is correcting and $R_{n_0}(\alpha(A), 1; \alpha_S(S(A)), 1) = \emptyset$ for some $n_0 \geqslant 1$. Then Corollary 6 replaces $R_{n_0}(\alpha(A), 1; \alpha_S(S(A)), 1)$ by $\alpha_{n_0}(R_{n_0}(A, \alpha; S(A), \alpha_S))$. But, as noted before, $\alpha_{n_0}(R_{n_0}(A, \alpha; S(A), \alpha_S)) = \emptyset$ iff $R_{n_0}(A, \alpha; S(A), \alpha_S) = \emptyset$ and the theorem follows.

It is natural to expect that if (A, f) is an indexed set, (A, α_f) is the corresponding gauged set, and $(S(A), \alpha_S)$ is the gauged set determined above, then there exists an index f_S on $S(A)$ such that the gauged set $(S(A), \alpha_{f_S})$ corresponding to $(S(A), f_S)$ is just $(S(A), \alpha_S)$. This is indeed the case and we provide the details now; the definition of f_S is essentially due to Calabi.

For $x \in S(A)$ we let $m(x) = \max \{\rho(x, y) : y \in [x]\}$ and for $x \in S(A)$ and $a \in A$ we let $F_S(x, a) = \min \{m(x), f(a)\}$. Finally, we define $f_S(x) = \max \{F_S(x, a) : a \in A \text{ and } x \in S(\{a\})\}$. Notice that there always exists some $a \in A$ such that $ux = A$ and such that $f_S(x) = F_S(x, a) = \min \{m(x), f(a)\}$. Clearly, f_S is an index on $S(A)$.

THEOREM 13. If (A, f) is an indexed set, (A, α_f) is the corresponding gauged set, and $(S(A), \alpha_S)$ is the gauged set induced by (A, α_f), then for each $x \in S(A)$, $\alpha_S(x) = \alpha_{f_S}(x)$ where f_S is the index on $S(A)$ defined above. Hence $(S(A), \alpha_S) = (S(A), \alpha_{f_S})$.

Proof. We show that $\alpha_S(x) \subset \alpha_{f_S}(x)$ for each $x \in S(A)$. Suppose $y \in \alpha_S(x)$. By the definition of $\alpha_S(x)$, $y \in [x] \cap S(\alpha(a))$ for some $a \in A$ such that $x \in S(\{a\})$. Hence $a = ux$ for some u and $u'y \in \alpha_f(a)$ for some u'. But then $ux \in \alpha_f(a)$, $u'y \in \alpha_f(a)$ and so $0 \leqslant \rho(ux, u'y) = \rho(u, u') + \rho(x, y) \leqslant f(a)$, in particular, $\rho(x, y) \leqslant f(a)$. But clearly $\rho(x, y) \leqslant m(x)$ and so $\rho(x, y) \leqslant F_S(x, a) \leqslant f_S(x)$ and $y \leqslant \alpha_{f_S}(x)$.

To show that $\alpha_{f_S}(x) \subset \alpha_S(x)$ for each $x \in S(A)$, we pick $y \in \alpha_{f_S}(x)$. Then $\rho(x, y) \leqslant f_S(x)$ by definition. From our previous remark, there exists an $a \in A$ such that $\rho(x, y) \leqslant f_S(x) = F_S(x, a) = \min\{m(x), f(a)\} \leqslant f(a)$ and $a = ux$ for some u. But then $\rho(ux, uy) \leqslant f(a)$ and so $uy \in \alpha_f(a)$ and hence $y \in \alpha_S(x)$. This completes the proof.

5. APPLICATION OF THE TESTS TO EXAMPLE CODES

In order to show how the tests provided by the theorems of the last section apply to particular codes, we give some simple examples which indicate the essential notions involved. For convenience, we letter the examples.

(a) If we apply our construction to the code of Example 1 we find that $R_1(A, \imath; A, \imath) = \emptyset$. Hence, by I, $(A, \imath)$ is correcting, and by II, $(A, \imath)$ is decodable. However, $(A, \imath)$ is not synchronizable because $R_3(A, \imath; S(A), \imath) = R_{n+3}(A, \imath; S(A), \imath) = \{10\} \neq \emptyset$ for all $n \geqslant 0$.

(b) We check the code of Example 2 for correcting ability using Theorem 7, parts (1) and (2). Earlier we computed $A_1 = \{0, 10\}$ with $\alpha_1(0) = \{0, 1\}$ and $\alpha_1(10) = \{10, 01\}$. We then went on to compute $A_2 = \{01, 010, 1010, 1, 10\}$. However, $010 \in \alpha(a)$ and $1010 \in \alpha(b)$ and so $\alpha(A) \cap A_2 \neq \emptyset$ and (A, α) is not correcting.

(c) A similar check of the code of Example 3 reveals again that $\alpha(A) \cap A_2 \neq \emptyset$ and hence the code is not correcting.

(d) We now give an example to indicate the utility of the index functions f_n on the A_n. We let $A = \{a, b\}$ were $a = 010110$, $b = 01001101$, $f(a) = f(b) = 1$ and restrict the function ρ to be the Hamming distance. Then we have

$\alpha(a)$	$\alpha(b)$
010110	01001101
110110	11001101
000110	00001101
011110	01101101
010010	01011101
010100	01000101
010111	01001001
	01001111
	01001100

We check to see if a is compatible with b using Theorem 1. Now $|a| \neq |b|$, $F(a, b) = f(a) + f(b) - \rho(a, b) = 1 + 1 - 2 \geqslant 0$ and so a is compatible with b and $R_1(A, \alpha_f; A, \alpha_f) = \{r(a, b)\} = \{01\} = A_1$. We then have that $f_1(01) = M(a, b) = \min\{S(a, b), F(a, b)\} = 0$.

We now check the compatibility of a with 01 and b with 01. Again $|a| \neq |01|$, $F(a, 01) = f(a) + f_1(01) - \rho(a, 01) = 1 + 0 - 0 = 1 \geqslant 0$, a is compatible with 01, and hence $r(a, 01) = 0110 \in A_2$. In a similar fashion, $|b| \neq |01|$, $F(b, 01) = f(b) + f_1(01) - \rho(b, 01) = 1 + 0 - 0 = 1 \geqslant 0$ and hence b is compatible with 01 and $r(b, 01) = 001101 \in A_2$. It follows that $A_2 = \{0110, 001101\}$. The index f_2 on A_2 is given by

$$f_2(0110) \quad = M(a, 01) = \min\{1, 1\} = 1,$$
$$f_2(001101) = M(b, 01) = \min\{1, 1\} = 1.$$

For convenience, we give a table of what we have done:

A	$f(x)$ for $x \in A$	A_1	$f_1(u)$ for $u \in A_1$	A_2	$f_2(u)$ for $u \in A_2$
$a = 010110$	1	01	0	0110	1
$b = 01001101$	1			001101	1

Clearly, 010110 is not compatible with 001101 so we need only compute

$$F(010110, 0110) = f(010110) + f_2(0110) - \rho(010110, 0110)$$
$$= \quad 1 \quad + \quad 1 \quad - \quad 2 \geqslant 0$$

$$F(01001101, 0110) = f(01001101) + f_2(0110) - \rho(01001101, 0110)$$
$$= 1 \quad + \quad 1 \quad - \quad 1 = 1 \geqslant 0$$
$$F(01001101, 001101) = f(01001101) + f_2(001101) - \rho(01001101, 001101)$$
$$= 1 \quad + \quad 1 \quad - \quad 4 < 0.$$

Then 010110 is compatible with 0110, and $r(010110, 0110) = 10 \in A_2$; similarly, 01001101 is compatible with 0110 and $r(01001101, 0110) = 1101 \in A_3$. Hence we have $A_3 = \{10, 1101\}$ with f_3 given by $f_3(10) = \min\{1, 0\} = 0$ and $f_3(1101) = \min\{1, 1\} = 1$. Therefore we have the table:

A_3	$f_3(u)$ for $u \in A_3$
10	0
1101	1

and we again check for compatibility.

$F(a, 10) = 1 + 0 - \rho(a, 10) = 1 - 2 < 0$ and so a is not compatible with 10.

$F(a, 1101) = 1 + 1 - \rho(a, 1101) = 1 + 1 - 1 \geqslant 0$ and so a is compatible with 1101 and $r(a, 1101) = 10 \in A_4$.

$F(b, 10) = 1 + 0 - \rho(b, 10) = 1 - 2 < 0$; not compatible.

$F(b, 1101) = 1 + 1 - \rho(b, 1101) = 1 + 1 - 2 \geqslant 0$; hence compatible and $r(b, 1101) = 1101 \in A_4$. Then $A_4 = \{10, 1101\}$, and $f_4(10) = \min\{1, 1\} = 1$, $f_4(1101) = \min\{1, 0\} = 0$ and so we have another table:

A_4	$f_4(u)$ for $u \in A_4$
10	1
1101	0

At the next step we obtain the results that

$$F(a, 10) \quad = 1 + 1 - 2 \geqslant 0, \quad r(a, 10) = 0110 \in A_5$$
$$F(a, 1101) = 1 + 0 - 1 \geqslant 0, \quad r(a, 1101) = 10 \in A_5$$
$$F(b, 10) \quad = 1 + 1 - 2 \geqslant 0, \quad r(b, 10) = 001101 \in A_5$$
$$F(b, 1101) = 1 + 0 - 2 < 0, \quad \text{not compatible.}$$

It follows that $A_5 = \{10, 0110, 001101\}$ and we have the table:

A_5	$f_5(u)$ for $u \in A_5$
10	0
0110	0
001101	0

At the next step we find that

$$F(a, 10) \quad = 1+0-2 < 0, \quad \text{not compatible}$$
$$F(a, 0110) = 1+0-1 \geqslant 0, \quad r(a, 1101) = 10 \in A_6$$
$$F(b, 10) \quad = 1+0-2 < 0, \quad \text{not compatible}$$
$$F(b, 0110) = 1+0-2 < 0, \quad \text{not compatible}$$
$$F(b, 001101) = 1+0-4 < 0, \quad \text{not compatible.}$$

We then have $A_6 = \{10\}$ with $f_6(10) = 0$ and hence the table:

A_6	$f_6(u)$ for $u \in A_6$
10	0

Checking compatibility, we find that $F(a, 10) < 0$ and $F(b, 10) < 0$, hence there are no compatible pairs and $A_7 = \emptyset = R_7(A, \alpha_f; A, \alpha_f)$.

It is routine to check that $\alpha(A) \cap A_i = \emptyset$ for $i = 1, 2, \ldots, 6$, hence $\alpha(A) \cap A_n = \emptyset$ for all $n \geqslant 1$. It then follows from Theorem 8 that (A, α_f) is decodable because (A, α_f) is correcting and $R_7(A, A) = \emptyset$.

It can be shown that (A, α_f) is not synchronizable but we shall not carry out the details. We shall illustrate the synchronizability test with another somewhat simpler example.

(e) Let $A = \{a, b\}$, $a = 010$, $b = 110111$, $f(a) = 1$, and $f(b) = 0$. We then have

$\alpha_f(a)$	$\alpha_f(b)$
010	110111
110	
000	
011	

We compute directly that $Q(\alpha_f(a), \alpha_f(b)) = \{111\}$ and so $A_1 = R_1(A, \alpha_f; A, \alpha_f) = \{111\}$, $\alpha_1(111) = \{111\}$. At the next stage of the construction $Q(\alpha_f(a), \alpha_1(111)) = Q(\alpha_f(b), \alpha_1(111)) = \emptyset$, hence $A_2 = R_1(A, \alpha_f; A, \alpha_f) = \emptyset$. It follows immediately that (A, α_f) is decodable.

We now apply Theorem 12 to check the synchronizability of (A, α_f). In view of the extensive computations of example (d), we give only a tabular presentation of the results of the test. Ignoring the gauges involved, we have the following scheme:

1. (A, f) gives $(S(A), f_S)$ by Theorem 13

2. (A, f) and $(S(A), f_S)$ give (A_1, f_1) by the construction

3. (A, f) and (A_1, f_1) give (A_2, f_2) by the construction

$\qquad \vdots \qquad\qquad \vdots \qquad\qquad \vdots \qquad\qquad \vdots$

$n+2.$ (A, f) and (A_n, f_n) give (A_{n+1}, f_{n+1}) by the construction

$\qquad \vdots \qquad\qquad \vdots \qquad\qquad \vdots \qquad\qquad \vdots$

It is clear that if (A_n, f_n) is the same as (A_{n+1}, f_{n+1}) for some $n \geqslant 1$, then (A_n, f_n) is the same as (A_{n+k}, f_{n+k}) for all $k \geqslant 0$. If $(A_n, f_n) = (A_{n+1}, f_{n+1})$ and $A_n \neq \emptyset$, then (A, α_f) is not synchronizable. Our table shows that $(A_2, f_2) = (A_3, f_3)$ and hence that our code is not synchronizable.

Synchronization Test Table for the Code (A, α_f)

A	f	$S(A)$	f_S	A_1	f_1	A_2	f_2	A_3	f_3	$\cdots$
010	1	010	1							
110111	0	110111	0							$\cdots$
		0	1	0	0	0	0	0	0	
		1	0	1	0	1	0	1	0	
		10	1	10	1	10	1	10	1	
		11	0	—	–	—	–	—	–	
		111	0	111	0	—	–	—	–	
		0111	0	0111	0	0111	0	0111	0	$\cdots$
		10111	0	10111	0	10111	0	10111	0	

ON A FAMILY OF ERROR CORRECTING
AND SYNCHRONIZABLE CODES

T. HATCHER

EDITORIAL NOTE

Desirable codes for information transmission for a real channel should have two properties: they should correct errors as long as the channel behaves as expected and they should limit the effect of noise which causes temporary violation of the presumed error pattern. In earlier terminology, they should be error-correcting and error-limiting. The painful problem in construction of desirable codes is the proof that the manufactured codes actually have these properties. This problem can at times be circumvented by a clever use of theorems which permit the utilization of known literature results concerning codes with the properties. In the paper (February 1968), the author employs this technique to provide a family of desirable codes and gives quantitative findings about some of their characteristics.

This paper appeared in *IEEE Transactions on Information Theory* IT-15 (1969) 620–623 in a somewhat shortened form.

1. INTRODUCTION

In [23] Neumann gave algorithms for the construction of variable length error limiting codes. These codes are error limiting in the sense that should an error occur its influence is only local and the message may be decoded correctly, but for the loss of some words. We prefer to call such a code synchronizing. We have used the ideas of Neumann to construct codes which, in addition to being synchronizing, also correct a certain number of errors. Our construction is based on the following ideas. Suppose we have a channel which makes at most one error per word; then, instead of the correct word, we may receive any sequence which differs from the correct word in one place. Thus, for any one word we have a set of possible sequences which may be received. If the various sets of sequences are disjoint, it will always be possible to decode correctly. Our idea is to select a code so that the union of the resulting sets form a synchronizing

W. E. Hartnett (ed.), Foundations of Coding Theory, 173–192. *All Rights Reserved.*
Copyright © 1974 by D. Reidel Publishing Company, Dordrecht-Holland.

code; in particular we have required the union to be a subset of a Neumann code.

The reader will realize that these codes must satisfy rather stringent conditions. Notice what is needed. First of all we must be able to find the correct word endings, and having done this, to decode the words correctly. The finding of word endings, or supposed endings, we term synchronization. If we wish to state that true endings and only true endings are found, we say that the code synchronizes correctly (or properly). The codes we have constructed synchronize correctly, even – and this is the important difference – if as many as v additive errors occur per word. Not only that, but they can correct these errors, which is to say these codes are also v-error correcting. Furthermore, if a burst of more than v errors should occur in some words, correct synchronization may be lost temporarily, but as soon as a word is found with v or fewer errors, synchronization is again correct. We refer the reader to the examples for some ideas as to average lengths, etc.

2. DEFINITIONS

In order to better understand the reasons for the definitions to follow, we briefly discuss the ideas of Neumann [23]. Simply stated, each word of the code has a unique suffix or, at least, forms a recognizable pattern when in concatenation with other words of the code. Such a configuration effectively determines the location of the end of a word irrespective of what precedes it. A formal definition of a Neumann code generated by a single sequence, s, is given by Definition 1. Note that we use $\emptyset$ to denote a void sequence.

Definition 1. A Neumann code, $N(s)$, generated by a single binary sequence s is a set of binary sequences with the property that for each $t_i \in N(s)$

   (0.1)   For any binary sequences x and y if $st_i = xsy$, then $x = \emptyset$ or $y = \emptyset$

and

   (0.2) $st_i = zs$ for some sequence z.

This form of the definition is very easily generalized to our purposes, and it is not difficult to see, in this special case, that the definition is the same as that of Neumann [23]. The formalism of the generalization is more apparent if we first observe that $st_1 = xsy$ can be written as $st_i \cap xsy \neq \emptyset$, and that $st_1 = zs$ for some z means $st_i \subset \sum_{|t_i|} s$. Here, and subsequently, we have used $|q|$ to denote the length of a sequence q, i.e., the number of terms in q, and $\sum_k$ to denote all sequences of length k. We will also use $d(s, t)$ for the (Hamming) distance between s and t. The i-th term of a sequence will generally be a subscripted Greek letter. As an example of such notation we may write,

$$d(s, t) = \sum_{i=1}^{\min(n, k)} \sigma_i \oplus \tau_i = \sum_{i=1}^{\min(n, k)} \sigma_i + \tau_i - 2\sigma_i \tau_i$$

where $s = \sigma_1, \sigma_2, ..., \sigma_n$, $t = \tau_1, \tau_2, ..., \tau_k$, and $\oplus$ is an 'exclusive or' operation. Another useful concept is that of a k-ball of radius v with center q denoted by $B_v^k(q)$; it is the set of all sequences of length k which have distance at most v from q. In case $k = |q|$ we write simply $B_v(q)$.

We generalize Definition 1 in two steps. First we define an N set, $N_v^\eta(s)$, generated by s, by replacing, in Definition 1, sequences by balls. The second step is to require disjointness for the sets of possible sequences. These two steps are represented by Definitions 2 and 3 respectively.

Definition 2. Given a sequence s, and non-negative integers v and η, the N-set, $N_v^\eta(s)$, is the set of all sequences t which satisfy the following two conditions:

(0.3)   For all sequences u and v such that $|usv| = |st|$,
          $u B_\eta(s) v \cap B_\eta(s) B_v(t) \neq \emptyset \Rightarrow u = \emptyset$ or $v = \emptyset$

and

(0.4) $B_\eta(s) B_v(t) \subset \sum_{|t|} B_\eta(s)$.

$N_v^\eta(s)$ is unique, for given s, η and v. It may of course be empty and, on the other hand, it is also frequently infinite.

Definition 3. A G-code, $G_v^\eta(s)$, is a subset of $N_v^\eta(s)$ with the property that for $t_1, t_2 \in G_v^\eta(s)$

(0.5) $B_v(t_1) \cap B_v(t_2) \neq \emptyset \Rightarrow t_1 = t_2$.

Notice that in contrast to $N_v^\eta(s)$, $G_v^\eta(s)$ is by no means unique. There are many subsets of $N_v^\eta(s)$ which have the required properties. By imposing an upper bound on the length of elements to be included, we could try to find a subset of N satisfying Definition 3 which has the maximum possible number of elements (a singularly difficult task), but there is no assurance this is in any way unique, since different maximal subsets may have the same number of elements.

3. CODE PROPERTIES

In this section we will show that the codes $G_v^\eta(s)$ are both synchronizing and v-error correcting. Strictly speaking, the G's have been defined with just the required properties, so that in a formal sense, there is nothing to prove. Therefore in this section the emphasis will be on the more intuitive aspects of these properties. Our point of view will be that of the receiver and decoder of a message which has been sent over some communication channel subject to substitution errors (that is, in a binary sequence, what was supposed to be a one might come over as a zero and vice versa; we do *not* consider errors which result in missing or inserted bits, although this too can be handled to some extent). We will envision the decoding process as a matching process. Dispensing with all aspects of implementation, we will simply assume that we have before us a message given as a long sequence of 'zeros' and 'ones', and that we have a unique synchronizing sequence s, and a code book or table for decoding each subsequence which we decide is a word. Suppose first that no errors have occurred; then decoding would proceed by 'sliding' the sequence s under the message sequence until a match occurs. The rightmost element of the matched portion would be the end of a word. The sequence between two consecutive ends would be a code word.

When errors are present, we must weaken our requirements by considering as a match, the achievement of a distance less than or equal to v. Further, if t_1 is the sequence between ends, it need not be a code word itself, but must be within distance v of one and only one entry in the code table. We will now show that our codes $G_v^\eta(s)$ are so constructed that (1) 'matches' occur at the right places and only at the right places, and (2) any word is distant enough from any other word in the code, so that no confusion can result when decoding in the presence of errors. Suppose we have a portion of a message which we represent as

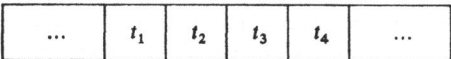

We must be able to tell where each t_i ends in order to decode properly, even with up to v errors present in each word. We will show that any subset of $N_v^\eta(s)$ has this property.

This is perhaps easiest to see when $v = \eta > 0$. In this case (0.4) becomes,

$$B_v(s)B_v(t) \subset \sum_{|t|} B_v(s)$$

for any $t \in N_v^\eta(s)$. Now, suppose that we are in the process of decoding and have located the end of a word. Then we have the following situation;

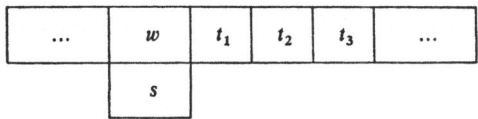

The sequence, w, immediately above s must be within distance v of s, in order for (0.4) to be satisfied. That is, $w \in B_v(s)$. Now slide s to the right under the message sequence.

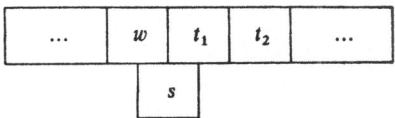

Requirement (0.4) guarantees a 'match', i.e., that the distance will be less than or equal to v, when s is at the end of t_1. That is, we know that some z with $|z| = |t_1|$ will satisfy $d(zs, wt_1) \leq v$. Thus, the distance, of s from the suffix of t_1 just above s, is less than v.

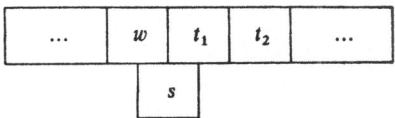

However, (0.4) is really a much stronger statement for it actually states that this matching occurs in spite of the presence of v errors in t_1. So that if $w \in B_v(s)$, $t_1^* \in B_v(t_1)$ then we will still have

$$d(wt_1^*, zs) \leq v$$

for an appropriate $z \in \sum_{|t_1|}$. Thus it is seen, that if (0.4) is satisfied we can find the end of each word even in the presence of v errors. This property alone is not enough, however, because it does *not* assure us that we will *not* find false endings in the middle of some words. This is the function of requirement (0.3). To see this, consider the following diagram.

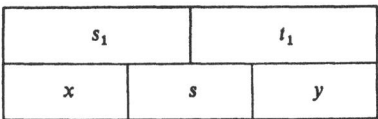

Suppose this were a match i.e., suppose, for some $s_1 \in B_v(s)$ and for non-empty x and y, that

$$d(s_1 t_1, xsy) \leqslant v,$$

then for some $s_2 \in B_v(s)$ we would have

$$d(s_1 t_1, x s_2 y) = 0.$$

But then, clearly, for these same x and y we would have

$$B_v(s) B_v(t) \cap x B_n(s) y \neq \emptyset.$$

This is equivalent to saying that (0.3) is not satisfied. Thus, if (0.3) is satisfied a false match cannot occur.

It should be pointed out that the delay involved is about as small as could be expected: one is able to find the end of a word as soon as one comes to it.

It is obvious that these properties remain if one considers only subsets of $N_v^\eta(s)$, and thus, will be true for any $G_v^\eta(s)$. The additional requirement which is made on G, i.e., that

$$B_v(t) \cap B_v(t_2) \neq \emptyset$$

clearly assures us that no ambiguity will occur once the word endings are ascertained.

The case $v < \eta$ is basically the same as the preceding; we will still be able to correct v errors per word at most but there is added generality in possible word endings, [cf. Theorem 2]. While we have usually taken $v = \eta$ in our examples, the theoretical development for $v < \eta$ has been included since little, if any, additional effort is required.

4. Properties of N-sets

Generally speaking, we will be concerned mostly with N-sets. To study them, it is useful to have an equivalent formulation in terms of distances. This is more easily written by making use of the abbreviated notation τ_r^s to denote the subsequence $\tau_r \tau_{r+1} \ldots \tau_s$ of the sequence $t = \tau_1 \tau_2 \ldots \tau_n$, note in particular, that $t = \tau_1^n$.

THEOREM 1. Let $t = \tau_1^n$, $s = \sigma_1^k$, then $t \in N_v^\eta(s)$, $v \leqslant \eta < k$, if and only if the sequence $\psi_1^{n+k} = x = st$ has the following properties for each r, $2 \leqslant r \leqslant n$:

(1.1) $d(\psi_r^{r+k-1}, s) \geqslant \eta + 1 + \min(v, r-1) + \min(\eta, \max(0, k-r+1))$

and

(1.2) $d(\psi_{n+1}^{n+k}, s) \leqslant \eta - \min(v, n) - \min(\eta, \max(0, k-n))$.

Before proving this result it might be good to give a schematic interpretation. Suppose that

$$x = \sigma_1 \sigma_2 \ldots \sigma_k \tau_1 \tau_2 \ldots \tau_n$$

represents a portion of a message we wish to synchronize. We could do this by putting $s = \sigma_1 \sigma_2 \ldots \sigma_k$ directly below x and slide it from left to right until its distance from the k terms above it is less than some number h. Since we wish this to happen only when σ_k alines with t_n it must be that for other positions of s the distances must exceed some number l. Clearly, inequalities of the type in Theorem 1 should hold, and we will show that the numbers h and l are respectively the right hand sides of (1.2) and (1.1).

The proof of Theorem 1 utilizes two simple lemmas which we now state and prove.

Lemma 1. Let s, t and w be sequences with $|w| = |st|$; then, for integers α, v and η

(1.3) $B_\alpha(s) B_v(t) \cap B_\eta(w) = \emptyset$

iff

(1.4) $d(st, w) \geqslant \min(\alpha, |s|) + \min(v, |t|) + \min(\eta, |w|) + 1$.

Proof. It is clearly possible to find sequences x and y such that $xy \in B_\alpha(s) B_v(t)$, $|x| = |s|$, and $|y| = |t|$, with $d(s, x) = \min(\alpha, |s|)$ and

$d(y, t) = \min(v, |t|)$. If (1.3) is satisfied, then $xy \in B_\eta(w)$ which means $d(xy, w) \geqslant \min(\eta, |w|) + 1$. Thus

$$d(st, w) \geqslant d(st, xy) + d(xy, w)$$
$$= d(s, x) + d(t, y) + d(xy, w)$$
$$\geqslant \min(\alpha, |s|) + \min(v, |t|) + \min(\eta, |w|) + 1,$$

as was to be proved. The converse is obvious.

Lemma 2. If s, t and w are binary sequences such that $|w| = |st| \geqslant \eta + 1$, then

(1.5) $\quad B_\alpha(s) B_v(t) \subset B_\eta(w)$

iff

(1.6) $\quad d(st, w) \leqslant \eta - \min(\alpha, |s|) - \min(v, |t|).$

Proof. $B_\alpha(s) B_v(t) \subset B_\eta(w)$ iff $B_\alpha(s) B_v(t)$ is disjoint from the complement, $\overline{B_\eta(w)}$, of $B_\eta(w)$. But $\overline{B_\eta(w)} = B_{|w|-\eta-1}(\bar{w})$. Thus, $B_\alpha(s) B_v(t) \cap B_{|w|-\eta-1}(\bar{w}) = \emptyset$, which by Lemma 1 is equivalent to $d(st, \bar{w}) \geqslant \min(\alpha, |s|) + \min(v, |t|) + |w| - \eta$. But then

$$d(st, w) = |w| - d(st, \bar{w}) \leqslant \eta - \min(\alpha, |s|) - \min(v, |t|).$$

Proof of Theorem 1. Suppose that $t \in N_v^\eta(s)$ but that (1.1) is violated i.e., assume that for some integer r, satisfying $2 \leqslant r \leqslant n$,

(1.7) $\quad d(\psi_r^{r+k-1}, s) < \eta + 1 + \min(v, r-1) +$
$\quad\quad\quad \min(\eta, \max(0, k-r+1)).$

There are two cases: $2 \leqslant r \leqslant k$ and $r > k$.

Case 1. $2 \leqslant r \leqslant k$; in this case,

$$\psi_r^{r+k+1} = \sigma_r^k \tau_1^{r-1}$$

and

$$d(\psi_r^{r+k-1}, s) < \eta + 1 + \min(v, |\tau_1^{r-1}|) + \min(\eta, |\sigma_r^k|) =$$
$$\min(\eta, |s|) + 1 + \min(v, |\tau_1^{r-1}|) + \min(\eta, |\sigma_r^k|).$$

Using Lemma 1 this is equivalent to stating

$$B_\eta(\sigma_r^k) B_v(\tau_1^{r-1}) \cap B_\eta(s) \neq \emptyset.$$

But then

$$\sigma_1^{r-1} B_\eta(\sigma_r^k) B_v(\tau_1^{r-1}) \tau_r^n \cap \sigma_1^{r-1} B_\eta(s) \tau_r^n \neq \emptyset$$

whence

$$B_\eta(s) B_v(t) \cap \sigma_1^{r-1} B_\eta(s) \tau_r^n \neq \emptyset.$$

This last statement contradicts (0.3) since σ_1^{r-1} and τ_r^n are both assumed nonvoid.

Case 2. $n \geqslant r > k$. Notice that $k - r + 1 \leqslant 0$ and thus the inequality (1.7) reduces to

$$(1.8) \qquad d(\psi_r^{r+k-1}, s) < \eta + 1 + \min(v, r-1) = \eta + 1 + \min(v, k)$$

since $v < k \leqslant r - 1$. Also $\psi_r^{r+k-1} = \tau_{r-k}^{r-1}$. So that again using Lemma 1 we obtain

$$B_v(\tau_{r-k}^{r-1}) \cap B_\eta(s) \neq \emptyset.$$

Here, again, we see that

$$s\tau_1^{r-k+1} B_v(\tau_{r-k}^{r-1}) \tau_r^n \cap s\tau_1^{r-k-1} B_\eta(s) \tau_r^n \neq \emptyset$$

whence

$$B_\eta(s) B_v(t) \cap u B_v(s) v \neq 0$$

for $u = s\tau_1^{r-k-1}$ and $v = \tau_r^n$ both of which are clearly nonempty. We have therefore shown that if $t \in N_v^n(s)$, t must also satisfy (1.1).

Similarly suppose that (1.2) is not true for some $t \in N_v^n(s)$ then

$$d(\psi_{n+1}^{n+k}, s) > \eta - \min(v, \eta) - \min(\eta, \max(0, k-n)).$$

Once again we distinguish two cases: If $n \geqslant k$ then ψ_{n+1}^{n+k} is but a suffix of t, if $k > n$ all of t and a suffix of s is included.

Case 1. $k > n$. $k - n > 0$ and $\psi_{n+1}^{n+k} = \sigma_{n+1}^k t$, thus

$$d(\psi_{n+1}^{n+k}, s) > \eta - \min(v, |t|) - \min(\eta, |\sigma_{n+1}^k|)$$

and by Lemma 2 it follows

$$B_\eta(\sigma_{n+1}^k) B_v(t) \subset B_\eta(s).$$

This implies

$$\sum_n B_\eta(\sigma_{n+1}^k) B_\nu(t) \not\subset \sum_n B_\eta(s) \Rightarrow$$
$$B_\eta(s) B_\nu(t) \not\subset \sum_n B_\eta(s) = \sum_{|t|} B_\eta(s),$$

a contradiction of (0.4).

Case 2. $k \leqslant n$. $k - n \leqslant 0$ and $\psi_{n+1}^{n+k} = \tau_{n+1-k}^n$. A denial of inequality (1.2) then gives

$$d(\tau_{n+1-k}^n, s) > \eta - \min(\nu, |t|) \qquad \text{(note } \nu < k < n).$$

We may, in this form, use Lemma 2 to give

$$B_\nu(\tau_{n+1-k}^n) \not\subset B_\eta(s).$$

Then as before we get in succession

$$\sum_{|s\tau_1{}^{n-k}|} B_\nu(\tau_{n+1-k}^n) \not\subset \sum_{|s\tau_1{}^{n-k}|} B_\eta(s),$$
$$B_\eta(s) B_\nu(\tau_1^{n-k}) B_\nu(\tau_{n+1-k}^n) \not\subset \sum_{|t|} B_\eta(s),$$
$$B_\eta(s) B_\nu(t) \not\subset \sum_{|t|} B_\eta(s),$$

and we again obtain a contradiction.

We have succeeded in showing that if $t \in N_\eta^\nu(s)$ then (1.1) and (1.2) must be satisfied.

The proof of the converse is much the same. If $t \notin N_\eta^\nu(s)$, then either (0.3) or (0.4) fails to hold true. Suppose (0.3) fails, i.e., suppose there exists nonempty u and v such that

$$uB_\eta(s)v \cap B_\eta(s) B_\nu(t) \neq \emptyset$$

with $|s| = k$, $|t| = n$. Clearly then also

$$uB_\eta(s)v \cap uB_\eta(s_1) B_\nu(t_1)v \neq \emptyset$$

where s_1, a suffix of s, may be empty and $|s_1 t_1| = |s|$. But then

$$B_\eta(s) \cap B_\eta(s_1) B_\nu(t_1) \neq \emptyset,$$

which by Lemma 1, is equivalent to

$$(1.9) \qquad d(s_1 t_1, s) < \min(\eta, |s_1|) + \min(\nu, |t_1|) + \min(\eta, |s|) + 1.$$

It is also easily seen that $s_1 t_1$ must be identical with ψ_r^{r+k-1} for some r, $2 \leqslant r \leqslant n$, since x is nothing more than st. Since we have assumed $|s| = k > n$, (1.7) reduces to

$$d(\psi_r^{r+k-1}, s) < n + 1 + \min(\eta, |s_1|) + \min(v, |t_1|).$$

Noting that $|s_1| + |t_1| = k$, we distinguish two cases; suppose $r > k$ then $|s_1| = 0$, $|t_1| = k > v$ so we get $\min(\eta, |s_1|) = 0$, $\min(v, |t_1|) = v = \min(v, r-1)$. If $r \leqslant k$, then $s_1 = \sigma_r^k$ and $t_1 = \tau_1^n$ whence $|s_1| = k - r$, and $|t_1| = r - 1$, and

$$\min(\eta, |s_1|) = \min(\eta, k-r), \quad \min(v, |t_1|) = \min(v, r-1).$$

We can see that in either case the inequality

$$d(\psi_r^{r+k-1}, s) < \eta + 1 + \min(\eta, \max(0, k - r)) + \min(v, r-1)$$

is satisfied. Thus, if $t \notin N_v^\eta(s)$, then the inequality (1.1) cannot be satisfied.

If on the other hand t fails to be in $N_v^\eta(s)$ because (0.4) is not satisfied, it must be that either

$$B_\eta(s_1) B_v(t) \not\subseteq B_\eta(s)$$

or

$$B_v(t_1) \not\subseteq B_\eta(s)$$

in case $n = |t| < |s| = k$, or $n \geqslant k$ respectively, where

$$s_1 = \sigma_n^k \quad \text{and} \quad t_1 = \tau_{n-k+1}^n.$$

In the first case, by Lemma 2 the inequality

$$d(s_1 t, s) < \eta - \min(\eta, |s_1|) - \min(\eta, |t|)$$

holds, and in the second case,

$$d(t_1, s) < \eta - \min(v, |t_1|)$$

is satisfied. Now if $x = st$ these two inequalities can be combined to give

$$d(\psi_{n+1}^{n+k}, s) < \eta - \min(\eta, \max(0, k - n)) - \min(v, n)$$

thus (1.2) is not satisfied. The theorem is, therefore, proven.

This theorem is useful for computation purposes, in particular for computer implementation, but it may also be used to prove a result on the lengths of the words in $N_v^\eta(s)$, since it says, in essence, that for non-zero v, the words cannot be too short.

THEOREM 2. If $v \neq 0$, every $t \in N_v^\eta(s)$ must satisfy

(1.10) $|s| \leqslant |t| + \eta - \min(v, |t|)$.

In particular, if $\eta = v < |t|$, then

$|s| \leqslant |t|$.

Proof. Let $n = |t|$, $k = |s|$ and $\alpha = \eta - \min(v, n)$. Then from (1.2) there follows,

$0 \leqslant \alpha - \min(\alpha + \min(v, n), \max(0, k-n))$,

or in other words

$\min(\alpha + \min(v, n), \max(0, k-n)) \leqslant \alpha$.

Thus either $\alpha + \min(v, \eta) \leqslant \alpha$, and hence $v = 0$, (for nonempty t) or $\max(0, k-n) \leqslant \alpha$. Since $v = 0$ has been excluded, we must have $k - n \leqslant \alpha$, $k \leqslant n + \alpha$. That is,

$|s| \leqslant |t| + \eta - \min(v, |t|)$.

The result for $\eta = v < |t|$ is obvious.

For $\eta = v \neq 0$, then, there are no code words with length shorter than $|s|$. In fact, in such a case, (1.8) reduces to

$d(\psi_{n+1}^{n+k}, s) \leqslant 0$

whence $\psi_{n+1}^{n+k} = s$, and $t = ps$ for some prefix p. Stated more formally

Corollary. If $t \in N_v^v(s)$, $0 < v < |s|$, then $t = ps$ for some binary sequence p (possibly empty).

Another interesting result is the following.

THEOREM 3. If $tps \in N_v^\eta(s)$ then $tps \in N_v^\eta(ps)$.
Proof. Suppose $tps \notin N_v^v(ps)$, i.e., since (0.4) is obviously satisfied, for some nonempty u and v of appropriate length

$uB_\eta(ps)v \cap B_\eta(ps)B_v(tps) \neq \emptyset$.

Then there exists $p_1, p_2 \in B_\eta(p)$ such that

$$up_1 B_\eta(s)v \cap p_2 B_\eta(s)B_v(tps) \neq \emptyset$$

whence $up_1 = p_2 u_2$ for some non-void sequence u_2. But then

$$u_2 B_\eta(s)v \cap p_2 B_\eta(s)B_v(tps) \neq \emptyset,$$

a contradiction of the fact that $tps \in N_v^\eta(s)$. This proves the theorem.

In particular, this theorem tells us that if $ps \in N_v^\eta(s)$, ps must also belong to $N_v^\eta(ps)$. The general question of when $s \in N_v^\eta(s)$ is in itself interesting. One simple result for the case $v = \eta = 1$ is the following.

Lemma 3. $s \in N_1^1(s)$ iff s has distance at least 4 from each of its cyclic shifts.
Proof. The proof is rather obvious since when $x = ss$, ψ_r^{r+k-1} is a cyclic shift of s for $2 \leqslant r \leqslant n = k$.

In this particular case $v = \eta = 1$, $\min(v, r-1) = 1$ and $\min(\eta, \max(0, k-r+1)) = 1$, so the result follows from (1.1).

It is known, see [PML33], that the shortest sequences with the property of Lemma 3 have length 7. So one can state that all sequences in $N_1^1(s)$ have a length of at least 7.

Before giving some examples, we prove a theorem which will enable us, in many cases, to show that an N-set is infinite.

THEOREM 4. If $tr_1 r_2 r_3 p \in N_v^\eta(s)$, where $r_1 r_2 = r_2 r_3$ and $|r_1 r_2| \geqslant |s|$, then $tr_1 r_2 r_3 r_3 p \in N_v^\eta(s)$.
Proof. Since $r_1 r_2 = r_2 r_3$ it follows $r_1 r_1 r_2 r_3 = r_1 r_2 r_3 r_3$. In particular, to show that

$$B_\eta(s)B_v(tr_1 r_2 r_3 r_3 p) \subset \sum B_\eta(s)$$

we can as well show

$$B_\eta(s)B_v(tr_1 r_1 r_2 r_3 p) \subset \sum B_\eta(s);$$

a trivial consequence of the hypothesis.

To obtain a contradiction, we assume $w = tr_1 r_2 r_3 r_3 p \notin N_v^\eta(s)$. Since (0.4) of definition 2 is satisfied, this means that for some non-void u and v we have

$$(1.11) \quad uB_\eta(s)v \cap B_\eta(s)B_v(w) \neq \emptyset.$$

Then, for $s', s'' \in B_\eta(s)$, $w' \in B_\nu(w)$,

$$us'v = s''w'.$$

If $|v| \geqslant |r_3 p|$, let $w' = w_1' w_2'$ with $|w_2'| = |v|$; then there is a suffix w_2 of $tr_1 r_2 r_3 p$, of length $|w_2'| - |r_3|$, such that $w_1' w_2 \in B_\nu(tr_1 r_2 r_3 p)$ and that $us'w_2 = s''w_1'w_2$; that is,

$$uB_\eta(s)w_2 \cap B_\eta(s)B_\nu(tr_1 r_2 r_3 p) \neq \emptyset,$$

a contradiction. If $|v| < |r_3 p|$, then, since $|u| + |v| = |w|$,

$$|u| > |tr_1 r_2 r_3| = |tr_1 r_1 r_2| \geqslant |tr_1| + |s|.$$

Set $w' = w_1' w_2'$ with $|w_1'| = |u| - |s|$. Then there is a prefix w_1 of $tr_1 r_2 r_3 p$, of length $|w_1'| - |r_1|$, such that $w_1 w_2' \in B_\nu(tr_1 r_2 r_3 p)$ and that $(uw_1)s'v = s''w_1 w_2'$, that is again

$$uw_1 B_\eta(s)v \cap B_\eta(s)B_\nu(tr_1 r_2 r_3 p) \neq \emptyset.$$

With this contradiction the theorem is proved.

We stated earlier that this theorem can sometimes be used to show that an N-set is infinite. This is because if we can add on r_3 we may add any finite number, i.e., suppose $tr_1 r_2 r_3 p \in N_\nu^\eta(s)$, then $tr_1 r_2 r_3 r_3 p = tr_1 r_1 r_2 r_2 p$ also belongs to the N-set and we can apply the theorem again (with the new 't' equal to the previous tr_1) to get that $tr_1 r_1 r_2 r_3 r_3 p = tr_1 r_1 r_1 r_2 r_3 p$ also belongs, etc. Thus we have the following:

Corollary. If an N-set $N_\nu^\eta(s)$ contains a sequence of the form $tr_1 r_2 r_3 p$, with $r_1 r_2 = r_2 r_3$ and $|r_1 r_2| \geqslant |s|$, then $N_\nu^\eta(s)$ is infinite.

5. Examples

We give some examples of N-sets and codes obtained with the aid of an electronic computer. Using the program NCD3 (see [PML54]) we were able to verify earlier hand computations which showed that no s of length less than 7 generates a non-empty N-set for $\nu = \eta = 1$. There are exactly 30 sequences of length 7 which generate nonempty $N_1^1(s)$'s. Of these, however, only 8 are non-trivial N-sets, (we call an N-set trivial if $s = N_\nu^\eta(s)$), and of these eight, four are complements respectively of the other four. We give the first few words of each of these four essentially different N-sets in Table I.

TABLE I

$N_{\bar{1}}^{1}((0011101)$

			0011	101
		00	0011	101
		000	0011	101
		0000	0011	101
	0	0000	0011	101
	0	0100	0011	101
	00	0000	0011	101
	00	1000	0011	101
	000	0000	0011	101
	000	1000	0011	101
	001	0000	0011	101

.
.

$N_{\bar{1}}^{1}((0110100)$

				0110	100
	0111	1110	1110	0110	100
0	1111	1110	1110	0110	100
01	1111	1110	1110	0110	100
011	1111	1110	1110	0110	100
0111	1110	1110	0110	0110	100
0111	1110	1110	1110	0110	100
0111	1111	1110	1110	0110	100

.
.

$N_{\bar{1}}^{1}(0110111)$

		0110	111
	000	0110	111
	0000	0110	111
0	0000	0110	111
00	0000	0110	111

.
.
.

$N_{\bar{1}}^{1}(0100111)$

		0100	111
	0000	0100	111
0	0000	0100	111
00	0000	0100	111
01	0000	0100	111
000	0000	0100	111
010	0000	0100	111

.
.
.

Each of these four N-sets are infinite as can be shown using the Corollary to Theorem 4. The set, $N_1^1(0011101)$, is the one most likely to be of any practical use, and an example of a G-code formed from its complement is given in Table III. However, $N_1^1(0110100)$ certainly raises some questions of theoretical interest. Notice that the shortest word in $N_1^1(s)$ aside from s itself, has length 19, more than twice the length of s. Indeed at first it seemed that $N_1^1(0110100)$ was trivial because we had not tried long enough sequences. The question then is: is there a reasonable bound on the length of sequences we must test to conclude that an N-set is empty or trivial? A (possibly) related question is: are there non-trivial but finite N-sets? Here indications are that the answer is no, but we have yet to find proof. With respect to the first question, we remark that only a few hand calculations are necessary to show $N_1^1(0001011)$ is trivial; whereas we have been able to conclude that $N_1^1(1101000)$ is trivial only after computer calculations and a rather involved argument.

All sequences of length 8 have been tested, in the case $\eta = v = 1$, and 120 of them give nonempty N-sets. We did not attempt to test all sequences of length 9. We did, however, attempt to find an example of a nonempty N-set for $\eta = v = 2$. The first few words of one such N-set are given in Table II. Notice that s has length 13, and the shortest word in $N_2^2(s)$ has length 19. While these words are rather long, it must be remembered that a code formed from such an N-set will synchronize properly in the presence of up to 2 errors per word, and will correct these errors. In addition, should synchronization be lost due to a 'burst' of errors, resynchronization will occur as soon as the first word with 2 or fewer errors is received.

TABLE II

$N_2^2(1011000100001)$

```
     111 1011 0110 0010 0001
  11 1101 1111 0110 0010 0001
     111 1011 1011 0110 0010 0001
    1111 0101 0101 0110 0010 0001
                 .
                 .
```

TABLE III

A code obtained from $N_1^1(1100010)$

Letter	Probability	Sequence	Length	Length Probability
	0.1859	110 0010	7	1.3013
E	0.1031	1 1110 0010	9	0.9278
T	0.0796	11 1110 0010	10	0.7960
A	0.0642	111 1110 0010	11	0.7062
O	0.0632	1111 1110 0010	12	0.7584
I	0.0575	1 1111 1110 0010	13	0.7475
N	0.0574	11 1111 1110 0010	14	0.8035
S	0.0514	111 1111 1110 0010	15	0.7710
R	0.0484	1111 1111 1110 0010	16	0.7744
H	0.0467	1 1011 1101 1110 0010	17	0.7938
L	0.0321	1 1110 1111 1110 0010	17	0.5457
D	0.0317	11 0111 1011 1110 0010	18	0.5705
U	0.0228	11 1101 1111 1110 0010	18	0.4104
C	0.0218	111 1011 1101 1110 0010	19	0.4141
F	0.0208	110 1111 0111 1110 0010	19	0.3952
M	0.0198	111 1101 1111 1110 0010	19	0.3762
W	0.0175	1111 0111 1011 1110 0010	20	0.3500
Y	0.0164	1101 1110 1111 1110 0010	20	0.3280
G	0.0152	1111 1011 1111 1110 0010	20	0.3040
P	0.0152	1 1111 0111 1101 1110 0010	21	0.3191
B	0.0127	1 1110 1111 1011 1110 0010	21	0.2667
V	0.0083	1 1011 1110 1111 1110 0010	21	0.1742
K	0.0049	1 1111 1011 1111 1110 0010	21	0.1028
X	0.0013	11 0111 1011 1101 1110 0010	22	0.0285
J	0.0008	11 1111 0111 1101 1110 0010	22	0.0175
Q	0.0008	11 1110 1111 1011 1110 0010	22	0.0175
Z	0.0005	11 1101 1111 0111 1110 0010	22	0.0109

The average length is 13.012

We consider next some encodings of the English alphabet. These are given in Tables III and IV, which are self-explanatory. Since, to our knowledge, no examples of codes which are both synchronizing and correcting have been published, no direct average length comparisons are available. However, in order to correct one error per word, a block code of 27 or more characters must have words of length 9 at least.

TABLE IV

A code obtained from $N_1^1(00111101)$

Letter	Probability	Sequence	Length	Length Probability
	0.1859	0011 1101	8	1.4872
E	0.1031	0 0011 1101	9	0.9278
T	0.0796	00 0011 1101	10	0.7960
A	0.0642	001 0011 1101	11	0.7062
O	0.0632	0001 0011 1101	12	0.7584
I	0.0575	0 0001 0011 1101	13	0.7475
N	0.0574	00 0010 0011 1101	14	0.8035
S	0.0514	00 1001 0011 1101	14	0.7196
R	0.0484	000 0100 0011 1101	15	0.7260
H	0.0467	000 1001 0011 1101	15	0.7005
L	0.0321	001 0011 0011 1101	15	0.4815
D	0.0317	0001 0100 0011 1101	16	0.5072
U	0.0228	0000 1010 0011 1101	16	0.3648
C	0.0218	0010 0001 0011 1101	16	0.3488
F	0.0208	0001 0011 0011 1101	16	0.3328
M	0.0198	0 0001 0100 0011 1101	17	0.3366
W	0.0175	0 0100 0010 0011 1101	17	0.2975
Y	0.0164	0 0010 1110 0011 1101	17	0.2788
G	0.0152	0 0010 0001 0011 1101	17	0.2584
P	0.0152	0 0100 1001 0011 1101	17	0.2584
B	0.0127	0 0001 0011 0011 1101	17	0.2159
V	0.0083	00 0011 0000 0011 1101	18	0.1493
K	0.0049	00 1001 1000 0011 1101	18	0.0881
X	0.0013	00 1000 0100 0011 1101	18	0.0234
J	0.0008	00 0101 1100 0011 1101	18	0.0143
Q	0.0008	00 1100 0010 0011 1101	18	0.0143
Z	0.0005	00 0010 1110 0011 1101	18	0.0089

The average length is 12.352

A Neumann code which synchronizes but does no correcting can have average length as short as 4.2645. On the other hand a variable length code, which corrects one error but does not synchronize, has an average length of 7.6846 (see [PML35]). Thus a value of 12 or 13 does not seem to be out of line for codes with both synchronization and correcting properties.

TABLE V

$N_1^1(00111101)$ itself used as a code

Letter	Probability	Sequence	Length	Length Probability
	0.1859	0011 1101	8	1.4872
E	0.1031	00 0011 1101	10	1.0309
T	0.0796	000 0011 1101	11	0.8755
A	0.0642	001 0011 1101	11	0.7062
O	0.0632	0000 0011 1101	12	0.7584
I	0.0575	0001 0011 1101	12	0.6900
N	0.0574	0010 0011 1101	12	0.6887
S	0.0514	0 0000 0011 1101	13	0.6682
R	0.0484	0 0001 0011 1101	13	0.6292
H	0.0467	0 0010 0011 1101	13	0.6071
L	0.0321	0 0100 0011 1101	13	0.4173
D	0.0317	00 0000 0011 1101	14	0.4437
U	0.0228	00 0001 0011 1101	14	0.3192
C	0.0218	00 0010 0011 1101	14	0.3051
F	0.0208	00 0100 0011 1101	14	0.2911
M	0.0198	00 1000 0011 1101	14	0.2772
W	0.0175	00 1001 0011 1101	14	0.2450
Y	0.0164	00 1100 0011 1101	14	0.2295
G	0.0152	000 0000 0011 1101	15	0.2279
P	0.0152	000 0001 0011 1101	15	0.2279
S	0.0127	000 0010 0011 1101	15	0.1904
V	0.0083	000 0100 0011 1101	15	0.1244
K	0.0049	000 1000 0011 1101	15	0.0734
X	0.0013	000 1001 0011 1101	15	0.0194
J	0.0008	000 1010 0011 1101	15	0.0120
Q	0.0008	000 1100 0011 1101	15	0.0120
Z	0.0005	001 0000 0011 1101	15	0.0075

The average length is 11.565

Another comparison can be made with Table V where we have used the shortest words of $N_1^1(00111101)$ to encode the alphabet. Such an encoding will of course not correct errors but will synchronize correctly in the presence of one error per word. This could be useful in cases where the text of the message is redundant enough to supply corrections by other means.

Finally, we give in Table VI a comparison of N and G with regard to sequences of given length. This comparison gives some indication of the effect of requirement (0.5).

TABLE VI

A comparison of the number of sequences of a given length for a typical N and G

Length	No. in $N_1^1(111001000)$	No. in $G_1^1(111001000)$
9	1	1
10	1	1
11	2	1
12	2	1
13	3	1
14	6	2
15	13	3
16	22	5
17	39	6
18	63	11

A FAMILY OF CODES FOR
THE CORRECTION OF SUBSTITUTION
AND SYNCHRONIZATION ERRORS

L. CALABI AND W. E. HARTNETT

EDITORIAL NOTE

The completion of our work on the classical models posed the obvious suggestion that the class of models considered be broadened. There were two modifications immediately available: (1) a change of the per word stipulation and (2) a change in the kinds of allowable errors. Because our past results were so intimately tied to the standard model, any change meant a re-examination of all the definitions and proofs of theorems already given and even a cursory examination showed that substantial alterations in viewpoint would become necessary. As a beginning step we developed models which allowed certain substitution and synchronization (= gain or loss of symbols) errors in each set of $t > 0$ consecutive words of a sentence. The resulting models thus embodied both kinds of changes.

For such models we were able to give sufficient conditions that a block code be decodable, where the definition of decodability was formally the same as our definition for the classical models. Using literature results, we were then able to construct families of codes decodable for these new models. The techniques of proof were different from those used before and the necessity of fashioning them forced us to look at the basic problems of Coding Theory in another light. Our major concern at this time was the problem of construction not of definitions or characterizations.

The paper appeared in *IEEE Transactions on Information Theory* **15** (1969) 102–106.

1. INTRODUCTION

Many different kinds of codes have been devised to combat the effect of noise. Most common are the codes capable of correcting a certain number of substitution (or additive) errors in each word. Great progress has also been made in the study of 'error limiting' (or synchronizable) codes (see e.g. [28]); these are codes which are able to limit the effect of the noise so that, after a message distortion, decoding can resume without having to wait for the message's end. Error limiting codes are normally considered for channels in which synchronization errors (i.e., deletions or insertions of digits) are expected. Recently codes have been found which are capable of correcting substitution errors *and* of limiting the effect of synchronization errors (e.g. [6], [PML55], [30]).

Some codes should properly be called correcting for synchronization errors: every message can be reconstructed in its entirety even when certain patterns of synchronization errors have occurred (e.g. [27], [16], [17], [31], [32]). In addition, the codes introduced in [27] and [16] have also some capability of correcting substitution errors. So do the codes A_n^c presented here and in [PML57].

For each pair of integers $n \geqslant 4$ and $c = 0, 1, \ldots, 2n-1$, A_n^c is a binary block code of length n designed to combat noise whose effect on any one word depends upon the effects on (a finite number of) preceding words. Such an assumption on the channel behavior is realistic; and while it may introduce some complications in the study and in the decoding of the codes, it also permits a very modest redundancy. Similar 'contextual' error patterns have been considered also in [22], for variable length codes, but only for substitution errors.

In more detail, our codes have the following error correcting capability: given any integer $t \geqslant 3$, A_n^c can correct, in every t consecutive words, *either* one substitution error in each one of at most $t-2$ words, *or* at most one synchronization error (but not both). The integer t can be chosen independently of n, c and may be changed by the decoder to suit the channel conditions. For example, if the probability of deletions or insertions is very small, one would choose large values of t, yielding the possibility of correcting one substitution error in almost every word. At the other extreme, taking $t = 3$ allows the correction of one synchronization error every 3 words.

Since we do not assume that the noise affects successive words independently, it is generally not possible to decode one word at a time. After having received, at most, $nt+1$ digits, the decoder can split off the first $rn-1$, rn or $rn+1$ digits and determine uniquely the first r words, for some integer r with $1 \leqslant r \leqslant t$ (as long as only correctable error patterns have occurred). That procedure is then repeated to exhaustion. Extending the terminology of [14], we may then say that the codes A_n^c are 'decodable with bounded delay'.

The construction of the codes A_n^c, described in Section 2 below, does not require the insertion of special synchronization sequences between words, a technique used very often. The error-correcting capability and the decoding technique are established in Section 3 for a large class of block codes; Section 4 shows that the codes A_n^c belong to that class.

2. THE CODES A_n^c

Following Levenshtein [16], we associate to every binary sequence $x = \xi_1 \xi_2 ... \xi_n$ of length n and with terms, or digits, $\xi_1, \xi_2, ..., \xi_n$, an integer $\sigma(x)$, defined by $\sigma(x) = \sum_i \xi_i$. If $0 \leqslant c < 2n$, we then denote by K_n^c the set of those sequences x of length n for which $\sigma(x) \equiv c \bmod 2n$. Further we let K_n be the set of those sequences of length n which are constant ((000...0) and (111...1)) or which

– if $n = 2h + 1$, have exactly h terms equal to 'one', except for first term, which is arbitrary;

– if $n = 2h$, have exactly h terms equal to 'one'.

For $n \geqslant 4$ we then set $A_n^c = K_n^c \backslash K_n$, that is A_n^c is that subset of K_n^c obtained by removing all the sequences belonging to K_n. Examples are given in Tables I and II; one example for each n between 4 and 13 may be found in [PML57].

TABLE I

Three examples of codes A_n^c. The set K_8^8 contains besides A_8^8,
also the sequences 00100111, 00011011

$A_7^6 (= K_7^6)$	$A_7^7 (= K_7^7)$	A_8^8
1110000	1111110	00000001
1011101	1101000	10000010
1000100	1100111	01000100
0000010	1011011	00101000
1101011	1000010	11001000
0011011	0000001	10110000
0100111	0010111	11000111
0101000	0011000	10101011
0111110	0100100	01110011
	0111101	01101101
		10011101
		11110101
		01011110
		11101110

TABLE II

Description of some codes A_n^c. The values of c are chosen to maximize
the number of elements (compare the last two columns)

n	c	Delete from K_n^c	No. of Elements	Average Size
8	9	00010111	15	11.5
	11	11101000	15	11.5
9	13	100001111	27	20.6
	14	011110000	27	20.6
10	17	0010001111	46	38.5
		0001010111		
		0000111011		
		1111001000		
		1110110000		
	18	5 sequences	46	38.5
11	21	7 sequences	86	70.1
12	2	20 sequences	150	134.
	3	22 sequences	150	134.
13	6	30 sequences	285	265.

Notice that K_n contains

$$2 + \binom{2h}{h} \text{ elements if } n = 2h$$

$$2 + 2\binom{2h}{h} \text{ elements if } n = 2h + 1.$$

Also observe that every sequence of length n belongs to exactly one of
the sets $K_n, A_n^0, A_n^1, \ldots, A_n^{2n-1}$. Thus each A_n^c contains, on the average,
a number of elements given by

$$\frac{2^n - 2 - \binom{2h}{h}}{2n} \quad \text{if} \quad n = 2h$$

$$\frac{2^n - 2 - 2\binom{2h}{h}}{2n} \quad \text{if} \quad n = 2h + 1.$$

If the redundancy of a binary block code of m words of length n is defined as $(n - \log_2 m)/n$, then we can show that the redundancy of the A_n^c of average size is larger than $(1 + \log_2 n)/n$ but less than $(2 + \log_2 n)/n$ (cf. [32]). Assuming $n = 2h$, we may prove that statement as follows:

$$1 + \log_2 n = n - \log_2(2^n) + \log_2(2n) \leqslant$$

$$n - \log_2\left(2^n - 2 - \binom{2h}{h}\right) + \log_2(2n) =$$

$$n - \log_2 \frac{2^n - 2 - \binom{2h}{h}}{2n} \leqslant$$

$$n - \log_2(2^{n-1}) + \log_2(2n) = 2 + \log_2 n$$

where the last inequality holds because $n \geqslant 4$. A similar proof may be given when $n = 2h + 1$.

The exact size of each A_n^c can be computed using the following approach. Since $1 \cdot \xi_1, 2 \cdot \xi_2, \dots, i \cdot \xi_i, \dots, n \cdot \xi_n$ is a partition of the integer $\sigma(x)$ into unequal parts not exceeding n, we find that the number of elements of K_n^c is given by $\sum p(c + m \cdot 2n, n)$ where the summation is extended from $m = 0$ to the largest integer m for which $c + m \cdot 2n \leqslant n(n + 1)/2$ and where $p(r, k)$ is the number of partitions of r into unequal parts not exceeding k. In a similar fashion, the number of elements of $K_n \cap K_a^c$ is given by

$$\sum p(c + m \cdot 2n, h, n) \quad \text{if} \quad n = 2h$$
$$\sum p(c + m \cdot 2n - h, h, n - 1) + \sum p(c + m \cdot 2n - h - 1, h, n - 1)$$
$$\text{if} \quad n = 2h + 1$$

where the summation ranges are as before and $p(r, h, k)$ is the number of partitions of r into exactly h unequal (and positive) parts not exceeding k. The number of elements of A_n^c is then obtained. The fourth column of Table II gives the size of the largest A_n^c for some pairs (n, c). A comparison with the average size given in the fifth column indicates the importance of a proper choice of c.

3. SOME GENERAL RESULTS

In this section we consider binary block codes A of length $n \geqslant 4$ and
let t be an integer satisfying $t \geqslant 3$. The sequences in A we call *words* and
any juxtaposition $a_1 a_2 \ldots a_k$ of words $a_1, a_2, \ldots, a_k$ of A a *message* (*over A*).
It is also convenient here to call a (r, s, t)-*neighbor* of a message $m =
a_1 a_2 \ldots a_k$ any sequence which may be obtained from m by making in
each t consecutive words $a_{i+1}, a_{i+2}, \ldots, a_{i+t}$ $(i = 0, 1, \ldots, k-t)$ one
substitution error in each one of at most r words, and no synchronization
errors; or one synchronization error in each one of at most s words, and
no substitution errors. For example we obtain a $(2, 1, 3)$-neighbor of
$a_1 a_2 a_3 a_4 a_5$ by making a synchronization error in a_1 and a substitution
error in each one of a_4 and a_5; or by making a substitution error every
second word; or by making a synchronization error every third word.

We say that a code A is (r, s, t)-*correcting* if every sequence is the
(r, s, t)-neighbor of at most one message over A. A code is further called
(r, s, t)-*decodable* (*with delay at most p*) if it is (r, s, t)-correcting and
if there exists an integer p with the following property: if a message m of
at least p words has a (r, s, t)-neighbor which is the prefix of a (r, s, t)-
neighbor of some message m', then the first word of m and that of m'
are equal. We will be concerned here only with the case $r = t - 2$ and $s = 1$;
for this case we shall give in the theorem below a set of sufficient conditions
for A to be $(t-2, 1, t)$-decodable with delay at most t.

In order to formulate those conditions, we first recall that the Hamming
distance between two (equally long) sequences may be defined as the
smallest number of substitutions necessary to transform the one into
the other. In [16] a new distance function has been introduced, which we
call *Levenshtein distance* and denote by D: for any two sequences x, y (of
equal or different length), $D(x, y)$ is the smallest number of substitutions,
deletions and insertions necessary to transform x into y (see Table III).
The usual properties hold, namely: $D(x, y) = 0$ if and only if $x = y$;
$D(x, y) = D(y, x)$; $D(x, y) \leqslant D(x, z) + D(z, y)$. If a code is capable of
correcting up to e errors (substitution and/or synchronization) in any
one word a, it is necessary for a to have Levenshtein distance at least
$2e + 1$ from any other word. As already remarked in [16], this condition
is however not sufficient, because of the length changes caused by
synchronization errors.

TABLE III

Some examples of Levenshtein distances

x	y	$D(x, y)$
00000	00000000	3
00000	01100100	3
01010	10101	2

The following are all the sequences y with $D(x, y) = 1$ when $x = 00101$:

0101	10101	000101	100101
0001	01101	001001	010101
0011	00001	001010	001101
0010	00111		001011
	00100		

In our case the first condition to consider is then:

(1) $D(a, a') \geqslant 3$ for $a, a' \in A, a \neq a'$.

Observe that if, for some sequences u, v of length h, $ua = a'v$, then certainly $D(a, a') \leqslant 2h$. Thus, if (1) holds, $h \geqslant 2$. In order to limit the effects of length changes due to insertions or deletions, we have found it convenient to eliminate also the case $h = 2$. Our second condition is then:

(2)   If $ua = a'v$ for $a, a' \in A$ and some sequences u, v, then the length of u is not 2.

In other words, $D(a, a') = 4$ is allowed as long as we cannot transform a into a' by deleting the last two digits of a and inserting (or prefixing) the first two of a'. We turn now to the proof that (1) and (2), together, imply that A has all the desired properties.

The set of all the $(t-2, 1, t)$-neighbors of the message $a_1 a_2 ... a_k$ of $X = (a_1, a_2, ..., a_k)$, where $a_i \in A$, will be denoted $\alpha_t(X)$. Such a k-tuple X of words of A may be called a *sentence* (*over A*) and k its *length* $|X|$. Similarly the length of any sequence x will be denoted by $|x|$; n is the length of the words of A. With this notation A is $(t-2, 1, t)$-correcting if and only if $\alpha_t(X) \cap \alpha_t(Y) = \emptyset$ whenever X, Y are different sentences.

We show now that if $\alpha_t(X)w \cap \alpha_t(Y) \neq \emptyset$ for some sequence w, then the lengths of X and Y are related in the obvious fashion. It will then follow that if $\alpha_t(X) \cap \alpha_t(Y) \neq \emptyset$, A has property (1), and X has at most t words, then $X = Y$.

Lemma 1. Suppose X and Y are sentences over A and $\alpha_t(X)w \cap \alpha_t(Y) \neq \emptyset$ for some sequence w.

(a)   If $|Y| \leqslant t$, then $|X| \leqslant |Y| \leqslant t$; hence if w is the empty sequence, $|X| = |Y|$ and X and Y have the same number of words.

(b)   If $|X| \geqslant t$, then $|Y| \geqslant t$.

Proof. By assumption, there exists an $x \in \alpha_t(X)$ and $y \in \alpha_t(Y)$ such that $xw = y$. If $|Y| = k$ and $|X| = h$, we assume that $k < h$ and derive a contradiction. For $y \in \alpha_t(Y)$, $nk - 1 \leqslant |y| \leqslant nk + 1$ and for $x \in \alpha_t(X)$, $nh - [h/t] - 1 \leqslant |x| \leqslant nh + [h/t] + 1$ where $[h/t]$ is the greatest integer less than or equal h/t.

Letting $s = [h/t]$, we claim that with $h - k \geqslant 1$, $s + 2 < 4(h - k)$ for all s. Clearly, the inequality holds for $s = 0$ and $s = 1$. If $s \geqslant 2$, then obviously $st \leqslant h$ and $s + 2 < 12(s - 1)$. Hence $s + 2 < 12(s - 1) = 4 \cdot 3(s - 1) \leqslant 4(s - 1)t = 4(st - t) \leqslant 4(st - k) \leqslant 4(h - k)$ because $k \leqslant t$. If follows that $s + 2 < 4(h - k)$ for all s and hence that $s + 2 < n(h - k)$.

It is now routine to compute that

$$nk + 1 < nh - [h/t] - 1 = nk + n(h - k) - [h/t] - 1$$

contradicting the assumption that $xw = y$ for some $x \in \alpha_t(X)$ and $y \in \alpha_t(Y)$. Hence $h = |X| \leqslant |Y| = k \leqslant t$ as we asserted. The second part of (a) follows from the first; if $\alpha_t(X) \cap \alpha_t(Y) \neq \emptyset$ and $|Y| \leqslant t$, then $|X| \leqslant |Y| \leqslant t$. But then $\alpha_t(X) \cap \alpha_t(Y) \neq \emptyset$ and $|X| \leqslant t$; hence $|Y| \leqslant |X| \leqslant t$ and $|X| = |Y|$.

For (b) we observe that if $|Y| < t$, then (a) applies and $|X| \leqslant |Y| \leqslant t$ contradicting the assumption that $|X| \geqslant t$.

Lemma 2. Suppose A satisfies (1), X and Y are sentences over A with $|X| \leqslant t$ and $\alpha_t(X) \cap \alpha_t(Y) \neq \emptyset$. Then $X = Y$.
Proof. Since $|X| \leqslant t$, Lemma 1(a) tells us that necessarily X and Y have the same number of words. Let $X = (a_1, a_2, \ldots, a_k)$, $Y = (b_1, b_2, \ldots, b_k)$ and $z \in \alpha_t(X) \cap \alpha_t(Y)$, with $z = x_1 x_1 \ldots x_k = y_1 y_2 \ldots y_k$ where x_i, y_i are

obtained from a_i, b_i respectively, that is, $x_i \in \alpha_t(a_i)$ and $y_i \in \alpha_t(b_i)$. If no synchronization errors occur, then $x_i = y_i$ for each i and $D(a_i, b_i) \leqslant D(a_i, x_i) + D(y_i, b_i) \leqslant 2$; that is $a_i = b_i$ for each i and $X = Y$. If z is the result of an insertion (or a deletion) in X, then it must be the result of an insertion (or a deletion) in Y; if such an error occurs, it is then easy to check that, again, $D(a_i, b_i) \leqslant 2$ and hence that $X = Y$.

Lemma 3. Suppose A satisfies (1) and (2). Then A satisfies

(3)   If $ua = a'v$ for $a, a' \in A$ and some sequences u, v, then $|u| \neq 1$.

Proof. If $ua = a'v$ with $|u| = 1$, then $D(a, a') \leqslant 2$ and $a = a'$ because of (1). If $a = \xi_1 \xi_2 \ldots \xi_n$, $ua = av$, and u and v are single bits, then $u = \xi_1 = \xi_2 = \ldots = \xi_n = v$. But then a violates (2).

Lemma 4. Suppose that A satisfies (2) and (3). Then A satisfies

(4)   If X and Y are sentences over A with $|X| \geqslant t$ and $\alpha_t(X)w \cap$
           $\cap \alpha_t(Y) \neq \emptyset$, it follows that X and Y may be written as
           $X = X_1 X_2$, $Y = Y_1 Y_2$ with $0 < |X_1| \leqslant t$, $\alpha_t(X_1) \cap \alpha_t(Y_1) \neq \emptyset$ and
           $\alpha_t(X_2)w \cap \alpha_t(Y_2) \neq \emptyset$.

Moreover, if A satisfies also (1), then $X_1 = Y_1$.
Proof. Let $X = (a_1, a_2, \ldots, a_k)$, $Y = (b_1, b_2, \ldots, b_h)$ and $z \in \alpha_t(X)w \cap \alpha_t(Y)$. Because $k \geqslant t$, it follows from Lemma 1(b) that also $h \geqslant t$. With the notation already introduced, let $z = x_1 x_2 \ldots x_k w = y_1 y_2 \ldots y_h$. If there is an $i \leqslant t$ such that $x_1 x_2 \ldots x_i = y_1 y_2 \ldots y_i$, then the sentences $X_1 = (a_1, \ldots, a_i)$, $X_2 = (a_{i+1}, \ldots, a_k)$, $Y_1 = (b_1, \ldots, b_i)$, $Y_2 = (b_{i+1}, \ldots, b_h)$ satisfy the requirements of our lemma. If such a subscript i does not exist, we have in particular $|x_1| \neq |y_1|$; and since we limit ourselves to consideration of only the first t words of X and of Y, we may assume $|y_1| < |x_1|$ without any loss of generality. Then x_1 is obtained by an insertion in a_1, or y_1 is the result of a deletion in b_1, or both. If both, then $x_1 a_2 a_3 \ldots a_t x_{t+1} \ldots x_k w = y_1 b_2 b_3 \ldots b_t y_{t+1} \ldots y_h$ and $ua_2 = b_2 v$ with $|u| = 2$, contradicting (2). If $|y_1| = |b_1| < |x_1|$, there is at least one subscript $j \leqslant t$ such that $y_j = b_j$, $x_j = a_j$ and $ua_j = b_j v$ with $|u| = 2$ (if y_2 is obtained by a deletion in b_2) or $|u| = 1$ because there are substitution errors in at most $t-2$ words. In any case a contradiction. If $|y_1| < |x_1| = |a_1|$ the conclusion is the same.

Thus (2) and (3) imply $x_1 x_2 \ldots x_i = y_1 y_2 \ldots y_i$ for some $i \leqslant t$ and A has property (4). The last statement now follows from Lemma 2.

Observe now that A is $(t-2, 1, t)$-decodable with delay at most t if and only if, besides being $(t-2, 1, t)$-correcting, A has the following property:

> (5)   If X and Y are sentences of A with $|X| \geqslant t$ and $\alpha_t(X)w \cap$
> $\cap \alpha_t(Y) \neq \emptyset$ it follows that the first word of X is the first word of Y.

We then have:

THEOREM. Suppose that A has properties (1) and (2). Then A is $(t-2, 1, t)$-decodable with delay at most t.

Proof. We first show that A is $(t-2, 1, t)$-correcting. Assume $\alpha_t(X) \cap$ $\cap \alpha_t(Y) \neq \emptyset$. If $|X| \leqslant t$, $X = Y$ by Lemma 2. If $|X| \geqslant t$, by Lemma 4 $(w = \emptyset)$ $X = X_1 X_2$ and $Y = Y_1 Y_2$ with $X_1 = Y_1$, $\alpha_t(X_2) \cap \alpha_t(Y_2) \neq \emptyset$, and $|X_2| < |X|$. By repeating this reasoning we eventually reach the equality $X = Y$. Hence A is correcting. Decodability with delay at most t follows now from Lemma 4, since (1) and (4) imply (5).

The deductive pattern developed in this section is generally applicable to codes with correction of synchronization errors and to variable-length codes. The following considerations then seem warranted. For any sentence X over an arbitrary code A let $\alpha(X)$ denote the set of those sequences which, when received, should be decoded into X. Let us call A *t-separating for* α if $|X| \leqslant t$ and $\alpha(X) \cap \alpha(Y) \neq \emptyset$ imply $X = Y$; and let us say that A is *t-exact for* α if $|X| \geqslant t$ and $\alpha(X)w \cap \alpha(Y) \neq \emptyset$ imply that $X = X_1 X_2$, $Y = Y_1 Y_2$ such that $0 < |X_1|$, $\alpha(X_1) \cap \alpha(Y_1) \neq \emptyset$ and $\alpha(X_2)w \cap$ $\cap \alpha(Y_2) \neq \emptyset$. Then the proof of our theorem shows that a code which is *t*-separating and *t*-exact for α is decodable for α with delay at most *t*. In this terminology, Lemma 2 has shown that (1) implies *t*-separating for α_t; and Lemma 4 that (2) and (3) imply (4) and hence that our codes are *t*-exact for α_t.

4. THE CODES A_n^c HAVE PROPERTIES (1) AND (2)

That the sets K_n^c, and hence their subsets A_n^c, have Levenshtein distance at least 3 (property (1)) is already known [16], but for completeness we sketch a proof.

To show that from x, $y \in K_n^c$ follows $D(x, y) \geqslant 3$, we show that if $D(x, y) < 3$ for two different sequences of length n, then $\sigma(x) \not\equiv \sigma(y)$ mod $2n$. Let $x = \xi_1\xi_2\ldots\xi_n$, $y = \eta_1\eta_2\ldots\eta_n$ and assume $D(x, y) = 1$. Then $y = \xi_1\ldots\xi_{i-1}\bar{\xi}_i\xi_{i+1}\ldots\xi_n$, where $\bar{\xi}$ denotes the complement of ξ. Consequently, since $\xi_i - \bar{\xi}_i = \pm 1$ and $0 < i \leqslant n$, $\sigma(x) - \sigma(y) = i(\xi_1 - \bar{\xi}_i) = \pm i \not\equiv 0$ mod $2n$. If $D(x, y) = 2$ we have three cases:

(a)　　　$y = \xi_1 \ldots \bar{\xi}_i \ldots \bar{\xi}_j \ldots \xi_n$

(b)　　　$y = \xi_1 \ldots \xi_{i-1}\xi_{i+1} \ldots \xi_j \eta \xi_{j+1} \ldots \xi_n$

(c)　　　$y = \xi_1 \ldots \xi_i \eta \xi_{i+1} \ldots \xi_{j-1}\xi_{j+1} \ldots \xi_n.$

In case (a), we obtain $\sigma(x) - \sigma(y) = \pm i \pm j \not\equiv 0 \bmod 2n$ as above. In case (b)

$$\sigma(x) - \sigma(y) = \sum_{i}^{j-1} h(\xi_h - \xi_{h+1}) + j(\xi_j - \eta) =$$

$$= i\xi_i + \sum_{i+1}^{j} \xi_h - j\eta$$

that is, $-n \leqslant \sigma(x) - \sigma(y) \leqslant n$. The only case of interest is $\sigma(x) - \sigma(y) = 0$; but then $\xi_i = \xi_{i+1} = \ldots = \xi_j = \eta$ and $x = y$, though $D(x, y) = 2$. Finally, case (c) is similar.

We show now that many subsets of K_n^c, in particular A_n^c, have property (2). To do so we prove:

Lemma 5. If x, $y \in K_n^c$ and $ux = yv$ with $|u| = 2$, then $y \in K_n$.
Proof. Let $ux = \xi_1\xi_2\ldots\xi_n\xi_{n+1}\xi_{n+2}$ so that $x = \xi_3\xi_4\ldots\xi_{n+2}$ and $y = \xi_1\xi_2\ldots\xi_n$. Because x, $y \in K_n^c$ we have, mod $2n$,

$$0 \equiv \sigma(y) - \sigma(x) = \sum_1^n i\xi_i - \sum_3^{n+2} (i - 2)\xi_i$$

that is

$$\xi_1 + 2\sum_2^n \xi_i \equiv (n - 1)\xi_{n+1} + n\xi_{n+2}.$$

Both sides of this last relation are nonnegative and have value at most $2n - 1$, hence we have an equality. We treat cases:

(a)　　　If $\xi_{n+1} = \xi_{n+2} = 0$, then $\xi_1 = \xi_2 = \ldots = \xi_{n+2} = 0$ and hence $x = y$ and $y \in K_n$.

If $\xi_{n+1} = \xi_{n+2} = 1$, then $\xi_1 = \xi_2 = \ldots = \xi_{n+2} = 1$ and again $x = y$ and $y \in K_n$.

(b)   If $\xi_{n+1} = 0$, $\xi_{n+2} = 1$, and $n = 2h$, then $\xi_1 = 0$ and $\sum_2^n \xi_i = h$.
        If $\xi_{n+1} = 1$, $\xi_{n+2} = 0$, and $n = 2h$, then $\xi_1 = 1$ and $\sum_2^n \xi_i = h - 1$.
        Hence if $n = 2h$, then $y \in K_n$.

(c)   If $\xi_{n+1} = 0$, $\xi_{n+2} = 1$, and $n = 2h + 1$, then $\xi_1 = 1$
        and $\sum_2^n \xi_i = h$.
        If $\xi_{n+1} = 1$, $\xi_{n+2} = 0$, and $n = 2h + 1$, then $\xi_1 = 0$
        and $\sum_2^n \xi_i = h$.
        Hence if $n = 2h + 1$, then $y \in K_n$.

Notice that we have actually proved more than the statement of Lemma 5. Indeed, we have shown that one of the following two situations occurs when $ux = yv$ and $|u| = 2$:

(a) $x = y = \text{constant}$

(b) $y = (\xi_1, \ldots, \xi_n) \in K_n$ and $x = (\xi_3, \ldots, \xi_n, 0, 1)$ if $\xi_1 = 0$ and $n = 2h$ or $\xi_1 = 1$ and $n = 2h + 1$;
        $x = (\xi_3, \ldots, \xi_n, 1, 0)$ if $\xi_1 = 1$ and $n = 2h$ or $\xi_1 = 0$, and $n = 2h + 1$.

EPILOGUE

The material of this book represents only a beginning, the beginning of a theory. It is sufficiently well developed to provide a new framework for the four problems of Coding Theory. But it is a long way from being adequate enough to generate codes with pre-assigned properties. It may be unreasonable to demand such behavior for Coding Theory regardless of its stage of sophistication. It would be pleasant, however, to have such facility.

More realistically one might be moderately content to achieve two goals: first, find ways to apply some of the results about the standard model to construct good error-limiting or comma-free codes and second, discover how to deal more adequately with models which permit both substitution and synchronization errors. One reason for undertaking the extensive study of the standard model was the feeling that the results derived would gracefully yield the constructive procedures necessary to generate desirable codes. As things turned out we never seriously tried to carry out that part of our proposed program. Actually we did not explicitly plan to construct the family of codes given in Chapter 11. When we began to move to the more general models we constructed a variety of examples and studied them to see what changes we would have to make in our standard model treatment. The more we pondered the examples the more convinced we became that a suitable construction was possible. It was, of course, but it was not supported by any elaborate theoretical basis such as we had available before. Hence, the neglected portion of our program is still available to any and all who might be interested.

The second goal grew out of our last two papers and represents a (now) obvious extension of our former work. So far we have only been able to begin a serious study of the model. The question of correcting seems to be more or less settled but more can be done on decodability not to mention error-limitation and comma-freedom. For example, we do not even have an adequate definition of comma-freedom for the general model which guarantees that most or all comma-freedom codes are also error-limiting. Then too we would like to develop more experience with what happens when one allows both kinds of errors to occur simultaneously in some profusion. Unfortunately, the problems seem to be rather difficult, both to formulate and solve.

It would be possible but probably not good manners to list all of the things that we would like to know but still do not know about coding. Suffice to say that the diligent and courageous reader who finishes the book can surely furnish his own list, which will be longer than ours in all likelihood. It may then happen that he will settle some of the problems which have puzzled us during the last few years. We would be most grateful if he does.

SELECTED BIBLIOGRAPHY ON CODING THEORY
(1957–1968)

Parke Mathematical Laboratories, Incorporated,
Carlisle, Massachusetts

Publications of the PML Coding Group are of three kinds: Technical Memoranda (TM) which are preliminary versions of work in progress, Scientific Reports (SR) which are polished versions of material selected from earlier memoranda – they almost always contain additional results, and Papers which normally have been prepared from past reports – occasionally a paper appeared with a different title. The list which follows traces the evolution of our ideas on general error-correcting codes. The first publication which moved explicitly in this direction was TM-6-7493, written in 1962.

1957
[1] June   H. Weinitschke, 'One Some Upper Bounds of Importance in Slepian's Theory of Coding', TM-15-1396.

1958
[2] Sept.   PML Staff, 'A Catalogue of Binary Systematic Codes', TM-7-3471.

1959
[3] Aug.   PML Staff, 'A Catalog of Binary Systematic Codes Supplement', TM-13-3471.
[4] Feb.   L. Calabi and H. G. Haefeli, 'A Class of Binary Systematic Codes Correcting Errors at Random and in Bursts', SR-1-3471. Appeared in *IRE Transactions on Information Theory*, IT-5 (1959) 79–94.

1960
[5] Sept.   P. J. Sally, 'Some Results Concerning the Probability Distribution of the Length of Error Bursts', TM-21-3471.
[6] Sept.   H. G. Haefeli, Subcontractor, 'An Extension of Kautz's Work on Error-Correcting Codes', SR-4-3471.
[7] Dec.   L. Calabi, 'A New Approach to the Study of Binary Systematic Codes', SR-6-3471.

1961
[8] Jan.   H. G. Haefeli, Subcontractor, 'Rules for Correcting Single and Double Errors Using $K_4{}^6$ (3, 2, 2, 2, 2, 2)', TM-22-3471.
[9] July   L. Calabi, 'New Tools for Coding Theory', TM-1-7493. Appeared as 'A Note of Rank and Nullity in Coding Theory', *Information and Control* 4 (1961) 359–363.
[10] Aug.   L. Calabi and R. Darst, 'A Study of the Sum and the Product of Two Codes', SR-3-7493.
[11] Dec.   PML Staff, 'An Annotated Bibliography on Error Correcting Codes', SR-4-7493.

1962
[12] Aug.   L. Calabi, 'On Variable-Length Binary Codes', TM-6-7493.

W E. Hartnett (ed.), Foundations of Coding Theory, 207–209. All Rights Reserved.
Copyright © 1974 by D. Reidel Publishing Company, Dordrecht-Holland.

1963

[13] April   L. Calabi and J. A. Riley, 'On Variable-Length Binary Codes, II', TM-9-7493.

[14] May   H. G. Haefeli, Subcontractor, 'The Checking Digits as Explicit Functions of the Information Digits in Kautz's Codes', TM-10-7493.

[15] May   L. Calabi, 'On Variable-Length Binary Codes, III', TM-11-7493.

[16] June   L. Calabi, 'On Variable-Length Binary Codes, IV', TM-13-7493.

[17] Aug.   L. Calabi and H. G. Haefeli, 'On Variable-Length Binary Codes, V', TM-14-7493.

[18] Sept.   D. Julin and W. Newsom, III, 'On Variable-Length Binary Codes, VI', TM-15-7493.

[19] March   L. Calabi and E. Myrvaagnes, 'On the Weights of the Elements of Binary Group Codes', SR-5-7493.

[20] March   L. Calabi and H. G. Haefeli, 'Decoding Rules for Certain Product Codes', SR-6-7493.

[21] March   L. Calabi and E. Myrvaagnes, 'On the Minimal Weight of Binary Group Codes', SR-7-7493. Appeared in *IEEE Transactions on Information Theory* IT-**10** (1964) 385–387.

[22] Oct.   H. G. Haefeli, Subcontractor, 'Decoding Rules for Kautz's Codes', SR-8-7493.

[23] Dec.   L. Calabi, 'On Error-Correcting, Variable-Length Codes', SR-9-7493.

[24] Oct.   E. Myrvaagnes, 'On Maximum-Weight Codes', *IEEE Transactions on Information Theory* IT-**9** (1963) 289–290.

1964

[25] Dec.   L. Calabi, appendix by J. A. Riley, 'Combinatorial Properties of Variable-Length Error-Correcting Codes', SR-2-3826.

[26] April   J. A. Riley, 'An Upper Bound for the Word Lengths of a Binary Code', TM-2-3826.

[27] March   L. Calabi, 'On Variable-Length Codes, VII', TM-1-3826.

[28] April   J. A. Riley, 'Combinatorial Forms of the Basic Coding Problems', TM-3-3826.

[29] June   E. Myrvaagnes, 'The Weight Distributions of Two Cyclic Codes of Length 73', TM-4-3826. Appeared in *IEEE Transactions on Information Theory* IT-**11** (1965) 316.

[30] Sept.   T. Hatcher, 'On Minimal Distance, Shortest Length and Greatest Number of Elements for Binary Group Codes', TM-6-3826.

[31] Nov.   D. Julin, 'Two Improved Block Codes', TM-8-3826. Appeared in *IEEE Transactions on Information Theory*, IT-**11** (1965) 459.

1965

[32] July   E. Myrvaagnes, 'Eighteen Hundred Selected Two-Word Codes', SR-3-3826.

[33] Oct.   E. Myrvaagnes, 'Some Binary Codes for Error-Correction and Synchronization', SR-4-3826.

[34] Nov.   J. A. Riley, 'The Sardinas/Patterson and Levenshtein's Theorems', SR-5-3826. Appeared in *Information and Control* **10** (1967) 120–136.

[35] Nov.   L. Calabi and L. K. Arquette, 'Basic Properties of Error-Correcting Codes', SR-6-3826.

[36] Feb.   L. Calabi and J. A. Riley, 'On Variable-Length Codes VIII', TM-10-3826.

[37] May   J. A. Riley, 'A Proof of the Sardinas/Patterson Theorem', TM-12-3826.
[38] May   L. K. Arquette, 'Variable-Length Error-Correcting Codes', TM-13-3826.
[39] July   L. K. Arquette and L. Calabi, 'Basic Properties of Codes', TM-14-3826.
[40] Aug.   L. Calabi and L. K. Arquette, 'Some Fundamental Properties of Error-Correcting Codes', TM-15-3826.
[41] Nov.   W. E. Hartnett, 'Graph Products and Codes', TM-17-3826.

1966
[42] June   W. E. Hartnett, 'Generalization of Tests for Certain Properties of Codes', SR-7-3826. Appeared as 'Generalization of Tests for Certain Properties of Variable Length Codes', *Information and Control* **13** (1968) 20–45.
[43] Aug.   L. Calabi and L. K. Arquette, 'A Study of Error-Correcting Codes: I', SR-8-3826.
[44] Nov.   L. K. Arquette and W. E. Hartnett, 'A Study of Error-Correcting Codes, II: Decodability Properties', SR-9-3826.
[45] Aug.   L. Calabi and W. E. Hartnett, 'Code-Related Properties', TM-21-3826.
[46] Dec.   L. Calabi, L. Arquette, and W. E. Hartnett, 'A Study of Error Correcting Codes, III: Synchronizability and Comma Freedom', SR-1-0030.

1967
[47] Feb.   L. Calabi and W. E. Hartnett, 'A Study of Error-Correcting Codes, IV: Code Properties and Unambiguous Sets', SR-2-0030.
[48] Oct.   L. Calabi and W. E. Hartnett, 'A Family of Codes for the Correction of Substitution and Synchronization Errors', SR-3-0030. Appeared in *IEEE Transactions on Information Theory*, IT-**15** (1969) 102–106.
[49] Feb.   W. E. Hartnett, 'Generalization of Codes and Strong Code Properties', TM-1-0030.
[50] March   H. G. Haefeli, 'A Family of Code Compositions', TM-2-0030.
[51] Aug.   L. Calabi and H. G. Haefeli (Subcontractor), 'On Binary Synchronizable Codes of Minimal Cost', TM-7-0030.
[52] Sept.   L. Calabi and E. Myrvaagnes, 'On Error Probabilities After Decoding', TM-8-0030
[53] Oct.   L. Calabi, 'On the Computation of Levenshtein's Distances' TM-9-0030.
[54] Nov.   T. Hatcher, 'The Program NCD3 and the Subroutine STXCK', TM-10-0030.

1968
[55] Feb.   T. Hatcher, 'On a Family of Error Correcting and Synchronizable Codes', SR-4-0030. Appeared in *IEEE Transactions on Information Theory*, IT-**15** (1969) 620–623.
[56] March   L. Calabi, 'A Corrected List of Relatively Large Cyclic Codes', TM-12A-0030.
[57] April   T. Hatcher, 'The Number of Sequences in A_n^c for $0 \leqslant c \leqslant 2n$, $0 \leqslant n \leqslant 13$, and Listings of Selected A_n^c-Codes', TM-13-0030.
[58] July   W. E. Hartnett, 'Code Properties for Generalized Models', TM-14-0030.
[59] Nov.   L. Calabi and W. E. Hartnett, 'Some General Results of Coding Theory with Applications to the Study of Codes for the Correction of Synchronization Errors', SR-5-0030. Appeared in *Information and Control* **15** (1969) 235–249.

REFERENCES

[1] N. Abramson, *Information Theory and Coding*, McGraw-Hill, New York (1963).

[2] R. Ash, *Information Theory*, Interscience, New York (1965).

[3] G. Bandyopadhyay, 'A Simple Proof of the Decipherability Criterion of Sardinas and Patterson', *Information and Control* 6 (1963) No. 4, 331–336.

[4] R. Banerji, 'On Constructing Group Codes', *Information and Control* 4 (1961) 1–14.

[5] E. K. Blum, 'Free Subsemigroups of a Free Semigroup', *Michigan Math. J.* 12 (1965) 179–182.

[6] R. C. Bose and J. G. Caldwell, 'Synchronizable Error-Correcting Codes', *Information and Control* 10 (1967) No. 6, 616–630.

[7] R. Chien, 'Group Codes for Prescribed Error Patterns', *IRE Convention Record*, Part 4, 125–134 (1960).

[8] P. M. Cohn, 'On Subsemigroups of Free Semigroups', *Proc. AMS* 13 (1962) 347–351.

[9] S. Even, 'Tests for Unique Decipherability', *IEEE Transactions on Information Theory*, IT-9 (1963) No. 2, 109–112.

[10] S. Even, 'Test for Synchronizability of Finite Automata and Variable Length Codes', *IEEE Transactions on Information Theory* IT-10 (1964) 185–189.

[11] E. N. Gilbert and E. F. Moore, 'Variable-Length Binary Encodings', *Bell System Technical Journal*, XXXVIII (1959) No. 4, 933–967.

[12] S. Golomb and B. Gordon, 'Codes with Bounded Synchronization Delay', *Information and Control* 8 (1965) 355–372.

[13] S. Golomb, B. Gordon, and L. Welch, 'Comma-Free Codes', *Canad. J. Math.* 10-2 (1958) 202–209.

[14] V. Levenshtein, 'Certain Properties of Code Systems', *Soviet Physics Doklady*, 6 (1962) No. 10, 858–860.

[15] V. Levenshtein, 'Some Properties of Coding and Self-Adjusting Automata for Decoding Messages', *Problemy Kiberneticki* 11 (1964) 63–121.

[16] V. Levenshtein, 'Binary Codes with Correction of Deletions, Insertions and Substitution of Symbols', *Doklady Akad. Nauk, SSSR* 163 (1965) No. 4, 845–848.

[17] V. Levenshtein, 'Binary Codes Capable of Correcting Spurious Insertions and Deletions of Ones', *Probl. Peredachi Inform.* 1 (1965) No. 1, 12–25.

[18] E. S. Ljapin, *Semîgroups*, Am. Math. Soc., Translations of Math. Monographs, No. 3 (1963).

[19] R. C. Lyndon and M. P. Schutzenberger, 'The Equation $a^m = b^n c^p$ in a Free Group', *Michigan Math. J.* 9 (1962) 289–298.

[20] A. A. Markov, 'Alphabet Coding', *Soviet Math. Doklady* 1 (1960) No. 3, 596–598.

[21] A. A. Markov, 'On Alphabet Coding', *Soviet Physics Doklady* 6 (1962) No. 7, 553–554.

[22] A. A. Markov, 'Non-Block Error-Correcting Codes', *Problemy Kiberneticki* 12 (1964) 137–153.

[23] P. Neumann, 'On a Class of Efficient Error-Limiting Variable-Length Codes', *IRE Trans.* IT-8 (1962) s260–s266.

[24] M. Nivat, 'Eléments de la théorie générale des codes', in *Automata Theory*, (Ed. E. R. Cainaniello) Academic Press, N.Y. pp. 278–294 (1966).

[25] A. Sardinas and G. Patterson, 'A Necessary and Sufficient Condition for Unique Decomposition of Coded Messages', *IRE Convention Record*, Part 8, 104–108 (1953).

[26] M. P. Schutzenberger, 'On an Application of Semigroups Methods to Some Problems in Coding', *IRE Trans*. IT-2 (1956) 47–60.

[27] F. F. Sellers, Jr. 'Bit Loss and Gain Correction Codes', *IRE Trans*. IT-8 (1962) No. 1, 35–38.

[28] R. A. Sholtz, 'Codes with Synchronization Capability', *IEEE Trans*. IT-12 (1966) No. 2, 135–142.

[29] D. Slepian, 'A Class of Binary Signaling Alphabets', *Bell Telephone System Technical Journal*, 35 (1956) 205–234.

[30] J.J. Stiffler, 'Synchronization of Telemetry Codes', *IRE Trans. SET* 8 (1962) No. 2, 112–117.

[31] J. D. Ullman, 'Near Optimal Single Synchronization Error Correcting Codes', *IEEE Trans*. IT-12 (1966) No. 4, 418–424.

[32] J.D. Ullman, 'On the Capability of Codes to Correct Synchronization Errors', *IEEE Trans*. IT-13 (1967) No. 1, 95–105.

[33] J. Wolfowitz, *Coding Theorems of Information Theory*, Springer-Verlag and Prentice Hall (1961).

ADDITIONAL REFERENCES

The following books and reports were not specifically used in our work but they represent outstanding sources of information about many aspects and problems of Coding Theory.

[34] W. H. Kautz and K. N. Levitt, 'A Survey of Progress in Coding Theory in the Soviet Union', *IEEE*, IT-15 (Part II), 197–245 (January 1969).

[35] W. W. Peterson and E. J. Weldon, Jr., *Error-Correcting Codes*, MIT Press, Second Edition (1972).

[36] E. Berlekamp, *Algebraic Coding Theory*, McGraw-Hill, New York (1968).

INDEX OF AUTHORS

INDEX OF SUBJECTS